★ ★ ★ ★ ★

the *Virgin* book of FILM RECORDS

The Authors

Phil Swern

Is a leading authority on film and pop.
A former record producer, he now
produces Pick of the Pops and
The Bob Harris Show for Radio 2.
Already well-established in the world
of pop, he also became known for
his vast knowledge of film with the
publication of The Guinness Book of
Box Office Hits in 1995.

Toby Rowan

Is a keen film buff, and was
appointed by the author to share
the momentous task of researching
material for this fact-filled volume.
He now works as a researcher full time.
This is his first book project.

First published in Great Britain by
Virgin Publishing Limited
Thames Wharf Studios,
Rainville Road,
London W6 9HT.

A catalogue record for this book
is available from the British Library.

ISBN 0 7535 0367 0

Text pages designed by Michael Bell Design.

Printed and bound in Great Britain.

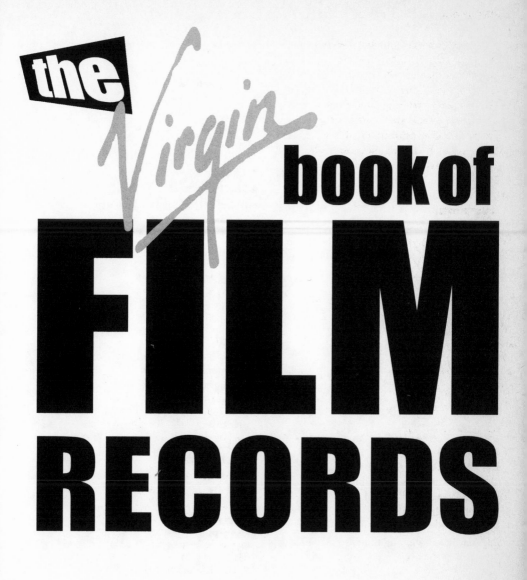

the Virgin book of FILM RECORDS

Virgin

**PHIL SWERN
AND TOBY ROWAN**

Contents

Introduction

In 1995, cinema celebrated its centenary and this book covers films from the early days right up to the turn of the millennium, documenting some of the more fascinating achievements, facts, statistics, trivia and information brought about through the hundreds of successes, flops and extravagances made possible by the decisions of the often misguided movie men.

Most of the facts contained within, you will find in list form, this has always been regarded as the easiest way to digest information. This collection contains the humorous, the quirky and the more serious movie facts; the bitchy things one star has said about another; those darling little children that made it to the big screen; the real names of the famous; and those impressive taglines that you read on the posters of newly publicised films for which promotion companies get paid small fortunes.

With the tens of thousands of movies currently available, it would have been impossible to come up with definitive lists; so, rather than always focusing on the most obvious, we've chosen to concentrate upon the more interesting material. No doubt there will be arguments and controversy over some of the choices and omissions, but the compilations have been achieved through painstaking research and the most accurate information available – not to mention the endless hours of discussion about what goes and what stays. So please forgive us if your favourite doesn't appear. However, we're always happy to hear from you if you have any ideas, embellishments or improvements for future volumes.

Now that you've read this far then you clearly have more than a passing interest in the world of cinema and there's bound to be something here for you, so why not reach into your pocket, buy this book and absorb at your leisure? Then, in no time at all, you'll be astounding your friends and colleagues with your amazing knowledge and insight into the world of film making.

Chapter 1
The Color of Money

PRETTY WOMAN (1990)

Big-Name Cheapies

1. *Rashomon* (1950),
Akira Kurosawa – $40,000

2. *Breathless* (1959),
Jean-Luc Godard – $120,000

3. *Shadows* (1959),
John Cassavetes – $40,000

4. *Night of the Living Dead* (1968),
George A Romero – $114,000

5. *Pink Flamingos* (1972),
John Waters – $12,000

6. *She's Gotta Have It* (1986),
Spike Lee – $114,333

7. *Slacker* (1991),
Richard Linklater – $23,000

8. *El Mariachi* (1992),
Robert Rodriguez – $7,000

9. *Clerks* (1994),
Kevin Smith – $26,685

10. *Pi* (1998),
Darren Aronofsky – $60,000

Contractual Excess

★ Jim Carrey insisted upon two personal chefs during the filming of *Ace Ventura: When Nature Calls* – one for himself, the other for his pet iguana!

★ While filming *Mary Reilly* in New York, Julia Roberts had the producers TriStar keep a jet on permanent standby, just in case she should ever feel the urge to visit Los Angeles.

★ Kim Basinger will use only mineral water to wash her hair in.

★ Mickey Rourke likes his carrot juice fresher than fresh: it has to be juiced no earlier than six minutes before the drink reaches his fair hand.

★ John Travolta, while working in Paris on Roman Polanski's *The Double*, insisted that the producers, Mandalay, fly over his personal entourage of over a dozen people, including chefs, bodyguards and personal trainers. Mandalay succumbed to the star's demands, only for Travolta to walk off the set as a result of 'creative differences' with Polanski.

★ Problems arose on set during the filming of 1992's *A Few Good Men*, when Demi Moore (known in the trade as 'Gimmee Moore') expressed her displeasure at having her double trailer further from the set than Tom Cruise, who was also starring in the film. Apparently, Cruise's contract stipulated that his trailer be the nearest one to the set. Negotiations ensued to have Tom's trailer moved back!

★ It is a stipulation of Sharon Stone's contract that she keep all the clothes that she wears during her films.

★ Oh, and speaking of Sharon Stone, she has her own personal manicurist, who charges the film studios a nail-biting-inducing rate of $75 per nail!

★ Sylvester Stallone, arriving at a New York hotel, to promote *Demolition Man*, was horrified to discover that the intended interview suite had light-yellow walls. Stallone wouldn't allow himself to be photographed against a yellow background. The walls were hastily repainted to Stallone's liking – peach!

★ The film producer Don Simpson favoured black Levi's; he wore them every day – a different pair that is!

★ Geena Davis once flew a make-up assistant from Los Angeles to Malta, where she was filming *Cut Throat Island*, to put powder on her 'upper chest'.

★ Demi Moore, while providing voiceovers for Disney's *The Hunchback of Notre Dame*, insisted that the studio provide transport so that she could attend a PTA meeting. The studio obliged and duly sent a car to drive Moore from the studio in Burbank to the meeting at her daughter's school. Only one problem: good old Demi omitted to mention that the meeting was actually in a different state, namely Idaho. In order to appease Ms Moore, the studio had no choice but to charter a private jet, at a cost of about $4,500 per hour, and fly her home.

★ Today's movie stars just can't seem to manage without their own private army of helpers – and guess who foots the bill. The studios, of course. Demi Moore, having finished filming of *The Scarlet Letter*, promptly billed the studio $877,000 in 'entourage costs'. Melanie Griffith, ever the economiser, billed Disney $589,000 for *Born Yesterday*, and Julia Roberts billed *I Love Trouble* a 'Mooresque' $841,000.

★ While we're on the subject of entourage costs, take a look at the costs incurred by Universal as a result of having Kevin Costner star in the 1999 baseball saga, *For Love of the Game*: trainer-nutritionist, $4,500 a week while on location; on-set trailer for wardrobe, hair and make-up personnel, $50,000; personal assistant, $800 per week during production; body double, $3,000 a week. And what did Costner's last film gross? $18 million! How much did it cost to make? $80 million! Well, all in all, it seems like money well spent. NOT!

Money Isn't Everything!

★ Not one to fly economy, Mel Gibson apparently books first-class when he and his family visit their Australian home. Oh, did we forget to mention? That's the whole of first-class!

★ Mel Gibson, Danny Glover and the producers of *Lethal Weapon 3* all received brand new Range Rovers as reward for their efforts.

★ Charlie Sheen, a baseball fanatic, once purchased all 2,615 seats behind the left-field fence at Anaheim Stadium, for a game between the Angels and the Tigers, at a cost of $6,537, in the hope of improving his chances of catching a home-run ball.

★ Arnold Schwarzenegger apparently paid $38 million for a Gulfstream Jet in 1997.

★ The late Don Simpson, producer of such box-office smashes as *Top Gun* and *Beverly Hills Cop*, just couldn't stand to follow. He had to lead. So much so that, when Ferrari launched its *first* all-black Testarossa, Simpson had an assistant be at the San Diego docks at six in the morning, with a cashier's cheque for a $100,000, so that he could have the first black Testarossa in Hollywood! Of course, within hours of Simpson's receiving his, the remainder of the shipment had been delivered. Oh well, he was still the first to have one and nobody could take that away from him.

It Could Have Been Yours...

Ever dreamt of owning a piece of movie history? A light sabre from *Star Wars* perhaps, or how about Oddjob's steel-rimmed bowler? Well, believe it or not, these and many more items of movie memorabilia have previously been offered for sale by the London auctioneers Christie's.

Indeed, a veritable treasure trove of items has passed through their hands. The following are all drawn from Christie's sales that took place during the 1990s, in either their 'Film and Entertainment' sale or 'Vintage Film Posters' sale.

It should be noted that all prices realised include a buyer's premium of 15 per cent. The date of the sale is indicated in brackets after the item's sale price.

★ 2001: A Space Odyssey
A grey cotton jumpsuit, labelled on the front 'Bowman D.L.', as made for and worn by Keir Dullea, in the 1968 film, *2001: A Space Odyssey*. It could have been yours for £2,200 (12/94).

★ Air Force One
A Cerruti 1881 two-piece suit, complete with 'special effects' bullet holes and bloodstains, as worn by Harrison Ford, playing the President of the United States of America, in the 1996 movie, *Air Force One*. It could have been yours for £1,800–£2,200 (estimated price) (12/97)

★ Aliens
Perspex dog tags, as worn by Michael Biehn, playing Corporal D Hicks in the 1986 movie *Aliens*. It could have been yours for £345 (12/98)

★ Aliens
A grotesque alien head, made of polyurethane foam, of the type worn by stuntmen during the scene where aliens break through the ceiling and fall down upon Ripley and the others, in the 1986 movie. It could have been yours for £1,725 (12/98).

★ Aliens
An alien egg, from the Queen's hatching chamber, as featured in the 1986 film, *Aliens*. It could have been yours for £920 (12/97).

★ Back to the Future Part II
A Mattel Hoverboard, complete with one appropriately futuristic Nike Mag training shoe, as made for, and used in the 1989 movie, *Back to the Future Part II*. It could have been yours for £2,640 (12/91).

★ Barbarella
An Italian poster, 79 x 55 in., made to promote the 1968 film, *Barbarella*. It could have been yours for £146 (11/96).

★ Batman Returns
A Batman cowl of moulded black rubber, complete with pointed ears and chest plate, as made for and worn by Michael Keaton in the 1992 film, *Batman Returns*. It could have been yours for £5,625 (12/95).

★ Ingrid Bergman
A signed piece of paper, together with a photograph of the actress. It could have been yours for £103 (12/98).

★ James Bond
Car registration number 0007, including registration rights. It could have been yours for £32,200 (09/98).

★ Breakfast at Tiffany's
A British poster, 30 x 40 in., to promote the 1961 film, *Breakfast at Tiffany's*. It could have been yours for £920 (11/96).

★ Yul Brynner
The black wool stetson, as worn by Yul Brynner while playing the part of Chris in the 1960 movie, *The Magnificent Seven*. It could have been yours for £5,175 (12/97).

★ Charlie Chaplin
A full-length publicity photograph of Charlie Chaplin, dressed as the Tramp, and signed on the reverse. It could have been yours for £1,955 (12/98).

★ Charlie Chaplin
A bowler hat and bamboo cane, as used by Charlie Chaplin, in many films from 1916 onwards. It could have been yours for £44,750 (12/95).

★ A Clockwork Orange
A silk-lined bowler hat, as worn by Malcolm McDowell (the hat is also signed by the actor), in the infamous 1971 movie, *A Clockwork Orange*. It could have been yours for £1,980 (12/91).

★ Conan the Barbarian
A prop dagger in the form of two entwined serpents with hissing heads, as made for, and used in the 1981 film, *Conan the Barbarian*. The dagger is used in the scene where King Ostric dispatches Conan and his accomplices, to rescue his daughter from Thulsa Doom. It could have been yours for £805 (12/97).

★ Tom Cruise
A one-sheet poster for the 1994 film, *Interview with the Vampire*, signed by Tom Cruise. It could have been yours for £219 (11/96).

★ Diamonds Are Forever

A black wool dress suit, as made for and worn by Sean Connery, playing James Bond, in the 1971 film, *Diamonds Are Forever*. It could have been yours for £9,777 (12/97).

★ Die Hard

A black rubber prop gun, moulded from a Kalashnikov 9mm machine gun. Made for and used in the 1988 film, *Die Hard*. It could have been yours for £345 (11/96).

★ The Empire Strikes Back

A one-sheet poster for the 1980 movie *The Empire Strikes Back*; the poster is signed by the following cast members: Harrison Ford, David Prowse, Billy Dee Williams, Carrie Fisher, Mark Hamill, Peter Mayhew, Anthony Daniels, Kenny Baker and George Lucas. It is believed that only three posters, each with a different image, were signed by the cast. It could have been yours for £935 (12/91).

★ The Empire Strikes Back

A 'light sabre', as made for and used by Mark Hamill, playing Luke Skywalker in the 1980 movie, *The Empire Strikes Back*. It could have been yours for £3,000–£4,000 (estimated price) (12/95).

★ The Empire Strikes Back

A black/grey fibreglass skull helmet, as made for and used by the character Darth Vader in the 1980 film, *The Empire Strikes Back*. It could have been yours for £4,620 (12/94).

★ The Enforcer

An Italian poster, 55 x 39 in., to promote the 1950 film *The Enforcer/La Citta E Salva*, starring Humphrey Bogart. It could have been yours for £1,380 (11/96).

★ Excalibur

The principal prop sword, in medieval style, as made for, and used in the 1981 film, *Excalibur*. It could have been yours for £1,380 (12/97).

★ Errol Flynn

The prop cavalry officer's sabre, as made for and used by Errol Flynn as Major Geoffrey Vickers, in the 1936 Warner Bros film, *The Charge of the Light Brigade*. It could have been yours for £4,000–£6,000 (estimated price) (12/98).

★ Forrest Gump

A prop chocolate box, labelled 'Russell Stover Candies', as made for the 1994 movie, *Forrest Gump*. It could have been yours for £460 (12/97).

★ From Russia With Love

A British poster, 30 x 40 in., made to promote the 1963 film, *From Russia With Love*. It could have been yours for £731 (11/96).

★ From Russia With Love

A prop knuckle-duster, as made for and used by the character Rosa Klebb, played by Lotte Lenya, in the 1963 film, *From Russia With Love*. It could have been yours for £1,495 (11/96).

★ GoldenEye

A sky-blue, 767cc, Gaz economy saloon, as driven by the CIA agent Jack Wade (Joe Don Baker) in the 1995 film, *GoldenEye*. It could have been yours for £4,830 (09/98).

★ Goldfinger

A black bowler hat, with customised metal rim, the brim cut on either side to reveal metal blades, as made for and worn by Harold Sakata, playing Oddjob in the 1964 film, *Goldfinger*. It could have been yours for £62,000 (09/98).

★ Goldfinger

A prop 'grappling-hook' gun, as made for and used by Sean Connery as James Bond in the 1964 film, *Goldfinger*. It could have been yours for £5,750 (09/98).

★ Goldfinger

Three blue perspex, prop hotel door signs, each marked 'Please Do Not Disturb', as made for, and used in the 1964 film, *Goldfinger*. It could have been yours for £2,530 (09/98).

★ Gone With the Wind

A bodice of printed lilac cotton in a pattern of scrolling leaves and flowerheads, as worn by Vivien Leigh, playing Scarlett O'Hara, in the 1939 film *Gone With the Wind*. It could have been yours for £7,475 (11/96).

★ Hellraiser

A wooden cube, with applied gilt decoration, as made for, and used in the 1987 film, *Hellraiser*. It could have been yours for £600–£800 (estimated price) (12/94).

★ Audrey Hepburn

A black-and-white portrait photograph, signed and dedicated by the actress. It could have been yours for £403 (11/96).

★ Hook

A polished metal hook, the base engraved with fleur-de-lis decoration, as made for, and worn by Dustin Hoffman, playing Captain Hook, in the 1991 film, *Hook*. It could have been yours for £2,500–£3,500 (estimated price) (12/97).

★ Judge Dredd

A prop 'Lawgiver' gun, as made for, and used in the 1994 movie, *Judge Dredd*. It could have been yours for £368 (12/97).

★ Lawrence of Arabia

A full-length desert robe of fine wool, decorated with gold brocade, as made for and worn by Peter O'Toole, in the title role of the 1962 film, *Lawrence of Arabia*. It could have been yours for £12,375 (12/95).

★ Live and Let Die

A specially adapted Rolex Oyster Perpetual Submariner wristwatch, as made for and worn by Roger Moore as James Bond, in the 1973 film *Live and Let Die*. It could have been yours for £21,850 (09/98).

★ Bela Lugosi

A signed, half-length publicity photo, circa 1932. It could have been yours for £264 (12/98).

★ Madonna

A portrait poster of Madonna as Eva Perón, as made for the 1996 film *Evita*, signed by Madonna. It could have been yours for £1,380 (11/96).

★ Moonraker

A futuristic prop space-marine laser gun of wood, metal and resin, as made for, and used in the 1979 film, *Moonraker*. It could have been yours for £1,150 (11/96).

★ Octopussy

A brown shooting waistcoat, as made for Roger Moore in the 1988 film, *Octopussy*. It could have been yours for £1,725 (11/96).

★ One Flew Over the Cuckoo's Nest

A white cotton straitjacket, signed by Jack Nicholson, as made for and featured in the 1975 film, *One Flew Over the Cuckoo's Nest*. It could have been yours for £2,070 (11/96).

★ On Her Majesty's Secret Service

A brass wall plaque, engraved 'Universal Exports (London) Ltd' (the cover name for M's operation), as made for and used in the 1969 film *On Her Majesty's Secret Service*. It could have been yours for £3,680 (09/98).

★ River Phoenix

A colour publicity photograph, signed by the actor. It could have been yours for £184 (11/96).

★ Raiders of the Lost Ark

A hand-made bull whip of kangaroo hide, as made for and used by Harrison Ford, as Indiana Jones, in the 1981 film, *Raiders of the Lost Ark*; it can also be seen in the sequels. It could have been yours for £2,000–£3,000 (estimated price) (12/95).

★ Robocop

A replica Robocop costume, made to promote the 1987 film, *Robocop*. It could have been yours for £2,300 (12/97).

★ The Seven Year Itch

A British poster, 30 x 20 in., made to promote the 1955 film, *The Seven Year Itch*. It could have been yours for £1,013 (11/96).

★ The Spy Who Loved Me

A 1977 Lotus Esprit S1 submarine shell, white, as made for, and used in the 1977 film, *The Spy Who Loved Me*. It could have been yours for £29,900 (09/98).

★ Star Wars

A gilt-finished medallion, as made for the presentation ceremony, which follows the destruction of the Death Star, in the 1977 movie *Star Wars*. It could have been yours for £1,760 (12/93).

★ Star Wars

A replica Stormtrooper costume, complete with prop 'blaster gun', black leather holster and white leather boots. As made to promote the 1977 film, *Star Wars*. It could have been yours for £3,680 (11/96).

★ Jimmy Stewart

A typed and signed letter from the actor to a fan, dated 28 February 1968. It could have been yours for £161 (12/98).

★ The Sting

A two-piece brown wool suit, as made for and worn by Robert Redford in the 1973 Universal movie, *The Sting*. It could have been yours for £1,500–£2,500 (estimated price) (12/98).

★ Supergirl

A four-piece outfit comprising a blue leotard with appliquéd yellow-and-black 'S' logo, a scarlet cape, miniskirt and tights. Made for and worn by Helen Slater in the title role of the 1984 film, *Supergirl*. It could have been yours for £4,025 (11/96).

★ Superman

A piece of 'Kryptonite' (actually green-tinted perspex), as made for the 1978 movie *Superman*. It could have been yours for £920 (12/98).

★ The Terminator

A pair of futuristic, black plastic and metal sunglasses, as made for and worn by Arnold Schwarzenegger in the 1984 film, *The Terminator*. It could have been yours for £800–£1,200 (estimated price) (12/94).

★ Terminator 2: Judgment Day

A distressed, black leather jacket as worn by Arnold Schwarzenegger in the 1991 film, *Terminator 2: Judgment Day*. It could have been yours for £3,500–£4,500 (estimated price) (12/94).

★ John Wayne

A full-length black-and-white publicity photo, signed by the actor. It could have been yours for £483 (12/98).

★ Zulu

Two prop 'Zulu' shields complete with prop spears, as used in the 1964 film *Zulu*, which starred Stanley Baker, Jack Hawkins and Michael Caine. It could have been yours for £230 (12/98).

Thirty Years of Number 1 Movies

UK Box Office

1969

		Weeks at Number 1
11 July	The Most Dangerous Man in the World	1
18 July	Oliver!	1
25 July	Three Into Two Won't Go	1
01 August	Oliver!	4
29 August	The Wild Bunch	4
26 September	Battle of Britain	4
31 October	Virgin Soldiers	1
07 November	Battle of Britain	7
26 December	On Her Majesty's Secret Service	1

1970

02 January	On Her Majesty's Secret Service	5
06 February	Battle of Britain	2
20 February	Butch Cassidy and the Sundance Kid	1
27 February	Battle of Britain	1
06 March	Butch Cassidy and the Sundance Kid	2
20 March	Anne of the Thousand Days	6
01 May	Airport	6
12 June	Paint Your Wagon	1
19 June	M*A*S*H	4
17 July	Woodstock	1
24 July	Cromwell	8
18 September	Lawrence of Arabia	1
25 September	Kelly's Heroes	1
02 October	Lawrence of Arabia	1
09 October	Cromwell	1
16 October	Tora! Tora! Tora!	3
06 November	Waterloo	5
11 December	Scrooge	3

1971

01 January	Scrooge	3
22 January	Murphy's War	1
29 January	Song of Norway	5
05 March	The Music Lovers	1
12 March	Death in Venice	1

19 March	**Love Story**	13
18 June	**Valdez is Coming**	1
25 June	**Little Big Man**	2
09 July	**Sunday Bloody Sunday**	2
23 July	**Le Mans**	1
30 July	**The Devils**	8
24 September	**Carnal Knowledge**	2
08 October	**The Go-Between**	3
29 October	**Bedknobs and Broomsticks**	4
27 November	**Traffic**	1
04 December	**Straw Dogs**	1
11 December	**Nicholas and Alexandra**	2
25 December	**Fiddler on the Roof**	1

1972

01 January	**Nicholas and Alexandra**	1
08 January	**Diamonds Are Forever**	10
18 March	**The French Connection**	1
25 March	**Diamonds Are Forever**	2
08 April	**Mary, Queen of Scots**	5
13 May	**A Clockwork Orange**	1
20 May	**The Hospital**	2
03 June	**Frenzy**	1
10 June	**Cabaret**	5
15 July	**What's Up Doc?**	2
29 July	**Young Winston**	5
02 September	**The Godfather**	13
02 December	**Lady Caroline Lamb**	3
23 December	**Alice's Adventures in Wonderland**	2

1973

06 January	**Alice's Adventures in Wonderland**	1
13 January	**Lady Caroline Lamb**	1
20 January	**The Valachi Papers**	2
03 February	**The Getaway**	5
10 March	**Travels with my Aunt**	2
24 March	**Last Tango in Paris**	8
19 May	**Hitler – The Last Ten Days**	1
26 May	**Last Tango in Paris**	2
09 June	**A Touch of Class**	1
16 June	**Last Tango in Paris**	1
23 June	**Day of the Jackal**	3

14 July	**Live and Let Die**	10
22 September	**Scorpio**	4
20 October	**Don't Look Now**	7
08 December	**Paper Moon**	2
22 December	**Magnum Force**	1
29 December	**Robin Hood**	1

1974

05 January	**Robin Hood**	1
12 January	**The Sting**	1
19 January	**Enter the Dragon**	2

ENTER THE DRAGON (1974)

02 February	**The Sting**	2
16 February	**The Way We Were**	1
23 February	**The Sting**	2
09 March	**The Way We Were**	2
23 March	**The Exorcist**	9
25 May	**Great Gatsby**	8
20 July	**The Exorcist**	2
03 August	**For Pete's Sake**	2
17 August	**Chinatown**	4
14 September	**Gold**	2
28 September	**Thunderbolt and Lightfoot**	1
05 October	**Gold**	2

12 October	**Emmanuelle**	2
26 October	**The Odessa File**	4
23 November	**Emmanuelle**	1
30 November	**Murder on the Orient Express**	1
07 December	**Earthquake**	3
28 December	**The Man with the Golden Gun**	1

1975

04 January	**The Man with the Golden Gun**	5
08 February	**The Towering Inferno**	7
29 March	**Funny Lady**	1
05 April	**Tommy**	7
24 May	**The Godfather, Part II**	5
28 June	**Tommy**	5
02 August	**French Connection II**	1
09 August	**Tommy**	2
23 August	**The Drowning Pool**	1
30 August	**The Eiger Sanction**	2
13 September	**Rollerball**	3
04 October	**Three Days of the Condor**	4
01 November	**Jungle Book**	3
22 November	**Lisztomania**	2
06 December	**Lenny**	2
20 December	**Barry Lyndon**	2

1976

03 January	**Jaws**	9
06 March	**One Flew Over the Cuckoo's Nest**	7
24 April	**Shout at the Devil**	1
01 May	**One Flew Over the Cuckoo's Nest**	1
08 May	**All the President's Men**	10
17 July	**The Missouri Breaks**	2
31 July	**Bugsy Malone**	1
07 August	**The Message**	1
14 August	**The Outlaw Josey Wales**	2
28 August	**Family Plot**	1
04 September	**Murder By Death**	2
18 September	**Drum**	1
25 September	**The Omen**	6
06 November	**Return of a Man Called Horse**	1
13 November	**Emmanuelle 2**	6
25 December	**The Pink Panther Strikes Again**	1

1977

01 January	**The Pink Panther Strikes Again**	5
05 February	**Silent Movie**	1
12 February	**The Pink Panther Strikes Again**	1
19 February	**Cross of Iron**	1
26 February	**Network**	1
05 March	**The Last Tycoon**	1
12 March	**The Pink Panther Strikes Again**	3
02 April	**A Star is Born**	1
09 April	**The Eagle Has Landed**	1
16 April	**Airport '77**	2
30 April	**Rocky**	3
21 May	**A Star is Born**	6
02 July	**A Bridge Too Far**	2
16 July	**The Spy Who Loved Me**	10
24 September	**Exorcist II: The Heretic**	1
01 October	**New York, New York**	2
15 October	**Valentino**	2
29 October	**The Spy Who Loved Me**	3
19 November	**Salon Kitty**	2
03 December	**The Spy Who Loved Me**	1
10 December	**Golden Rendezvous**	2
24 December	**The Deep**	2

1978

07 January	**Star Wars**	11
25 March	**Close Encounters of the Third Kind**	15

CLOSE ENCOUNTERS OF THE THIRD KIND (1978)

08 July	**Game of Death**	1
15 July	**Close Encounters of the Third Kind**	1
22 July	**Revenge of the Pink Panther**	8
16 September	**Heaven Can Wait**	1
23 September	**Grease**	6
04 November	**Death on the Nile**	6
16 December	**Force 10 from Navarone**	1
23 December	**Superman**	2

1979

06 January	**Superman**	9
10 March	**The Deer Hunter**	3
31 March	**California Suite**	3
21 April	**Battlestar Galactica**	1
28 April	**California Suite**	2
12 May	**The Deer Hunter**	1
19 May	**The Warriors**	2
02 June	**Escape to Athena**	1
09 June	**The Lady Vanishes**	1
16 June	**The World is Full of Married Men**	1
23 June	**Doctor Zhivago**	1
30 June	**Players**	1
07 July	**Moonraker**	10
15 September	**Alien**	8
10 November	**Yanks**	1
17 November	**Monty Python's Life of Brian**	6
29 December	**Star Trek – The Motion Picture**	1

1980

05 January	**Star Trek – The Motion Picture**	1
12 January	**Apocalypse Now**	1
19 January	**Monty Python's Life of Brian**	2
02 February	**Escape from Alcatraz**	2
16 February	**10**	5
22 March	**The Electric Horseman**	1
29 March	**Kramer vs. Kramer**	7
17 May	**American Gigolo**	2
31 May	**The Empire Strikes Back**	11
16 August	**Airplane!**	4
13 September	**McVicar**	1
20 September	**Cruising**	2
04 October	**Dressed to Kill**	1

11 October	**The Shining**	2
25 October	**The Elephant Man**	2
08 November	**Caligula**	6
20 December	**Flash Gordon**	2

1981

03 January	**Flash Gordon**	4
31 January	**The Exterminator**	1
07 February	**The Jazz Singer**	3
28 February	**Raging Bull**	1
07 March	**Private Benjamin**	2
21 March	**Ordinary People**	2
04 April	**Stir Crazy**	1
11 April	**Ordinary People**	1
18 April	**Superman II**	4
16 May	**The Postman Always Rings Twice**	2
30 May	**Tess**	2
13 June	**The Postman Always Rings Twice**	2

THE POSTMAN ALWAYS RINGS TWICE (1981)

27 June	**Friday the 13th Part 2**	1
04 July	**For Your Eyes Only**	10
12 September	**Raiders of the Lost Ark**	2
26 September	**The Final Conflict**	1

03 October	**Raiders of the Lost Ark**	2
17 October	**History of the World Part 1**	2
31 October	**The French Lieutenant's Woman**	7
19 December	**Gallipoli**	1
26 December	**Arthur**	1

1982

02 January	**Arthur**	7
20 February	**Death Wish 2**	2
06 March	**Reds**	1
13 March	**Mad Max 2**	1
20 March	**Reds**	2
03 April	**Evil Under the Sun**	2
17 April	**Quest for Fire**	2
01 May	**The Border**	1
08 May	**Private Lessons**	2
22 May	**The Empire Strikes Back/Star Wars**	3
12 June	**Missing**	5
17 July	**Porky's**	1
24 July	**Pink Floyd The Wall**	1
31 July	**Rocky III**	1
07 August	**Pink Floyd The Wall**	4
04 September	**Conan the Barbarian**	1
11 September	**Who Dares Wins**	1
18 September	**Blade Runner**	1
25 September	**Poltergeist**	2
09 October	**Cat People**	1
16 October	**The Entity**	2
30 October	**Tron**	6
11 December	**Gandhi**	1
18 December	**E.T. – The Extra-Terrestrial**	2

1983

01 January	**E.T. – The Extra-Terrestrial**	4
29 January	**Airplane II – The Sequel**	1
05 February	**Gandhi**	2
19 February	**An Officer and a Gentleman**	1
26 February	**Gandhi**	8
23 April	**Sophie's Choice**	2
07 May	**Tootsie**	5
11 June	**Return of the Jedi**	5
16 July	**Octopussy**	1

23 July	**Return of the Jedi**	1
30 July	**Superman III**	1
06 August	**Octopussy**	3
27 August	**War Games**	5
01 October	**Staying Alive**	2
15 October	**Zelig**	2
29 October	**The Jungle Book/Mickey's Christmas Card**	7
17 December	**Trading Places**	1
24 December	**Never Say Never Again**	2

1984

07 January	**Never Say Never Again**	2
21 January	**Trading Places**	1
28 January	**Gorky Park**	1
04 February	**Sudden Impact**	1
11 February	**Scarface**	3
03 March	**To Be or Not to Be**	3
24 March	**Terms of Endearment**	4
21 April	**Greystoke: The Legend of Tarzan, Lord of the Apes**	4
19 May	**Against All Odds**	3
09 June	**Breakdance**	1
16 June	**Another Country**	1
23 June	**Indiana Jones and the Temple of Doom**	9
25 August	**Romancing the Stone**	4
22 September	**Paris, Texas**	1
29 September	**The Company of Wolves**	3
20 October	**The Woman in Red**	5
24 November	**1984**	2
08 December	**Give My Regards to Broad Street**	1
15 December	**Ghostbusters**	3

1985

05 January	**Ghostbusters**	3
26 January	**Water**	1
02 February	**Beverly Hills Cop**	5
09 March	**Dance with a Stranger**	1
16 March	**2010**	4
13 April	**A Passage to India**	5
18 May	**The Cotton Club**	2
01 June	**Witness**	3
22 June	**A View to a Kill**	11
07 September	**Rambo: First Blood Part II**	1

14 September	**Desperately Seeking Susan**	3
05 October	**Fletch**	1
12 October	**Pale Rider**	1

PALE RIDER (1985)

19 October	**Life Force**	1
26 October	**Mad Max Beyond Thunderdome**	2
09 November	**The Emerald Forest**	2
23 November	**Prizzi's Honor**	2
07 December	**Santa Claus**	1
14 December	**Back to the Future**	3

1986

04 January	**Back to the Future**	2
18 January	**A Chorus Line**	2
01 February	**Rocky IV**	5
01 March	**Commando**	2
15 March	**Out of Africa**	5
19 April	**Absolute Beginners**	2
03 May	**Out of Africa**	1
10 May	**The Jewel of the Nile**	3
31 May	**Down and Out in Beverly Hills**	1
07 June	**After Hours**	1
14 June	**A Room with a View**	5
19 July	**Police Academy III: Back in Training**	1
26 July	**Hannah and Her Sisters**	2

09 August	**Cobra**	1
16 August	**Hannah and Her Sisters**	3
06 September	**Aliens**	5
11 October	**Top Gun**	2

TOP GUN (1986)

25 October	**Mona Lisa**	1
01 November	**The Mission**	2
15 November	**Ruthless People**	2
29 November	**The Mission**	1
06 December	**Top Gun**	1
13 December	**Labyrinth**	1
20 December	**Crocodile Dundee**	2

1987

03 January	**Crocodile Dundee**	7
21 February	**The Fly**	3
14 March	**The Color of Money**	3
04 April	**The Fourth Protocol**	1
11 April	**Personal Services**	1
18 April	**The Voyage Home: Star Trek IV**	2
02 May	**Platoon**	6
13 June	**The Morning After**	3
04 July	**The Secret of My Success**	1

11 July	**The Living Daylights**	8
05 September	**Lethal Weapon**	1
12 September	**The Living Daylights**	1
19 September	**Full Metal Jacket**	1
26 September	**The Untouchables**	4
24 October	**Beverly Hills Cop II**	1
31 October	**The Witches of Eastwick**	5
05 December	**Cry Freedom**	4

1988

02 January	**Cry Freedom**	1
09 January	**Predator**	2
23 January	**Fatal Attraction**	3
13 February	**Robocop**	2
27 February	**Fatal Attraction**	1
05 March	**The Last Emperor**	5
09 April	**Three Men and a Baby**	4
07 May	**Wall Street**	8
02 July	**Crocodile Dundee II**	5
06 August	**Coming to America**	4
03 September	**Rambo III**	1
10 September	**Coming to America**	1
17 September	**Big Business**	1
24 September	**Buster**	2
08 October	**Good Morning Vietnam**	2
22 October	**A Fish Called Wanda**	7
10 December	**Who Framed Roger Rabbit?**	4

1989

07 January	**Who Framed Roger Rabbit?**	2
21 January	**Red Heat**	1
28 January	**Cocktail**	2
11 February	**Die Hard**	1
18 February	**Naked Gun From the Files of Police Squad**	3
11 March	**Scandal**	1
18 March	**Rain Man**	4
15 April	**Working Girl**	3
06 May	**My Stepmother is an Alien**	1
13 May	**Nightmare on Elm Street 4: The Dream Master**	1
20 May	**Mississippi Burning**	4
17 June	**Beaches**	1
24 June	**Licence to Kill (License to Kill in US)**	2

08 July	**Indiana Jones and the Last Crusade**	4
05 August	**Licence to Kill**	2
19 August	**Batman**	5
23 September	**Lethal Weapon 2**	2
07 October	**Dead Poets Society**	3
28 October	**Shirley Valentine**	5
02 December	**Back to the Future Part II**	3
23 December	**When Harry Met Sally**	2

1990

06 January	**When Harry Met Sally**	4
03 February	**Black Rain**	2
17 February	**Family Business**	1
24 February	**Sea of Love**	2
10 March	**Born on the Fourth of July**	1
17 March	**The War of the Roses**	4
14 April	**Look Who's Talking**	2
28 April	**The Hunt for Red October**	1
05 May	**The Krays**	2
19 May	**Pretty Woman**	8
14 July	**Dick Tracy**	1
21 July	**Back to the Future Part III**	1
28 July	**Dick Tracy**	1
04 August	**Total Recall**	3
25 August	**Die Hard 2: Die Harder**	3
15 September	**Memphis Belle**	3
29 September	**Another 48 Hrs**	1
06 October	**Presumed Innocent**	1
13 October	**Ghost**	8
08 December	**Teenage Mutant Ninja Turtles**	1
15 December	**Home Alone**	3

1991

03 January	**Home Alone**	1
11 January	**Arachnophobia**	1
18 January	**Cyrano de Bergerac**	2
01 February	**Rocky V**	1
08 February	**Kindergarten Cop**	1
15 February	**Three Men and a Little Lady**	3
08 March	**Green Card**	1
15 March	**The Godfather, Part III**	1
22 March	**Green Card**	1

29 March	**Dances With Wolves**	3
19 April	**Highlander II: The Quickening**	1
26 April	**Sleeping with the Enemy**	3
17 May	**Misery**	3
07 June	**The Silence of the Lambs**	4
05 July	**Naked Gun 2½: The Smell of Fear**	2
19 July	**Thelma and Louise**	1
26 July	**Robin Hood: Prince of Thieves**	2
09 August	**Backdraft**	2
23 August	**Terminator 2: Judgment Day**	7
11 October	**The Commitments**	3
01 November	**Dead Again**	1
08 November	**City Slickers**	1
15 November	**The Fisher King**	3
06 December	**Hot Shots!**	2
20 December	**The Addams Family**	2

1992

03 January	**The Addams Family**	2
17 January	**Delicatessen**	1
24 January	**Frankie and Johnny**	1
31 January	**JFK**	3
21 February	**Star Trek VI: The Undiscovered Country**	1
28 February	**Father of the Bride**	1
06 March	**The Prince of Tides**	1
13 March	**Cape Fear**	3
03 April	**Bugsy**	2
17 April	**Hook**	2
01 May	**The Hand that Rocks the Cradle**	2
15 May	**Basic Instinct**	4
12 June	**The Lawnmower Man**	1
19 June	**Basic Instinct**	1
26 June	**The Lover**	1
03 July	**The Player**	2
17 July	**Batman Returns**	3
07 August	**Universal Soldier**	1
14 August	**Far and Away**	1
21 August	**Lethal Weapon 3**	1
28 August	**Alien 3**	3
18 September	**Bob Roberts**	1
25 September	**Unforgiven**	1
02 October	**Patriot Games**	3

23 October	**Beauty and the Beast**	1
30 October	**1492: Conquest of Paradise**	1
06 November	**Strictly Ballroom**	1
13 November	**Last of the Mohicans**	1
20 November	**Peter's Friends**	1
27 November	**Sister Act**	2
11 December	**Death Becomes Her**	1
18 December	**Home Alone 2: Lost in New York**	2

1993

01 January	**The Bodyguard**	1
08 January	**A Few Good Men**	1
15 January	**Reservoir Dogs**	2
29 January	**A Few Good Men**	1
05 February	**Bram Stoker's Dracula**	4
05 March	**Under Siege**	1
12 March	**Malcolm X**	1
19 March	**Scent of a Woman**	1
26 March	**Orlando**	1
02 April	**The Distinguished Gentleman**	1
09 April	**Scent of a Woman**	1
16 April	**The Jungle Book**	1
23 April	**Accidental Hero**	1
30 April	**Sommersby**	2
14 May	**Groundhog Day**	1
21 May	**Indecent Proposal**	3
11 June	**Falling Down**	3
02 July	**Cliffhanger**	3
23 July	**Jurassic Park**	6
03 September	**In the Line of Fire**	2
17 September	**The Firm**	2
01 October	**The Fugitive**	5
05 November	**The Piano**	2
19 November	**Demolition Man**	1
26 November	**Aladdin**	6

1994

07 January	**Aladdin**	1
14 January	**Malice**	2
28 January	**Manhattan Murder Mystery**	1
04 February	**Mrs Doubtfire**	3
25 February	**Schindler's List**	2

11 March	Philadelphia	3
01 April	Schindler's List	5
06 May	Ace Ventura: Pet Detective	1
13 May	The Paper	1
20 May	Four Weddings and a Funeral	9
22 July	Maverick	1
29 July	The Flintstones	2
12 August	Sirens	1
19 August	True Lies	1
26 August	The Mask	1
02 September	Wolf	1
09 September	The Mask	1
16 September	True Lies	1
23 September	Clear and Present Danger	2
07 October	Speed	1
14 October	Forrest Gump	1
21 October	The Lion King	2
04 November	Pulp Fiction	1
11 November	Mary Shelley's Frankenstein	2
25 November	Pulp Fiction	3
16 December	Junior	2
30 December	The Specialist	1

1995

06 January	Stargate	2
20 January	Interview with the Vampire	3
10 February	Star Trek: Generations	2
24 February	Natural Born Killers	2
10 March	Disclosure	4
07 April	Dumb and Dumber	3
28 April	Legends of the Fall	2
12 May	Muriel's Wedding	1
19 May	Street Fighter	1
26 May	Rob Roy	1
02 June	Richie Rich	1
09 June	The Brady Bunch Movie	1
16 June	Bad Boys	2
30 June	Congo	1
07 July	First Knight	1
14 July	Batman Forever	2
28 July	Casper	2
11 August	Waterworld	1

18 August	**Die Hard with a Vengeance**	2
01 September	**While You Were Sleeping**	1
08 September	**Braveheart**	2
22 September	**Apollo 13**	3
13 October	**Pocahontas**	3
03 November	**French Kiss**	1
10 November	**Crimson Tide**	2
24 November	**GoldenEye**	3
15 December	**Babe**	3

1996

05 January	**Seven**	4
02 February	**Heat**	2
16 February	**Jumanji**	3
08 March	**Trainspotting**	1
15 March	**Get Shorty**	1
22 March	**Toy Story**	4

TOY STORY (1996)

19 April	**12 Monkeys**	2
03 May	**The Birdcage**	1
10 May	**Executive Decision**	2
24 May	**Spy Hard**	1
31 May	**From Dusk Till Dawn**	1
07 June	**Up Close and Personal**	2
21 June	**The Rock**	2
05 July	**Mission: Impossible**	3
26 July	**Twister**	2
09 August	**Independence Day**	7
27 September	**Last Man Standing**	1
04 October	**The Nutty Professor**	3
25 October	**Dragonheart**	2
08 November	**Michael Collins**	1
15 November	**The First Wives Club**	2
29 November	**The Long Kiss Goodnight**	1
06 December	**Jingle All the Way**	1
13 December	**101 Dalmatians**	3

1997

03 January	**Evita**	5
07 February	**Ransom**	3
28 February	**Mars Attacks!**	1
07 March	**Jerry Maguire**	2
21 March	**Star Wars (re-issue)**	3
11 April	**The Empire Strikes Back (re-issue)**	2
25 April	**Return of the Jedi**	1
02 May	**Liar Liar**	4
30 May	**Absolute Power**	1
06 June	**Con Air**	1
13 June	**The Fifth Element**	2
27 June	**Batman and Robin**	3
18 July	**The Lost World: Jurassic Park**	2
01 August	**Men in Black**	5
05 September	**The Full Monty**	9
07 November	**Face/Off**	1
14 November	**The Full Monty**	2
28 November	**Alien Resurrection**	2
12 December	**Tomorrow Never Dies**	2
26 December	**Spiceworld: The Movie**	1

1998

02 January	**Starship Troopers**	1
09 January	**The Jackal**	1
16 January	**Devil's Advocate**	1
23 January	**Titanic**	13
24 April	**US Marshals**	1
01 May	**Scream 2**	2
15 May	**Deep Impact**	3
05 June	**The Wedding Singer**	2
19 June	**City of Angels**	2
03 July	**Six Days, Seven Nights**	2
17 July	**Godzilla**	2
31 July	**Lost in Space**	1
07 August	**Armageddon**	2
21 August	**The X Files**	2
04 September	**Lock, Stock & Two Smoking Barrels**	1
11 September	**Saving Private Ryan**	2
25 September	**There's Something About Mary**	2
09 October	**The Truman Show**	2
23 October	**Small Soldiers**	1
06 November	**Antz**	4
04 December	**Rush Hour**	2
18 December	**The Mask of Zorro**	1
25 December	**Enemy of the State**	1

1999

01 January	**Star Trek: Insurrection**	2
15 January	**Meet Joe Black**	1
22 January	**Practical Magic**	1
29 January	**Shakespeare in Love**	1
05 February	**A Bug's Life**	5
12 March	**Patch Adams**	1
19 March	**Waking Ned**	1
26 March	**The Rugrats Movie**	3
16 April	**The Faculty**	1
23 April	**8MM**	1
30 April	**The Waterboy**	1
07 May	**I Still Know What You Did ...**	1
14 May	**Forces of Nature**	1
21 May	**She's All That**	1

All in a Day's Work!

It's no easy life being a movie star, just look at the mere pittance they get in their pay packets. How could any 'normal' superstar be expected to live on these salaries?

★ **Marlon Brando**
Superman (1978)
$4,000,000 (10 mins. screentime)

★ **Nicolas Cage**
Gone in 60 Seconds (2000 – expected)
$20,000,000
Snake Eyes (1998) $16,000,000
Face/Off (1997) $6,000,000

★ **Jim Carrey**
The Truman Show (1998) $12,000,000
The Cable Guy (1996) $20,000,000
Batman Forever (1995) $5,000,000
Mask (1994) $540,000

★ **George Clooney**
Out of Sight (1998) $10,000,000
Batman and Robin (1997) $10,000,000

★ **Sean Connery**
Robin Hood: Prince of Thieves (1991) $250,000

★ **Tom Cruise**
Mission: Impossible (1996) $20,000,000
Interview with the Vampire (1994) $15,000,000

★ **Macaulay Culkin**
Home Alone 2: Lost in New York (1992)
$5,000,000
Home Alone (1990) $100,000

★ **Matt Damon**
Rounders (1998) $600,000

★ **Robert De Niro**
Analyze This (1999) $8,000,000
Ronin (1998) $14,000,000

★ **Leonardo DiCaprio**
The Beach (1999) $20,000,000
Titanic (1997) $2,500,000
The Basketball Diaries (1995) $1,000,000

★ **David Duchovny**
The X Files (1998) $6,000,000

★ **Clint Eastwood**
A Fistful of Dollars (1964) $15,000

★ **Harrison Ford**
Air Force One (1997) $22,000,000

★ **Mel Gibson**
Lethal Weapon 4 (1998) $40,000,000
Conspiracy Theory (1997) $20,000,000
Mad Max (1979) $15,000 (Australian)

★ **Hugh Grant**
Notting Hill (1999) $1,000,000

★ **Tommy Lee Jones**
U.S. Marshals (1998) $10,000,000

★ **Val Kilmer**
At First Sight (1999) $9,000,000
Batman Forever (1995) $7,000,000

★ **Steve McQueen**
The Sand Pebbles (1966) $650,000
The Blob (1958) $3,000
Somebody Up There Likes Me (1956)
$50 per day

★ **Eddie Murphy**
The Nutty Professor II (2000) $20,000,000
Doctor Dolittle (1998) $17,000,000

★ **Mike Myers**
Austin Powers: The Spy Who Shagged Me
(1999) $7,000,000

★ **Jack Nicholson**
Batman (1989) $50,000,000

★ **Gary Oldman**
Lost in Space (1998) $4,000,000

★ **Brad Pitt**
Meet Joe Black (1998) $17,500,000

★ **Keanu Reeves**
The Devil's Advocate (1997) $8,000,000

★ Kurt Russell
Soldier (1998) $20,000,000
Stargate (1994) $7,000,000

★ Arnold Schwarzenegger
End of Days (1999) $25,000,000
Batman and Robin (1997) $25,000,000
Twins (1988) $35,000,000

★ Frank Sinatra
From Here to Eternity (1953) $8,000

★ Will Smith
Enemy of the State (1998) $14,000,000

★ Sylvester Stallone
Into Thin Air (1999) $20,000,000
Copland (1997) $60,000
Rambo 3 (1988) Gulfstream Jet (valued at $12,000,000)
Rocky (1976) $23,000

★ Patrick Stewart
Star Trek: Insurrection (1998) $9,500,000
Star Trek: First Contact (1996) $5,000,000

★ John Travolta
Face/Off (1997) $15,000,000
Pulp Fiction (1994) $140,000

★ Bruce Willis
Armageddon (1998) $14,800,000
Die Hard (1988) $5,000,000

★ Gillian Anderson
The X Files (1998) $3,000,000

★ Jennifer Aniston
Picture Perfect (1997) $2,000,000

★ Drew Barrymore
Ever After (1998) $3,000,000
Scream (1996) $500,000

★ Sandra Bullock
Hope Floats (1998) $11,000,000
Speed 2: Cruise Control (1997) $12,500,500
Speed (1994) $500,000

★ Jodie Foster
Anna (1999) $15,000,000
Contact (1997) $9,000,000

★ Sarah Michelle Gellar
Cruel Intentions (1999) $500,000

★ Elizabeth Hurley
Austin Powers: The Spy Who Shagged Me (1999) $3,000,000

★ Jennifer Lopez
Out of Sight (1998) $2,000,000

★ Demi Moore
G.I. Jane (1997) $11,000,000
Striptease (1996) $12,500,000

★ Julia Roberts
Notting Hill (1999) $15,000,000
Stepmom (1998) $17,000,000

★ Meg Ryan
You've Got Mail (1998) $10,500,000
City of Angels (1998) $8,500,000

★ Alicia Silverstone
Excess Baggage (1997) $3,300,000

★ Sharon Stone
Diabolique (1996) $6,000,000
Basic Instinct (1992) $750,000

★ Elizabeth Taylor
Cleopatra (1963) $1,000,000

★ Sigourney Weaver
Alien Resurrection (1997) $11,000,000
Alien (1979) $30,000

Chapter 2
The Family Way

DAYS OF THUNDER (1990)

40 Stars Who Got Married After Meeting On Set

1. **Lew Ayres** and **Ginger Rogers** –
Don't Bet on Love (1933)

2. **Alec Baldwin** and **Kim Basinger** –
The Marrying Man (1991)

3. **Ellen Barkin** and **Gabriel Byrne** –
Siesta (1987)

4. **Warren Beatty** and **Annette Bening** –
Bugsy (1991)

5. **Luc Besson** (director) and **Milla Jovovich** –
The Fifth Element (1997)

6. **Humphrey Bogart** and **Lauren Bacall** –
To Have and Have Not (1944)

7. **Ernest Borgnine** and **Katy Jurado** –
The Badlanders (1958)

8. **Richard Burton** and **Elizabeth Taylor** –
Cleopatra (1963)

9. **James Cameron** (director) and **Linda Hamilton** – *Terminator 2: Judgment Day* (1991)

10. **Tom Cruise** and **Nicole Kidman** –
Days of Thunder (1990)

11. **Tony Curtis** and **Christine Kauffman** –
Taras Bulba (1962)

12. **Brian De Palma** (director) and
Nancy Allen – *Carrie* (1976)

13. **Howard Deutch** (director) and **Lea Thompson** – *Some Kind of Wonderful* (1987)

14. **Howard Duff** and **Ida Lupino** –
Women in Hiding (1950)

15. **Blake Edwards** (director) and
Julie Andrews – *Darling Lili* (1970)

16. **Errol Flynn** and **Patricia Wymore** –
Rocky Mountain (1950)

17. **Jeff Goldblum** and **Geena Davis** –
The Fly (1986)

18. **Stewart Granger** and **Jean Simmons** –
Adam and Evelyn (1949)

19. **Cary Grant** and **Betsy Drake** –
Every Girl Should Be Married (1948)

20. **Tom Hanks** and **Rita Wilson** –
Volunteers (1985)

21. **Danny Huston** (director) and
Virginia Madsen – *Mr. North* (1988)

22. **Harry James** and **Betty Grable** –
Springtime in the Rockies (1942)

23. **Stanley Kubrick** (director) and
Christiane Harlan – *Paths of Glory* (1957)

24. **Lyle Lovett** and **Julia Roberts** –
The Player (1992)

25. **Tony Martin** and **Cyd Charisse** –
Till the Clouds Roll By (1946)

26. **Malcolm McDowell** and
Mary Steenburgen – *Time After Time* (1979)

27. Vincente Minnelli and **Judy Garland** – *The Clock* (1945)

28. Pat O'Connor (director) and **Mary Elizabeth Mastrantonio** – *The January Man* (1989)

29. Laurence Olivier and **Vivien Leigh** – *Fire Over England* (1937)

30. George Peppard and **Elizabeth Ashley** – *The Carpetbaggers* (1964)

31. Dennis Quaid and **Meg Ryan** – *Innerspace* (1987)

32. Ronald Reagan and **Jane Wyman** – *Brother Rat* (1938)

33. Nicolas Roeg (director) and **Theresa Russell** – *Bad Timing: A Sensual Obsession* (1980)

34. Roy Rogers and **Dale Evans** – *The Cowboy and the Senorita* (1944)

35. Roberto Rossellini (director) and **Ingrid Bergman** – *Stromboli* (1949)

36. Ron Shelton (director) and **Lolita Davidovich** – *Blaze* (1989)

37. Steven Spielberg (director) and **Kate Capshaw** – *Indiana Jones and the Temple of Doom* (1984)

38. Robert Taylor and **Barbara Stanwyck** – *His Brother's Wife* (1936)

39. James Threapleton and **Kate Winslet** – *Hideous Kinky* (1998)

40. Franchot Tone and **Joan Crawford** – *Today We Live* (1933)

It's Not What You Know: It's Who You Know

Keeping it in the family x 20

1. Sean Penn
Son of the director Leo Penn; brother of Christopher Penn

2. Carrie Fisher
Daughter of Debbie Reynolds and the singer Eddie Fisher

3. Nicolas Cage
Nephew of the director Francis Ford Coppola

4. Matt Dillon
Great-nephew of the cartoonist Alex Raymond, who created the comic strips 'Flash Gordon' and 'Jungle Jim'

5. Emilio Estevez
Son of Martin Sheen and brother of Charlie Sheen

6. Warren Beatty
Brother of Shirley MacLaine

7. Jamie Lee Curtis
Daughter of Tony Curtis and the star of Hitchcock's *Psycho*, Janet Leigh

8. Sigourney Weaver
Niece of the character actor Doodles Weaver

9. Alan Alda
Son of Robert Alda

10. Rosanna Arquette

Daughter of the actor Lewis Arquette, granddaughter of the comedian Cliff 'Charley Weaver' Arquette, sister of Patricia, Alexis and David Arquette (also actors)

11. Isabella Rossellini

Daughter of Ingrid Bergman and the Italian film director Roberto Rossellini

12. Jeff Bridges

Son of Lloyd Bridges, younger brother of Beau Bridges. All three starred in *The Thanksgiving Promise* (1986); Beau also directed

13. David Carradine

Son of John Carradine, stepbrother of Keith and Robert Carradine

14. Liza Minnelli

Daughter of Judy Garland and Vincente Minnelli

15. Bridget Fonda

Daughter of Peter Fonda, niece of Jane Fonda and granddaughter of Henry Fonda

16. Melanie Griffith

Daughter of Tippi Hedren and Peter Griffith

17. Jennifer Jason Leigh

Daughter of Vic Morrow and Barbara Turner

18. Maureen Reagan

Daughter of Ronald Reagan and Jane Wyman

19. Julia Roberts

Sister of Eric Roberts

20. Laura Dern

Daughter of Diane Ladd and Bruce Dern

Marriages / Celebrity Pairings x25

1. Woody Allen

1955 married a schoolteacher, Harlene Rosson; divorced 1960.

1966 (2 February) married a co-star of several films, Louise Lasser, divorced 1971.

Subsequently involved with another co-star, Mia Farrow, by whom he has children. Relationship came to an end in 1992 when, while involved in a custody battle for his and Farrow's three children, it was revealed that Allen was having an affair with Soon-Yi Previn, the adopted daughter of Farrow from her marriage to the composer André Previn.

2. Ursula Andress

1957 married the actor-director John Derek (the late husband of Bo Derek); they divorced in 1966.

3. Julie Andrews

1959 married the scenic director Tony Walton; Andrews filed for divorce on the grounds of mental cruelty in 1967.

1969 married the director-producer Blake Edwards.

4. Jean Arthur

1928 married the photographer Julian Anker: the marriage lasted for one day; it was annulled after Arthur stated that, contrary to her knowledge, her studio contract did not permit her to marry.

5. Lauren Bacall

1945 (21 May) married Humphrey Bogart (met while both were filming *To Have and*

Have Not); following Bogart's death from cancer in 1957 she married the actor Jason Robards Jr in 1961.

6. Brigitte Bardot

1952 married the director Roger Vadim (who directed Bardot in *And God Created Women*, 1956) at the age of 18. Divorced 1957. Vadim later married Jane Fonda.

7. Patricia Arquette

Married to Nicolas Cage.

8. Ellen Barkin

1988 married Gabriel Byrne, her co-star in *Sea of Love*

9. Kim Basinger

1980 married Ron Britton, a make-up man and painter; he filed for divorce in 1988. Basinger has since married the actor Alec Baldwin.

10. Ingrid Bergman

1937 married a dentist, Dr Petter Aron Lindstrom.

1949 she left her husband and daughter for the Italian film director Roberto Rossellini, whom she married in 1950. Marriage annulled in 1958; wed her third husband, the Swedish producer Lars Schmidt, in 1958.

11. Kenneth Branagh

1989 married Emma Thompson; subsequently divorced.

12. Richard Burton

1949 married Sybil Williams.

1964 married Elizabeth Taylor; they had both starred in *Cleopatra* (1963), during which time they had fallen in love. Sybil Williams divorced Burton in February of 1963.

13. Michael Caine

1955 married the actress Patricia Haines; 1957 following the birth of their daughter, the couple were divorced.

1973 married the actress Shakira Baksh, the Miss Guyana of 1967.

14. Phoebe Cates

1989 married the actor Kevin Kline.

CHER – MERMAIDS (1990)

15. Cher

1969 married the singer Sonny Bono; divorced 1975, 27 June.

1975 married the singer Gregg Allman on 30 June, only three days later. Since divorced.

16. Tom Cruise

1987, 9 May, married the actress Mimi Rogers; divorced 1990.

1990, 24 December, married the Australian actress Nicole Kidman.

17. Geena Davis

1981 married Richard Emmolo; divorced after eighteen months.

1987, 1 November, married the actor Jeff Goldblum; divorced in October 1990 as a result of irreconcilable differences.

18. Catherine Deneuve

1965, 18 August, married the photographer David Bailey; divorced 1970. Deneuve also has a son, Christian, born in 1963, by the French film director and former husband of Bardot, Roger Vadim.

19. Danny DeVito

1982, 8 January, married his long-time lover, the Cheers star Rhea Perlman; they had lived together since 1970.

20. Angie Dickinson

1952 the future star of Police Woman (1974–8) married a college football player, Gene Dickinson; divorced in 1959.

1965 married the composer Burt Bacharach; divorced 1981.

21. Faye Dunaway

1974, 7 August, married the rock singer Peter Wolf, of the J Geils Band; divorced 1977.

22. Mia Farrow

1966, 19 July, married Frank Sinatra at the age of nineteen; divorced 1968, 16 August.

1970, 11 September, married the composer and conductor André Previn; divorced 1979, 31 January.

Subsequently entered into a relationship with Woody Allen, which came to an end in 1992 (see above).

23. Farrah Fawcett

1973, 28 July, married the 'Bionic Man', Lee Majors; divorced 1982, 12 February.

1988, 18 June, married Ryan O'Neal.

24. Carrie Fisher

1983, August, married the rock singer Paul Simon; divorced in 1984.

25. Tatum O'Neal

1986 married the vitriolic tennis professional and Wimbledon champ John McEnroe; subsequently divorced.

Chapter 3
Crime Story

MARILYN MONROE

Hollywood's Alternative List of Law-School Graduates

★ Tim Allen

Santa Claus Tim was arrested for driving his Ferrari while under the influence of alcohol in 1997. Allen had previously been arrested for dealing cocaine in 1978, for which he spent 28 months in jail.

★ Tom Arnold

Arrested, aged 21, for streaking with two friends.

★ Daniel Baldwin

Arrested for possession of cocaine in 1998. He had overdosed on the drug in New York's Plaza hotel and been found naked and incoherent.

★ Emmanuelle Béart

Arrested in 1997 in Paris for her involvement in demonstrations supporting black illegal immigrants: the so-called *sans papiers*.

★ Gary Busey

Domestic violence, 1999.

★ Johnny Depp

Arrested in 1994 on a criminal-mischief charge, having trashed his $1,200-a-night New York hotel room.

★ Robert Downey Jr

It would seem that this son of an underground film maker takes some roles to heart: he played a cocaine addict in *Less Than Zero*. In 1996 Downey was arrested for driving while under the influence. He was also found to be in the possession of crack cocaine, powder cocaine and heroin, as well as an unloaded but concealed .357 Magnum. Less than a month later, he was found unconscious, under the influence of a controlled substance and, worse still, he wasn't even in his own house. He'd stumbled into a stranger's house some several blocks from his own. As a result Downey was placed on probation and ordered to attend a secure rehabilitation clinic; eventually Downey decided otherwise and checked out! This time he was sentenced to 180 days in jail for parole violation.

★ Jane Fonda

Arrested in 1970 for assault and battery following a scuffle that had broken out as a result of drugs, including Dexedrine (all of which were in fact legally prescribed), found upon Fonda's person.

★ Zsa Zsa Gabor

Arrested in 1994 for battery against a police officer, disobeying an officer, driving without a licence or registration and driving with an open container of alcohol. As a result of her oversights she spent 72 hours in jail.

★ Hugh Grant

Charged with lewd exposure in 1995. *The Four Weddings and a Funeral* star was apparently investigating the finer points of oral sex on Sunset Boulevard with the soon-to-be-world-famous Divine Brown. He was fined $1,180 and given two years' probation.

★ Woody Harrelson

Arrested in 1996, having climbed the cables of San Francisco's Golden Gate Bridge, to protest at proposals to cut down a redwood forest in northern California. Harrelson, who is also a pro-hemp campaigner, apparently couldn't resist getting just that little bit higher.

★ John Heard

The *Home Alone* dad was arrested for stalking and assault in 1996; now there's a role model for children the world over!

DENNIS HOPPER & PETER FONDA – EASY RIDER (1969)

★ Dennis Hopper

Of all things, Dennis was arrested and charged with traffic (cars, nothing more) offences: namely reckless driving, failing to report an accident and leaving the scene of an accident. Hopper was arrested at home following his identification by a member of the public.

★ Nastassja Kinski

Arrested in 1998 following a violent brawl with her ex-husband.

★ Martin Lawrence

The *Bad Boys* star was arrested for misdemeanour battery in 1997.

★ Robert Mitchum

Arrested for marijuana possession in 1948; served a total of 50 days in the slammer.

★ Dudley Moore

Arrested on suspicion of domestic violence in 1994.

★ Al Pacino

Arrested for carrying a concealed weapon, a .38 calibre pistol, in 1961.

★ Sean Penn

Served 32 days in jail for hitting an extra in 1987.

★ Brad Pitt

Rumour has it that Pitt was arrested for flashing at passing drivers while awaiting filming during the making of *Cutting Class* in 1988.

★ Keanu Reeves

The star of *Speed* was arrested for drunken driving in 1993. His mugshot apparently reminded him of his father, who was serving a ten-year sentence for narcotics possession at the time.

★ Paul 'Pee-Wee Herman' Reubens

Arrested in 1991 for showing everybody his 'pee-wee' while enjoying the feature presentation in a Florida porn cinema.

★ Eric Roberts

The 'black sheep' brother of *Pretty Woman* Julia was arrested in 1987 and charged with criminal trespass, attempted assault on a police officer, and possession of marijuana and cocaine.

★ Charlie Sheen

Sheen, like so many of his contemporaries, has more than tasted excess. In 1995 he was indicted for his involvement in the trial of the Hollywood madam Heidi Fleiss. In court it was revealed that Sheen's total expenditure with Madam Fleiss and her girls had been $53,000.

'Sheesh!' he joked upon hearing this. 'It's really starting to add up!' However, the life of excess continued, so much so that in May of 1998 the star narrowly survived a drugs overdose. Concerned for his son's wellbeing, his father Martin Sheen signed a warrant for Charlie's arrest only days later. Sheen fils is now on probation until June 2000 and enrolled on a drugs-rehabilitation programme.

★ OJ Simpson

Orenthal James Simpson was arrested and charged with the murder of his ex-wife, Nicole Brown Simpson, and her friend Ronald Goldman, on the night of 12 June 1994. Following a bungled trial he was acquitted of their murder on 3 October 1995.

★ Christian Slater

The James Dean of the 90s is, we suspect, not a good friend of American law-enforcement officers. In 1989 he was arrested for drink-driving. Slater didn't give in to arrest easily, though: he first attempted to outspeed police, and, upon crashing his Saab, he proceeded to climb the fence that stood between him and freedom, pausing only to kick the arresting officer. He subsequently spent ten days in a Los Angeles jail. Slater later remarked that, had he escaped, 'I would have kept drinking and died. So fortunately for me, I didn't get away with it.' His story didn't end there, though. In 1997 Slater was arrested following a particularly hard session of drugs and alcohol. He was sentenced to 180 days in jail.

★ Mae West

Arrested and jailed for ten days in 1926, having fallen foul of the obscenity laws with a play she had written entitled *SEX*.

Five Stars Who Were Murdered

1. Dominique Dunne (4/11/59–4/11/82)

Most memorable performance as the older daughter of Craig T Nelson and Jo Beth Williams in *Poltergeist* (1982); strangled by her estranged boyfriend when she declined his request for a reconciliation.

2. Sharon Tate (24/1/43–9/8/69)

The wife of Roman Polanski was murdered along with four others by the satanic Manson Family (the followers of Charles Manson). Tate was heavily pregnant at the time of the slaying.

3. Sal Mineo (10/1/39–12/2/76)

Remembered for his role as the flick-knife-wielding teen alongside James Dean in *Rebel Without a Cause* (1955); Mineo was stabbed to death by an unknown assailant – motive unknown.

4. Ramon Novarro (6/2/1899–31/10/68)

The 1920s screen idol was murdered at the hands of a male hustler and his brother.

5. Judith Barsi (6/6/77–27/7/88)

The child star of *Jaws: The Revenge* was shot along with her mother by her father. Judith's mother had informed her husband that she wished to take Judith to Hungary to meet her relatives. It would appear he didn't approve!

Five Stars Who Died as a Result of Drink or Drugs

1. River Phoenix (24/8/70–31/10/93)

The apparently clean-living star died from a lethal cocktail of Valium, marijuana, ephedrine, cocaine and heroin; he had been partying, perhaps a little too hard, at the Viper Room club (owned by Johnny Depp) with his brother, sister and girlfriend. He was aged 23.

2. John Belushi (24/1/49–5/3/82)

The highly talented 'Blues Brother' died as a result of acute toxicity from cocaine and heroin. This combination was administered by his friend Cathy Evelyn Smith to help ease his depression. She was subsequently charged with involuntary manslaughter.

3. Peter Lawford (7/9/23–24/12/84)

'Rat-packer' Lawford died of cardiac arrest, his body destroyed by years of overindulging could simply no longer cope.

4. Bela Lugosi (20/10/1882–16/8/56)

Addicted to painkillers as the result of a leg injury received during World War One; unable to overcome his addiction, he died of a heart attack, clutching the script for his next feature: *The Final Curtain*.

5. Gail Russell (23/9/24–6/8/61)

Reputed to have been the lover of John Wayne, Russell died following a four day vodka-drinking binge. The autopsy cited liver failure due to alcohol abuse as the cause of death.

Five Mysterious Deaths

1. Bruce Lee (27/11/40–20/7/73)

The martial-arts master died several hours after taking a prescribed painkiller, given to him by an actress friend. The coroner concluded that Lee had died as the result of a reaction to aspirin contained within the painkiller. Doubt has remained, though, surrounding the cause of death, some believing it to be a family curse, others the action of the Chinese Mafia or Triads.

2. Brandon Lee (1/2/65–31/3/93)

The son of Bruce Lee died during the filming of his big break *The Crow*. He had been filming a stunt scene in which a drug dealer, played by Michael Massee, shoots Lee in the chest: as Lee's opposite number fired, the star collapsed, bleeding profusely from the right side of his abdomen: Lee had been shot with a real bullet and not a blank!

3. Marilyn Monroe (1/6/26–5/8/62)

The official verdict is that Monroe died as the result of a lethal overdose of Nembutal and chloral hydrate. However, several factors, such as the lack of a suicide note, the absence of any glass or container with which to take water with the pills and the disappearance of Monroe's diary and telephone records, would all seem to point to foul play – a belief strengthened by her friendship with President John F Kennedy and his brother Robert.

4. Natalie Wood (20/7/38–29/11/81)

The female lead of *Rebel Without a Cause* (1955), and two-times wife of Robert Wagner, died from drowning after an evening aboard the couple's 55-foot yacht, the *Splendour*, accompanied by her husband and the actor Christopher Walken. Walken was Wood's co-star in the then forthcoming *Brainstorm*,

and some would say offscreen romantic
interest. Wood had apparently retired from
the party to get a change of clothes: her body
was found some hours later, face down in
the water. What truly happened aboard the
Splendour remains a mystery.

5. **Russ Columbo** (14/1/08–2/9/34)

The star of *Broadway Thru a Keyhole* (1933)
died (reputedly) while examining his collection
of pistols with a friend, the Hollywood
portrait photographer Lansing V Brown Jr.
Brown supposedly struck a match on one
of the pistols, causing an old charge to be
expelled from it. The charge ricocheted around
the room before hitting Columbo in the left
eye and causing his subsequent death.

Chapter 4
The Road to Glory

FROM HERE TO ETERNITY (1953)

The awards listings appear in the back of the book, but you may be in the mood for a little trivia. For example, why did the statuette come to be known as Oscar? Which films have received the most Oscar nominations? Which celebrities have hosted the Academy Awards ceremony the most? What have the winners and losers had to say about the big day? Well, read on as we reveal the answers to these questions and more.

Oscar-Related Words of Wisdom from the Heroes of Hollywood

'It means a lot to me, but next year it's going to be a Trivial Pursuit question.'

★ **Meg Tilly**, speaking of her 1985 Academy Award nomination for Best Supporting Actress, *Agnes of God*.

'It's like a wedding, except you have no idea if you'll be jilted at the altar, and he's only a nine-inch groom.'

★ **Helena Bonham Carter**, on being asked about her 1998 Oscar nomination.

'I feel for eight minutes on screen I should only get a little bit of him.'

★ **Dame Judi Dench**, on her Academy-Award-winning performance in *Shakespeare in Love* (1998).

'This is all very odd. I am essentially a strolling player, not a movie star. This kind of thing mustn't happen to you very often.'

★ **Dame Judi**, talking after her success with *Shakespeare in Love* (1998).

'I've been doing this work for over half my life and I finally got it right, I guess! Some you do for money, some you do for love. This was a love child.'

★ **James Coburn** on winning his first Oscar, aged 70, for his role in *Affliction* (1998).

'It's a load of rubbish [the Oscars, not his music], but we all love it. It's good fun. I'm here to have a good time.'

★ **Rod Stewart**

'I would like to be Jupiter! And kidnap everybody and lie down in the firmament making love to everybody, because I don't know how to express. It's a question of love.'

★ **Roberto Benigni**, on winning the Best Actor Oscar for *Life is Beautiful* (1998). In so doing Benigni became only the second person in the history of the Academy Awards to win an acting award for a foreign-language film. The other was Sophia Loren at the 1961 Awards, for her performance in *Two Women* (1961).

'I've been here three times before and lost. Basically, my odds before were the same as the Jamaican bobsled team's winning.'

★ **Robin Williams**, winner of Best Supporting Actor for *Good Will Hunting* (1997).

'It was, you know, the Oscars, and it was good.'

★ **Leonardo 'the philosopher' DiCaprio**

'I owe a lot of my performance to the corset I had to wear.'

★ **Emma Thompson**, on her Oscar-winning performance, in *Howards End* (1992).

'If you think you're a great actor 'cause you won an Oscar you're crazy.'

★ **Joe Pesci**, winner of the Best Supporting Actor Oscar, for his role in *GoodFellas* (1990).

'That's part of the sickness of America, that you have to think in terms of who wins, who loses ... We always think in extreme terms. What's the point?'

★ **Marlon Brando**, having been nominated for the Best Supporting Actor Oscar, for his role in *A Dry White Season* (1989).

'Being asked to perform at the Academy Awards is like being asked to the White House.'

★ **Rob Lowe**, on being asked to sing the Creedence Clearwater song 'Proud Mary' (with the new lyrics 'Rolling, rolling, keep the cameras rolling') at the 1988 Awards Ceremony.

'If you make a popular movie, you start to think, Where have I failed?'

★ **Woody Allen**, Oscar-winning director of *Hannah and Her Sisters* (1986).

'The first time I hardly felt it because it was all so new ... But now I feel it ... You like me! You like me!'

★ **Sally Field**, on winning her second Oscar, for *Places in the Heart* (1984).

'My mother polishes them to an inch of their lives until the metal shows. That sums up the Academy Awards – all glitter on the outside and base metal coming through. Nice presents for a day. But they don't make you any better.'

★ **Glenda Jackson**, two-times Oscar winner, for *Women in Love* (1970) and *A Touch of Class* (1973).

'I don't believe my wife has ever made love to an Academy Award winner before.'

★ **F Murray Abraham**, on winning Best Supporting Actor at the 1984 Awards for his performance in *Amadeus* (1984).

'It might mean I'd get more scripts without other actors' coffee stains on them.'

★ **Michael Caine**, having been nominated for an Oscar for Best Actor, *Educating Rita* (1983).

'It's Reagan's strongest attack on the arts since he signed with Warner Brothers.'

★ **Johnny Carson**, presenter of the 1980 Academy Awards, referring to the President's proposals to cut funding to the arts and humanities.

'As Joan Crawford once said, "I'll show ya a pair of Golden Globes".'

★ **Bette Midler**, accepting two Golden Globes, Best Actress in a Musical and Most Promising Female Newcomer, for her role in *The Rose* (1979).

'Oscar doesn't mean anything in England. They don't know quite what they are.'

★ **Maggie Smith**, winner of an Oscar for Best Supporting Actress, for her role in *California Suite* (1978).

'And I just want to say, what a night – the furs, the jewels, the glamour. Looks like the opening night of the Beverly Hills Taco Bell ... I haven't seen so much expensive jewellery go by since I watched Sammy Davis Jr's house sliding down *Coldwater Canyon* ...

★ **Bob Hope's** opening speech as presenter of the 1977 Academy Awards.

'To all the Rockys of the world, I love ya!'

★ **Sylvester Stallone's** closing remarks, as he leaves the podium, with the producer Irwin Winkler and Robert Chartoff, following three Oscar wins for 1976's *Rocky*.

'This couldn't have happened to a nicer fella.'

★ **Ben Johnson**, accepting his Oscar for Best Supporting Actor, *The Last Picture Show* (1971).

'The Oscars are some sort of masturbatory fantasy.'

★ **Elliott Gould**, nominated for Best Supporting Actor, *Bob & Carol & Ted & Alice* (1969).

'Raquel, you open the envelope, my eyes are busy.'

★ **Dean Jones**, co-presenter, along with Raquel Welch, of Best Sound at the 1966 Academy Awards.

'I need a drink.'

★ **Lila Kedrova** to the award presenter Karl Malden, having collected an Oscar for her role in *Zorba the Greek* (1964).

'This is the one night I wish I smoked and drank.'

★ **Grace Kelly**, speaking at a post-Awards bash, having just picked up an Oscar for her performance in *The Country Girl* (1954).

'Isn't it beautiful and shiny, Mr Disney?'
'Yes, I'm so proud of it, I'm going to burst.'
'Oh, don't do that Mr Disney!'

★ Exchange between a ten-year-old Shirley Temple, presenter of a Special Oscar at the 1938 Academy Awards, and the recipient of the award, Walt Disney.

'Thanks, but you gave it to me for the wrong picture.'

★ **Leo McCarey**, accepting the Best Director Oscar for *The Awful Truth* (1937); the director was still smarting at the poor reception of his other feature, *Make Way for Tomorrow* (1937).

The Host with the Most

Stars who've presented the Oscars more than once:

★ 19 Appearances

Bob Hope

★ 5 Appearances

Billy Crystal
Johnny Carson

★ 4 Appearances

Jack Lemmon

★ 3 Appearances

Whoopi Goldberg
Jane Fonda
Jerry Lewis
Conrad Nagel
David Niven
Frank Sinatra

★ 2 Appearances

Fred Astaire
Jack Benny
Frank Capra
Chevy Chase
Sammy Davis Jr
William DeMille
Goldie Hawn
Walter Matthau
Richard Pryor
James Stewart

Films with the Most Oscar Nominations

★ *Titanic* (1997)
11 Oscars; 14 Nominations.

★ *All About Eve* (1950)
6 Oscars; 14 Nominations.

★ *Gone With the Wind* (1939)
8 Oscars (and 2 special awards);
13 Nominations.

★ *From Here to Eternity* (1953)
8 Oscars; 13 Nominations.

★ *Shakespeare in Love* (1998)
7 Oscars; 13 Nominations.

★ *Mary Poppins* (1964)
5 Oscars; 13 Nominations.

★ *Who's Afraid of Virginia Woolf?* (1966):
5 Oscars; 13 Nominations.

★ *Forrest Gump* (1994)
6 Oscars; 13 Nominations.

★ *Ben-Hur* (1959)
11 Oscars; 12 Nominations.

★ *The English Patient* (1996)
9 Oscars; 12 Nominations.

★ *On the Waterfront* (1954)
8 Oscars; 12 Nominations.

★ *My Fair Lady* (1964)
8 Oscars; 12 Nominations.

★ *Dances With Wolves* (1990)
7 Oscars; 12 Nominations.

★ *Schindler's List* (1993)
7 Oscars; 12 Nominations.

★ *Mrs. Miniver* (1942)
6 Oscars; 12 Nominations.

★ *The Song of Bernadette* (1943)
4 Oscars; 12 Nominations.

★ *A Streetcar Named Desire* (1951)
4 Oscars; 12 Nominations.

★ *Reds* (1981)
3 Oscars; 12 Nominations.

★ *Johnny Belinda* (1948)
1 Oscar: 12 Nominations.

★ *Becket* (1964)
1 Oscar: 12 Nominations.

BEN HUR (1959)

Top Ten Oscar– Winning Films

★ *Titanic* (1997)
14 Nominations; 11 Awards.

★ *Ben-Hur* (1959)
12 Nominations; 11 Awards.

★ *West Side Story* (1961)
11 Nominations; 10 Awards.

★ *The English Patient* (1996)
12 Nominations; 9 Awards.

★ *Gigi* (1958)
9 Nominations; 9 Awards.

★ *The Last Emperor* (1987)
9 Nominations; 9 Awards.

★ *Gone With the Wind* (1939)
13 Nominations; 8 Awards (and 2 special awards).

★ *From Here to Eternity* (1953)
13 Nominations; 8 Awards.

★ *On the Waterfront* (1954)
12 Nominations; 8 Awards.

★ *My Fair Lady* (1964)
12 Nominations; 8 Awards.

★ *Cabaret* (1972)
10 Nominations; 8 Awards.

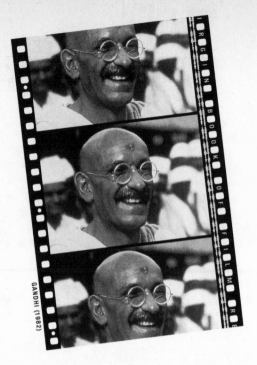

GANDHI (1982)

★ Gandhi (1982)
11 Nominations; 8 Awards.

★ Amadeus (1984)
11 Nominations; 8 Awards

SHAKESPEARE IN LOVE (1998)

★ *Shakespeare in Love* (1998), while receiving thirteen nominations, won only seven Oscars, and as such does not gain a place in the top ten.

The following films have also won seven Oscars

★ *Schindler's List* (1993)

★ *Dances With Wolves* (1991)

★ *Out of Africa* (1985)

★ *The Sting* (1973)

★ *Patton* (1970)

★ *Lawrence of Arabia* (1962)

★ *The Bridge on the River Kwai* (1957)

★ *The Best Years of Our Lives* (1946)

★ *Going My Way* (1944)

Essential Oscar Trivia

The Academy of Motion Picture Arts and Sciences became a legal corporation on 4 May 1927.

It was the brainchild of Louis B Mayer, the head of Metro-Goldwyn-Mayer.

The initial purpose of the Academy was the mediation of labour disputes. It's activities were quickly expanded, to include, among other things, the bestowal of 'awards of merit for distinctive achievement'. The first elected president was Douglas Fairbanks Sr.

The Oscar statuette was conceived by Cedric Gibbons, while he was attending an Academy meeting, at which talk was of the five branches of the Academy and the need for a strong public image for the film industry – his initial sketch showed a naked man plunging a sword into a reel of film with five holes.

The Oscar statuette was produced by an unemployed art school graduate, George Stanley, who was paid $500 for his efforts.

The Oscar statuette is thirteen and a half inches high, weighs six and three-quarter pounds, is made of tin and copper and plated in gold.

It is believed that the statuette came to be known as 'Oscar' after a secretary, following the first striking of the statuette, remarked, 'It reminds me of my Uncle Oscar.'

Of the statuette itself, an MGM screenwriter, Frances Marion, wrote, 'The little gold-washed statuette was thought, by sceptics and art lovers, a bit on the amateurish side, still, I saw it as a perfect symbol of the picture business: a powerful athletic body clutching a gleaming sword with half of his head, that part which held his brain, completely sliced off.'

The first award for Best Actor went to Emil Jannings for his performance in both *The Way of All Flesh* and *The Last Command*. However, Jannings, disillusioned with Hollywood life, asked that the award be sent to him prior to the ceremony. The Academy duly obliged, Jannings thanked them, took the trophy and ran – all the way back to his native Germany!

The first ever Academy Awards ceremony was held on 16 May 1929 at 8 p.m. in the Blossom Room of the Hollywood Roosevelt Hotel. The Awards were presented by Douglas Fairbanks and William C DeMille.

Chapter 5
Follow That Dream

MASK OF ZORRO (1940)

It's a known fact that the film industry is always on the lookout for new ideas and with the number of new films in production today, there's always a shortage of new scripts.
As a result it's little surprise that the big bucks are being invested in previously tried and tested storylines. Among the prime pickings are television spin-offs, remakes of classic movies, follow-ups to the big earners and of course adapting the works of lesser-known foreign directors.

The following chapter looks at some of the more interesting examples of the way in which the industry has borrowed from such sources.

Movie Screenplay Made Easy, Part 1

50 Films Based on Successful TV Series

★ *Here Come the Nelsons* (1952)

★ *Dragnet* (1954)

★ *The Lone Ranger* (1956)

★ *The Quatermass Experiment* (1956)

★ *Dr. Who and the Daleks* (1965)

★ *Munster, Go Home* (1966)

★ *A Man Called Flintstone* (1966) – feature-length cartoon version

★ *Batman* (1966)

★ *House of Dark Shadows* (1967)

★ *And Now for Something Completely Different* (1971)

★ *On the Buses* (1971)

★ *Dad's Army* (1971)

★ *Steptoe and Son* (1972)

★ *Nearest and Dearest* (1972)

★ *Man About the House* (1974)

★ *Callan* (1974)

★ *Sweeney!* (1976)

★ *Are You Being Served?* (1977)

★ *Star Trek – The Motion Picture* (1979)

★ *Porridge* (1979)

★ *The Muppet Movie* (1979)

★ *George and Mildred* (1980)

★ *The Blues Brothers* (1980) – based on a *Saturday Night Live* sketch

★ *Twilight Zone: The Movie* (1983)

★ *Smurfs and the Magic Flute* (1984)

★ *The Naked Gun* (1988)

★ *Jetsons: The Movie* (1990)

★ *Tales From the Dark Side: The Movie* (1990)

★ *The Addams Family* (1991)

★ *Wayne's World* (1992) – based on a *Saturday Night Live* sketch

★ *Twin Peaks – Fire Walk With Me* (1992)

★ *The Fugitive* (1993)

★ *The Beverly Hillbillies* (1993)

★ *The Flintstones* (1994) (1999)

★ *The Brady Bunch Movie* (1995)

★ *Flipper* (1996)

★ *Beavis and Butt-head Do America* (1996)

★ *Mission: Impossible* (1996) (1999)

★ *Sgt. Bilko* (1996)

★ *Bean* (1997)

★ *The Saint* (1997)

★ *Mr. Magoo* (1997)

★ *The Avengers* (1998)

★ *Lost in Space* (1998)

★ *The X Files* (1998)

★ *The Rugrats Movie* (1998)

★ *Inspector Gadget* (1999)

★ *My Favorite Martian* (1999)

★ *Wild Wild West* (1999)

★ *Charlie's Angels: The Movie* (2000)

Ten Movies that Started Life as Sketches on Saturday Night Live

★ *The Blues Brothers* (1980)

★ *Wayne's World* (1992)

★ *Wayne's World 2* (1993)

★ *Coneheads* (1993)

★ *Stuart Saves his Family* (1995)

★ *A Night at the Roxbury* (1998)

★ *Blues Brothers 2000* (1998)

★ *Office Space* (1999)

★ *Superstar* (1999)

★ *Sprockets* (2000)

Movie Screenplay Made Easy, Part 2

Remakes with the Same Title

★ *Little Lord Fauntleroy* (1921) (1936)

★ *Seventh Heaven* (1927) (1937)

★ *Little Women* (1933) (1949)

★ *Limelight* (1936) (1952)

★ *Ten Commandments* (1923) (1956)

★ *The Man Who Knew Too Much* (1934) (1956)

★ *A Tale of Two Cities* (1936) (1958)

★ *Ben-Hur* (1925) (1959)

★ *Kid Galahad* (1937) (1962)

★ *Lost Horizon* (1937) (1973)

★ *Ten Little Indians* (1966) (1975)

★ *A Star is Born* (1934) (1954) (1976)

★ *The Big Sleep* (1946) (1978)

★ *The Thirty-Nine Steps* (1935) (1959) (1978)

★ *The Lady Vanishes* (1938) (1979)

★ *The Jazz Singer* (1927) (1952) (1980)

★ *Cat People* (1942) (1982)

★ *Scarface* (1932) (1983)

★ *To Be or Not to Be* (1942) (1983)

★ *The Wicked Lady* (1945) (1983)

★ *Brewster's Millions* (1914) (1921) (1935) (1945) (1961) (1985)

★ *The Fly* (1958) (1986)

★ *We're No Angels* (1955) (1989)

★ *A Kiss Before Dying* (1956) (1991)

★ *Cape Fear* (1962) (1991)

★ *Father of the Bride* (1950) (1991)

★ *The Last of the Mohicans* (1936) (1992)

★ *Wuthering Heights* (1939) (1971) (1992)

★ *The Three Musketeers* (1921) (1931) (1939) (1948) (1993)

★ *Born Yesterday* (1950) (1993)

★ *Miracle on 34th Street* (1947) (1994)

★ *Love Affair* (1939) (1994)

★ *The Getaway* (1972) (1994)

★ *Little Women* (1933) (1994)

★ *Frankenstein* (1931) (1994)

★ *Village of the Damned* (1960) (1995)

★ *Sabrina* (1954) (1995)

★ *Kiss of Death* (1947) (1995)

★ *The Nutty Professor* (1963) (1996)

★ *Lolita* (1962) (1997)

★ *The Parent Trap* (1961) (1998)

★ *Psycho* (1960) (1998)

★ *Godzilla* (1954 a.k.a. *Gojira*) (1956) (1998)

★ *Gloria* (1980) (1999)

★ *Mighty Joe Young* (1949) (1998)

★ *The Out-Of-Towners* (1970) (1999)

★ *The Thomas Crown Affair* (1968) (1999)

★ *The Haunting* (1963) (1999)

★ *Fahrenheit 451* (1966) (2000)

★ *Gone in 60 Seconds* (1974) (2000)

50 Remakes Incognito

(Original movie on the second line)

★ *One Hour With You* (1932)
★ *The Marriage Circle* (1924)

★ *Satan Met a Lady* (1936)
★ *The Maltese Falcon* (1931)

★ *His Girl Friday* (1940)
★ *The Front Page* (1931)

★ *'Til We Meet Again* (1940)
★ *One Way Passage* (1932)

★ *The Man Who Talked Too Much* (1940)
★ *The Mouthpiece* (1932)

★ *Moon Over Miami* (1941)
★ *Three Blind Mice* (1938)

★ *Murder My Sweet* (1944)
★ *The Falcon Takes Over* (1942)

★ *Cross My Heart* (1946)
★ *True Confession* (1937)

★ *The Kid from Brooklyn* (1946)
★ *The Milky Way* (1936)

★ *A Song is Born* (1948)
★ *Ball of Fire* (1941)

★ *Three Godfathers* (1949)
★ *Three Bad Men* (1926)

★ *In the Good Old Summertime* (1949)
★ *The Shop Around the Corner* (1940)

★ *A Place in the Sun* (1951)
★ *An American Tragedy* (1930)

★ *Stop You're Killing Me* (1952)
★ *A Slight Case of Murder* (1938)

★ *How to Marry a Millionaire* (1953)
★ *The Greeks Had a Word For Them* (1932)

★ *House of Wax* (1953)
★ *Mystery of the Wax Museum* (1933)

★ *I Died a Thousand Times* (1955)
★ *High Sierra* (1941)

★ *Storm Over the Nile* (1955)
★ *Four Feathers* (1929) (1939)

★ *High Society* (1956)
★ *The Philadelphia Story* (1940)

★ *The King and I* (1956)
★ *Anna and the King of Siam* (1946)

★ *The Opposite Sex* (1956)
★ *The Women* (1939)

★ *An Affair to Remember* (1957)
★ *Love Affair* (1939)

★ *Silk Stockings* (1957)
★ *Ninotchka* (1939)

★ *Stage Struck* (1958)
★ *Morning Glory* (1933)

★ *The Gift of Love* (1958)
★ *Sentimental Journey* (1946)

★ *No Place Like Homicide* (1962)
★ *The Ghoul* (1933)

★ *Stolen Hours* (1963)
★ *Dark Victory* (1939)

★ *Move Over Darling* (1963)
★ *My Favourite Wife* (1940)

★ *The Eye Creatures* (1965)
★ *Invasion of the Saucer Men* (1957)

★ *Ten Little Indians* (1966)
★ *And Then There Were None* (1945)

★ *Farewell My Lovely* (1975)
★ *The Falcon Takes Over* (1942)

★ *Heaven Can Wait* (1978)
★ *Here Comes Mr. Jordan* (1941)

★ *The Happy Hooker Goes to Hollywood* (1980)
★ *Silent Movie* (1976)

★ *The Thing* (1982)
★ *The Thing From Another World* (1951)

★ *Never Say Never Again* (1983)
★ *Thunderball* (1965)

★ *The Bounty* (1984)
★ *Mutiny on the Bounty* (1935) (1962)

★ *Switching Channels* (1988)
★ *His Girl Friday* (1940)

★ *Always* (1989)
★ *A Guy Named Joe* (1943)

★ *Homeward Bound: The Incredible Journey* (1993)
★ *The Incredible Journey* (1963)

★ *Desperado* (1995)
★ *Il Mariachi* (1993)

★ *Father of the Bride Part II* (1995)
★ *Father's Little Dividend* (1951)

★ *The Preacher's Wife* (1996)
★ *The Bishop's Wife* (1946)

★ *Flubber* (1997)
★ *The Absent Minded Professor* (1961)

★ *Washington Square* (1997)
★ *The Heiress* (1949)

★ *The Jackal* (1997)
★ *The Day of the Jackal* (1973)

★ *A Perfect Murder* (1998)
★ *Dial M for Murder* (1954)

★ *You've Got Mail* (1998)
★ *The Shop Around the Corner* (1940)

★ *Meet Joe Black* (1998)
★ *Death Takes A Holiday* (1960)

★ *The Mask of Zorro* (1998)
★ *The Mark of Zorro* (1920) (1940)

★ *Anna* (1999)
★ *The King and I* (1956)

20 Successful Films and Their Sequels

★ *Angels With Dirty Faces* (1938)
★ *Angels Wash Their Faces* (1939)

★ *National Velvet* (1944)
★ *International Velvet* (1978)

★ *Cheaper By the Dozen* (1950)
★ *Belles on Their Toes*

★ *The Bad and the Beautiful* (1952)
★ *Two Weeks in Another Town* (1962)

★ *The Hustler* (1961)
★ *The Color of Money* (1986)

★ *The Pink Panther* (1964)
★ *Shot in the Dark* (1964)

★ *Night of the Living Dead* (1968)
★ *Zombies* (1979)

★ *True Grit* (1969)
★ *Rooster Cogburn* (1975)

★ *The Last Picture Show* (1971)
★ *Texasville* (1990)

★ *Dirty Harry* (1971)
★ *Magnum Force* (1972)

★ *Chinatown* (1974)
★ *The Two Jakes* (1990)

★ *All Creatures Great and Small* (1974)
★ *It Shouldn't Happen to a Vet* (1979)

★ *Every Which Way But Loose* (1978)
★ *Any Which Way You Can* (1980)

★ *Zombies* (1979)
★ *Day of the Dead* (1985)

★ *Where the Buffalo Roam* (1980)
★ *Fear and Loathing in Las Vegas* (1998)

★ *Romancing the Stone* (1984)
★ *The Jewel of the Nile* (1985)

★ *A Fish Called Wanda* (1988)
★ *Fierce Creatures* (1997)

★ *The Hunt for Red October* (1990)
★ *Patriot Games* (1992)

★ *Bad Channels* (1992)
★ *Dollman Vs. The Demonic Toys* (1993)

★ *Patriot Games* (1992)
★ *Clear and Present Danger* (1994)

Movie Screenplay Made Easy, Part 4 (and in English we say ...)

Remakes of foreign films (remake on the top line; original foreign title on the second line)

★ *Port of Seven Seas* (1938)
★ *Fanny* (1932)

★ Algiers (1938)
★ Pépé Le Moko (1937)

★ A Woman's Face (1941)
★ En Kvinnas Ansikte (1938)

★ Scarlet Street (1945)
★ La Chienne (1931)

★ The Long Night (1947)
★ Le Jour se Leve (a.k.a. Daybreak) (1939)

★ The Unfinished Dance (1947)
★ Ballerina (1938)

★ The Thirteenth Letter (1951)
★ Le Corbeau (a.k.a. The Raven) (1948)

★ Midnight Episode (1951)
★ Monsieur le Souris
(a.k.a. Midnight in Paris) (1947)

★ Human Desire (1954)
★ La Bête Humaine (a.k.a. The Human Beast;
Judas Was a Woman) (1938)

★ The Magnificent Seven (1960)
★ The Seven Samurai
(a.k.a. Shichinin no Samurai) (1954)

★ A Fistful of Dollars (1964)
★ Yojimbo (1961)

★ The Outrage (1964)
★ Rashomon (1951)

★ Games (1967)
★ Les Diaboliques (a.k.a. Diabolique)

★ Cop-Out (1968)
★ Les Inconnus dans la Maison
(a.k.a. Strangers in the House) (1949)

★ Sweet Charity (1969)
★ Nights of Cabiria
(a.k.a. Le Notti di Cabiria) (1957)

★ Which Way Is Up? (1977)
★ The Seduction of Mimi (a.k.a. Mimi
Metallurgico Ferito nell'Onore) (1972)

★ Sorcerer (1977)
★ The Wages of Fear
(a.k.a. La Salaire de la Peur) (1953)

★ Another Man, Another Chance (1977)
★ A Man and a Woman
(a.k.a. Un Homme et une Femme) (1996)

★ A Little Night Music (1978)
★ Smiles of a Summer Night
(a.k.a. Sommarnattens Leende) (1978)

★ Willie and Phil (1980)
★ Jules and Jim (a.k.a. Jules et Jim) (1961)

★ Buddy, Buddy (1981)
★ A Pain in the A— (a.k.a. L'Emmerdeur)
(1973)

★ The Toy (1982)
★ Le Jouet (1976)

★ Kiss Me Goodbye (1982)
★ Dona Flor and Her Two Husbands
(a.k.a. Dona Flor e Seurs Dois Maridos) (1977)

★ Breathless (1983)
★ À Bout de Soufflé (a.k.a. Breathless) (1960)

★ Blame It On Rio (1984)
★ One Wild Moment
(a.k.a. Un Moment D'Egarement) (1972)

★ The Woman in Red (1984)
★ Pardon Mon Affaire
(a.k.a. Elephant ça Troupe Enormement) (1976)

★ Crackers (1984)
★ Big Deal on Madonna Street
(a.k.a. I Soliti Ignoti) (1958)

★ The Man With One Red Shoe (1985)
★ The Tall Blond Man With One Black Shoe
(a.k.a. Le Grand Blond Avec Une Chaussure
Noire) (1972)

★ Down and Out in Beverly Hills (1986)
★ Boudu Saved From Drowning
(a.k.a. Boudu Sauvé des Eaux) (1932)

★ Three Men and a Baby (1987)
★ Three Men and a Cradle
(a.k.a. Trois Hommes et un Couffin) (1985)

★ Happy New Year (1987)
★ Happy New Year (a.k.a. La Nonne Anné;
The Happy New Year Caper) (1973)

★ *And God Created Woman* (1988)
★ *Et Dieu ... Créa La Femme*
(a.k.a. *And God Created Woman*) (1957)

★ *Dangerous Liaisons* (1988)
★ *Les Liaisons Dangereuses*
(a.k.a. *Dangerous Meetings*) (1959)

★ *Cousins* (1989)
★ *Cousin, Cousine* (1975)

★ *Three Fugitives* (1989)
★ *Les Fugitifs* (1986)

★ *Men Don't Leave* (1990)
★ *Continue* (a.k.a. *Life Goes On*) (1981)

★ *Pure Luck* (1991)
★ *Le Chevre* (a.k.a. *The Goat*) (1981)

★ *Paradise* (1991)
★ *The Big Road* (a.k.a. *Le Grand Chemin;
The Grand Highway*) (1987)

★ *Scent of a Woman* (1992)
★ *Profumo di Donna* (1974)

★ *Assassin* (1993)
★ *La Femme Nikita* (a.k.a. *Nikita*) (1991)

★ *The Vanishing* (1993)
★ *The Vanishing* (a.k.a. *Spoorloos*) (1988)

★ *Sommersby* (1993)
★ *The Return of Martin Guerre*
(a.k.a. *Le Retour de Martin Guerre*) (1982)

★ *True Lies* (1994)
★ *La Totale!* (1991)

★ *Nine Months* (1995)
★ *Neuf Mois* (1994)

★ *Diabolique* (1995)
★ *Diabolique* (1950)

★ *Birdcage* (1996)
★ *La Cage aux Folles* (1978)

★ *Jungle2Jungle* (1997)
★ *Little Indian, Big City*
(a.k.a. *Un Indien dans la ville*) (1994)

★ *Fathers' Day* (1997)
★ *Les Comperes* (1983)

★ *City of Angels* (1998)
★ *Wings of Desire*
(a.k.a. *Der Himmel Über Berlin*) (1987)

★ *Cruel Intentions* (1999)
★ *Les Liaisons Dangereuses*
(a.k.a. *Dangerous Meetings*) (1959)

★ *The Talented Mr. Ripley* (1999)
★ *Plein Soleil* (1960)

Chapter 6
The Young Ones

SID AND NANCY (1986)

It seems in Hollywood that people always want to be somebody else. Those who are happy to be themselves seem to be few and far between. Take method actors for example: disillusioned with the idea of merely acting, they seek to experience first-hand that which they are to portray on screen, so as to lend an air of credibility to their performance.

Perhaps little removed from this phenomenon are the stars who place themselves under the surgeon's knife, thereby embarking upon a personal transformation, ultimately induced by their involvement in the world of movies.

In this section we examine a variety of stars, from the method actors to the plastic-surgery disasters, not forgetting the baldness beaters. At the end of the day, though, they are all stars who share a common bond: a desire to be somebody else.

MARTIN SHEEN - APOCALYPSE NOW (1979)

Method Madness

★ 'It's as if they're trying to impose their psychiatric difficulties on the audience.'– Joan Crawford on method actors.

★ Stoned (1)

Prior to the filming of *Platoon* (1986), the director, Oliver Stone, had Charlie Sheen and his fellow cast members spend two weeks training in the Philippines, under the guidance of a former marine, so as to make them appear credible soldiers.

Charlie Sheen's ordeal didn't end there: at one point Stone insisted that Sheen be bare-chested for the shooting of a scene. Sheen, fearing the risk of injury from flying debris, was unwilling to comply with the director's wishes. Stone, hit back at the star with, 'Are you a little pussy from Malibu? Played too much volleyball all your life?' Sheen, angered by Stone's remarks, tore his shirt off, only to be hit by debris, causing scars that remained for some weeks.

★ Stoned (2)

Charlie's father Martin Sheen gives a truly convincing performance as a soldier on the edge of a breakdown, as Captain Willard in *Apocalypse Now* (1979). However, it seems Francis Coppola helped Sheen get into the part by placing him on a strict diet of marijuana and alcohol. Sheen subsequently suffered a heart attack during filming!

★ Ice Maiden

Coppola's at it again: apparently during filming of *The Rainmaker* (1997), he pushed ice cubes down Clare Danes's back in order to obtain a convincing reaction from the actress, during the scene where she is beaten by her husband.

★ Ice One, Tom!

Tom Hanks apparently acknowledged the assistance of a local ice-cream shop in getting ready for his part in *A League of Their Own* (1992). Following the shop's encouragement, Hanks had found it no problem to put on the required thirty pounds in weight.

★ Weighting for it

In order to transform himself into prizefighter Jake LaMotta, for the film *Raging Bull* (1980), Robert De Niro, had to gain 56 pounds in weight. As a result, the film's production shut down for four months to await De Niro's metamorphosis. LaMotta, who trained De Niro for the role, said of the actor, 'Bobby's a main-event fighter. I'm not kidding. He's thirty-five, but he moves and hits like a nineteen-year-old. Any time he wants to quit acting, I could easily make him into a champion, he's that good.'

★ Downsizing (1)

Truly a martyr for the cause, Matt Damon used a combination of extreme fasting and daily runs of thirteen miles in order to prepare for his role in *Courage Under Fire* (1996). As a result he lost three and a half stone and achieved a look bordering on anorexia.

★ Downsizing (2)

Gary Oldman starved himself in readiness for his part as Sid Vicious in *Sid and Nancy* (1986). He was subsequently treated for malnutrition.

★ Upsizing (1)

Mariel Hemingway had breast implants for her part in *Star 80* (1983).

★ Upsizing (2)

For his role in 1998's *Your Friends and Neighbours*, Aaron Eckhart gained 35 pounds; however, the extra poundage meant that Eckhart was frequently out of breath.

★ Aw!

The Paramount director, Norman Taurog, 'skilfully' coaxed his nephew, ten-year-old Jackie Cooper, into crying for another heart-warming scene of *Skippy* (1931). Taurog promised to shoot Cooper's pet dog if he didn't comply. Cooper proceeded to cry and the camera proceeded to roll!

★ Ow!

Nicolas Cage, in preparation for his role as a battle-scarred Vietnam veteran in Alan Parker's *Birdy* (1984), spent five weeks with his head wrapped in bandages. As if that were not bad enough, Cage also had two teeth extracted without anaesthetic in preparation for the same movie. Well, as they say, 'No pain: no gain!'

★ Hogging the Role

Nick Nolte made himself slaughter a Borneo pig for 1988's *Farewell to the King*.

★ What a waist!

Nicole Kidman wore a corset during filming of 1996's *The Portrait of a Lady*, in order to reduce her waist to a 'slim' nineteen inches. Ouch!

★ A Study in Genius

To ready herself for filming of *Hilary and Jackie* (1999), the biographical account of the cellist Jacqueline du Pré, Emily Watson not only learnt how to play the cello, but spent hours, accompanied by a movement coach, watching videos of du Pré playing. As a result, Watson convincingly recreates the violently sensual way in which du Pré drew music from her instrument.

Ultimately, du Pré lost her life to multiple sclerosis, a disease that first came into her life during her late twenties. Once again, in order to give the best performance that she could, Watson spent time studying the effects of the disease with both doctors and patients.

★ A Study in Hospital

Marlon Brando, the man responsible for making method acting fashionable, once spent a month in a hospital ward in order to gain first-hand experience in the treatment of paraplegics, in preparation for his role as an embittered paraplegic in *The Men* (1950).

Plastic-Surgery Disasters!

Why suddenly do we hear so much negative talk about the prospect of syn-thespians (computer-generated actors)? Judging by the number of times most Hollywood stars have been rebuilt it would seem that we already have them. Below we offer a piece-by-piece breakdown of the alleged plastic people.

★ **Pamela Anderson** – breasts (as if you hadn't noticed); breasts again, this time to make them appear more natural, i.e. smaller

★ **Roseanne Barr** – breasts, cheek implants, face, nose

★ **Cher** – buttocks, breasts, cheek implants, face, nose, stomach

★ **Catherine Deneuve** – face (supposedly her surgeon used the world's most expensive stitches – gold ones!)

★ **Michael Douglas** – face

★ **Faye Dunaway** – cheek implants, face

★ **Jane Fonda** – breasts, face

★ **Melanie Griffith** – breasts, lips

★ **Sophia Loren** – eyes, face

★ **Demi Moore** – hips, buttocks, breasts, nose, stomach

★ **Paul Newman** – face

★ **Michelle Pfeiffer** – cheek implants, nose

★ **Priscilla Presley** – face

★ **Burt Reynolds** – face

★ **Arnold Schwarzenegger** – face

★ **Barbra Streisand** – nose (yes, really!)

★ **Elizabeth Taylor** – face (several times)

★ **Raquel Welch** – breasts, face

Hair Today, Gone Tomorrow!

Shiny-topped leading men

★ **F Murray Abraham**

★ **Yul Brynner**

★ **Sean Connery**

★ **Danny DeVito**

★ **Robert Duvall**

★ **Hector Elizondo**

★ **Lou Gossett, Jr**

★ **Sidney Greenstreet**

★ **Ed Harris**

★ **Charlton Heston**

★ **Bob Hoskins**

★ **Ben Kingsley**

★ **Ida Lupino**

★ **John Malkovich**

★ **Burt Reynolds**

★ **Telly Savalas**

★ **Eli Wallach**

★ **John Wayne**

★ **Sigourney Weaver** (sorry, just kidding)

★ **Bruce Willis**

Chapter 7
The Sound of Music

AMADEUS (1984)

It's been said that movie stars make lousy musicians and musicians make lousy movie stars. Well, judge for yourself as we expose those who've felt it necessary to stray beyond their true vocation. We reveal the Hollywood stars who've gone for a song and the musicians with thespian aspirations.

And first, we list some of the great pieces of music, both popular and classical, to have featured in the movies over the years.

Name That Tune!

Movie classics

★ '10' – Boléro by Ravel

★ 2001: A Space Odyssey – Introduction, from Also sprach Zarathustra, Op. 30 by Richard Strauss

★ Amadeus – 'Requiem Aeternam', from Mass No. 19 in D Minor, K626 'Requiem' by Mozart.

★ The American President and Someone To Watch Over Me and True Romance – 'Viens, Mallika' a.k.a. 'Flower Duet', from Lakmés by Delibes

★ Apocalypse Now – 'Ride Of The Valkyries', from Die Walküre by Wagner

★ Awakenings and Moonstruck – 'O Soave Fanciulla', from La Bohème by Puccini

★ Babe – Presto, Symphony No. 3 ('Organ') by Saint-Saëns

★ Babette's Feast – 'Là Ci Darem La Mano', from Don Giovanni by Mozart

★ Brassed Off – Overture to William Tell by Rossini

★ Breaking Away – Saltarello Presto, from the Symphony No. 4 ('Italian'), fourth movement, by Mendelssohn

★ The Bridges of Madison County – 'Casta Diva', from Norma by Bellini

★ A Clockwork Orange – A march from Pomp and Circumstance, Op. 39/1, by Elgar

★ Dangerous Liaisons – Allegro from the Organ Concerto in F, 'The Cuckoo And The Nightingale', by Handel

★ Dark Eyes – 'Una Voce Poco Fa', from The Barber of Seville by Rossini

★ Dead Again and Groundhog Day and Somewhere In Time – Rhapsody on a Theme of Paganini for piano and orchestra, Op. 43, Var. 18, by Rachmaninov

★ Dead Poets Society – Allegro, from Water Music by Handel

★ Death in Venice – Adagietto, from the Symphony No. 5 by Mahler

★ The Deer Hunter – Cavatina by Myers

★ The Devil's Own – Frühlingsstimmen by Strauss

★ Die Hard II – Finlandia, Op. 26/7, by Sibelius

★ Driving Miss Daisy – 'Du Lieber Mond', from Rusalka by Dvořák

★ Excalibur and Glory and The Hunt for Red October – Carmina Burana by Orff

★ Face/Off – 'Pamina's Aria', from The Magic Flute by Mozart

★ Fame and Amadeus – Allegro, from Eine Kleine Nachtmusik by Mozart

★ Fantasia – 'Dance Of The Hours', from La Gioconda by Ponchielli; Toccata and Fugue in D minor by Bach

★ Fatal Attraction – 'Un Bel Dì Vedremo', from Madama Butterfly by Puccini

★ *Fifth Element, The* – 'Mad Scene', from Lucia di Lammermoor by Donizetti

★ *The Firm* – Adagio, from the Concerto in D Minor for Oboe and String Orchestra by Marcello

★ *Four Weddings and a Funeral* – 'Wedding March', from A Midsummer Night's Dream, by Mendelssohn

★ *Frankie and Johnny* – Clair de Lune by Debussy

★ *Gallipoli* – 'Au Fond Du Temple Saint', from The Pearl Fishers by Bizet

★ *G.I. Jane* – O Mio Babbino Caro by Puccini

★ *Greystoke: The Legend of Tarzan, Lord of the Apes* – Andante nobilmente e semplice, from the Symphony No. 1 in A Flat Major, Op. 55, by Elgar

★ *Guarding Tess* – 'madaina … Il Catalogo é Questo', from Don Giovanni by Mozart

★ *Hannah and Her Sisters* – 'Sola, Perduta e Abbandonata', from Manon Lescaut by Puccini

★ *Hard Target* – Finale, from the Piano Sonata No. 23 in F Minor, Op. 57, 'Appassionata' by Beethoven

★ *Hearts And Souls* – 'Ah! Si Ben Mio … Di Quella Pira', from Il Trovatore by Verdi

★ *Heat And Dust* – Fantasiestücke, Op. 12 ('Aufschwung'), by Schumann

★ *Henry V* – Touch Her Soft Lips and Part and Passacaglia – Death of Falstaff, both by Walton

★ *Howard's End* – Bridal Lullaby and Mock Morris; both by Grainger

★ *Hudsucker Proxy* – 'Habanera', from Carmeni by Bizet

★ *Immortal Beloved* – the Kyrie from the Missa Solemnis by Beethoven

★ *Indecent Proposal* – Concerto No. 8, Allegro, from L'estro armonico by Vivaldi

★ *In the Line of Fire* – 'Brindisi: Libiamo', from La Traviata by Verdi

★ *Jean de Florette* and *Manon of the Spring* – La Forza del destino by Verdi

★ *Jennifer 8* – 'Humming Chorus', from Madama Butterfly by Puccini

★ *JFK* – Rondo, from the Horn Concerto in E flat, K. 417, third movement, by Mozart

★ *The Lost World: Jurassic Park* – Adagio cantabile, from the sonata 'Pathétique' by Beethoven

★ *Kramer vs. Kramer* – Largo, from the Concerto for Mandolin, Strings and Cembalo in C major, RV 425 by Vivaldi

★ *L.A. Confidential* – Hebrides Overture by Mendelssohn

★ *Last Action Hero* and *Trading Places* – Overture, from The Marriage of Figaro by Mozart

★ *A League of Their Own* – Minuet by Boccherini

★ *Little Women* – 'Leila! Leila! Dieu puissant', from The Pearl Fishers by Bizet

★ *The Madness of King George* – 'Zadok The Priest', from the Coronation Anthem No. 1 by Handel

★ *Manhattan* – Rhapsody in Blue by Gershwin

★ *The Mission* – Theme by Ennio Morricone

★ *Mrs. Doubtfire* – 'Largo Al Factotum', from The Barber of Seville by Rossini

★ *The Music Lovers* – 1812 Overture by Tchaikovsky

★ *Ordinary People* – Canon in D by Pachelbel

★ *Out of Africa* – Adagio, from Clarinet Concerto in A major, KV 622 by Mozart

★ *The Peacemaker* – Nocturne in F minor by Chopin

★ *The People Vs. Larry Flynt* – 'Polonaise', from Rusalka by Dvořák

★ *Peter's Friends* – 'Can-Can', from Orpheus in the Underworld by Offenbach

★ *The Piano* – 'The Heart Asks Pleasure First/The Promise' by Michael Nyman

★ *Philadelphia* – 'La Mamma Morta', from Andrea Chenier by Giordano

★ *Platoon* and *Lorenzo's Oil* – Adagio for Strings, Op. 11, by Barber

★ *Pretty Woman* – 'Addio, Del Passato', from La Traviata by Verdi

★ *Primal Fear* – 'Lacrymosa', from Requiem by Mozart

★ *The Prince of Tides* – London Symphony No. 104 ('London'), 3rd Movement, minuet, by Haydn

★ *Priscilla, Queen of the Desert* – 'Sempre Libera', from La Traviata by Verdi

★ *Prizzi's Honor* – 'Una Furtiva Lagrima', from L'Elisir d'amore by Donizetti

★ *Raging Bull* and *The Godfather, Part 3* – Intermezzo, from Cavalleria rusticana by Mascagni

★ *Raising Cain* – 'Morning Mood', from Peer Gynt by Grieg

★ *Regarding Henry* – Andante, from the Piano Concerto No. 21 in C, KV 467 by Mozart

★ *Rollerball* – Allegro non troppo, from the Symphony No. 5 in D Minor, Op. 47, by Shostakovich

★ *A Room with a View* – 'Chi Il Bel Sogno Di Doretta', from La Rondine by Puccini

★ *Rosemary's Baby* – Für Elise by Beethoven

★ *Sammy And Rosie Get Laid* – 'Der Erlkönig' by Schubert

★ *Serpico* – 'E Lucevan Le Stelle', from Tosca by Puccini

★ *Seven* – 'Air On A "G" String' from the Suite No. 3 in D by Bach

★ *Shine* – 'Allegro Na Non Tanto', from the Piano Concerto No. 3 in D minor by Rachmaninov

★ *The Silence of the Lambs* and *The English Patient* – Goldberg Variations, BWV 988: Aria by Bach

★ *Slam Dance* – 'Mon Coeur S'Ouvre A Ta Voix' from Samson and Delilah by Saint-Saëns

★ *Sleeping With the Enemy* – 'Reveries – Passions', from Symphonie Fantastique by Berlioz

★ *Titanic* and *Cool Runnings* – The Blue Danube by Strauss

★ *The Untouchables* – 'Vesti La Giubba', from Pagliacci by Leoncavallo

★ *The Year of Living Dangerously* – 'Beim Schlafengehen' from Four Last Songs by Strauss

★ *Wall Street* – 'Questa O Quella', from Rigoletto by Verdi

★ *Wayne's World* – Romeo and Juliet overture, love theme, by Tchaikovsky

★ *Who Framed Roger Rabbit?* – Hungarian Rhapsody No. 2 by Liszt

★ *William Shakespeare's Romeo and Juliet* – Allegro con brio, from Symphony No. 25 in G minor, K 183, by Mozart

★ *The Witches of Eastwick* – 'Nessun Dorma', from Turandot by Puccini

★ *The Wizard of Oz* – Three Fantasies or Caprices, Op. 16, Scherzo, by Mendelssohn

Hollywood Sings!

Leading men who've gone for a song and the albums they recorded.

★ **John Wayne** – 'America, Why I Love Her'

★ **William Shatner** – 'The Transformed Man'

★ **George Segal** – 'The Yama Yama Man'

★ **Telly Savalas** – 'Who Loves Ya Baby'

★ **Burt Reynolds** – 'Ask Me What I Am'

★ **Anthony Quinn** – 'In My Own Way ... I Love You'

★ **Sidney Poitier** – 'READS Poetry Of The Black Man'

★ **Anthony (Psycho) Perkins** – 'On A Rainy Afternoon'

★ **Jack Palance** – 'Palance'

★ **Leonard Nimoy** – 'Mr Spock Presents Music From Outer Space'

★ **Eddie Murphy** – 'How Could It Be?'

★ **Robert Mitchum** – 'The Ballad of Thunder Road'

★ **Jack Lemmon** – 'A Twist Of Lemon'

★ **David Hemmings** – 'David Hemmings Happens'

★ **George Hamilton** – 'By George'

★ **Albert Finney** – 'Albert Finney's Album'

★ **Dick Van Dyke** – 'Songs I Like'

★ **Kenneth Connor** with **Glennis Beresford** – 'Much Ado About Love'

★ **Ian Carmichael** – 'Girl Crazy'

★ **Yul Brynner** (sings Gypsy Songs) – 'The Gypsy and I'

★ **Dirk Bogarde** – 'Lyrics For Lovers'

★ **Joe Pesci**, as Joe Ritchie – 'Little Joe Sure Can Sing'

★ **Roger Moore** – 'Where Does Love Go'

★ **James Dean** – 'Jungle Rhythm'

★ **Clint Eastwood** – 'Rowdy'

★ **Peter Fonda** – 'Bobby Ogden's Outlaw Blues'

★ **David McCallum** – 'Communication'

★ **Oliver Reed** – 'The Wild One'

★ **Robbie Coltrane** – 'New Orleans'

★ **John Mills** – 'Young At Heart'

★ **Vincent Price** – 'The Monster Mash'

★ **James Stewart** – 'Day After Day'

★ **Humphrey Bogart** – 'I've Got My Love To Keep Me Warm'

★ **Jack Nicholson** – 'Who Is There Among Us Who Knows?'

★ **Tyrone Power** – 'Chattanooga Choo-Choo'

★ **Cary Grant** – 'Did I Remember'

★ **Danny DeVito** – 'They Can't Take That Away From Me'

★ **Orson Welles** – 'You Made Me Love You'

★ **Rock Hudson** – 'Pillow Talk'

★ **Walter Pidgeon** – 'What'll I Do'

★ **Michael Caine** – 'Do You Wanna Touch Me (Oh Yeah)'

And let's not forget the leading ladies who've gone for a song.

★ **Mae West** – 'Way Out West', 'Great Balls Of Fire' to name but two

★ **Sissy Spaceck** – 'Hangin' Up My Heart'

★ **Hayley Mills** – 'Johnny Jingo'

★ **Virginia McKenna** – 'Two Faces Of Love'

★ **Cheryl Ladd** – 'Think It Over'

★ **Goldie Hawn** – 'Pitti Pitta'

★ **Diana Dors** – 'Swingin' Dors'

★ **Bette Davis** – 'Miss Bette Davis'

★ **Honor Blackman** – 'Everything I've Got'

★ **Brigitte Bardot** – 'Sidonie'

★ **Sophia Loren** – 'Bing, Bang, Bong'

★ **Gina Lollobrigida** – 'La Loa'

★ **Jayne Mansfield** – 'Little Things Mean A Lot'

★ **Cybil Shepherd** – 'I Told Ya I Love Ya, Now Get Out!'

★ **Jennifer Lopez** – 'If You Had My Love'

★ **Ava Gardner** – 'Loving' Dat Man'

★ **Susan Hampshire** – 'When Love Is True'

★ **Joan Collins** – 'Imagine'

★ **Sondra Locke** – 'I Seek The Night'

★ **Diana Rigg** – 'Forget Yesterday'

★ **Julie Walters** – 'Toy Boys'

★ **Joan Crawford** – 'How Long Will It Last?'

★ **Farrah Fawcett** (as Farrah Fawcett-Majors) – 'You'

★ **Cheryl Ladd** – 'Think It Over'

★ **Audrey Hepburn** – 'Moon River'

★ **Britt Ekland** – 'Do It To Me'

★ **Vanessa Redgrave** – 'Pink Angora'

★ **Elizabeth Taylor** – 'Send In The Clowns'

Forty No. 1 Hits from the Big Screen

Movies and music go together like peaches and cream – somehow, having one without the other just doesn't seem right. Whether we remember the movie because of the music, or the music because of the movie, there's no denying the power of music to rouse the emotions.

We've chosen forty hits, all of which reached number one in the British charts. As you read through the following list, ask yourself which you remember best: the song, or the sequence from the movie.

★ 'It's All In The Game' by Tommy Edwards – *Diner*

★ 'Dream Lover' by Bobby Darin – *Diner*

★ 'Unchained Melody' by the Righteous Brothers – *Ghost* (a number-one hit in the 90s!)

★ 'You've Lost That Loving Feeling' by the Righteous Brothers – *Top Gun*

★ 'King Of The Road' by Roger Miller – *Swingers*

★ 'Bad Moon Rising' by Creedence Clearwater Revival – *An American Werewolf in London*

★ 'There's Always Something There To Remind Me' by Sandie Shaw – *Letter To Brezhnev*

★ 'What A Wonderful World' by Louis Armstrong – *Good Morning Vietnam*

★ 'These Boots Are Made For Walking' by Nancy Sinatra – *Full Metal Jacket*

★ 'I Got You Babe' by Sonny and Cher – *Buster*

★ 'Sweets For My Sweet' by The Searchers – *Buster*

★ 'Stand By Me' by Ben E King – *Stand by Me* (reached number one in the 80s)

★ 'House Of The Rising Sun' by the Animals – *Casino*

★ 'San Francisco (Be Sure To Wear Some Flowers In Your Hair)' by Scott McKenzie – *Forrest Gump*

★ 'I Will Survive' by Gloria Gaynor – *Four Weddings and a Funeral*

★ 'Bohemian Rhapsody' by Queen – *Wayne's World* (also number one in the 90s)

★ 'Dancing Queen' by Abba – *Muriel's Wedding*

★ 'I've Never Been To Me' by Charlene – *Priscilla Queen of the Desert* (reached number one in 1982)

★ 'Make Me Smile (Come Up And See Me)' by Steve Harley & Cockney Rebel – *Velvet Goldmine*

★ 'Without You' by Nilsson – *Casino*

★ 'You're The First, The Last, My Everything' by Barry White – *Four Weddings and a Funeral*

★ 'Heart of Glass' by Blondie – *Donnie Brasco*

★ 'Pump Up The Volume' by M.A.R.R.S. – *My Stepmother Is An Alien*

★ 'When The Going Gets Tough The Tough Get Going' by Billy Ocean – *The Jewel of the Nile*

★ 'Into The Groove' by Madonna – *Desperately Seeking Susan*

★ 'A Groovy Kind Of Love' by Phil Collins – *Buster*

★ 'Eye Of The Tiger' by Survivor – *Rocky III*

★ 'I Just Called To Say I Love You' by Stevie Wonder – *The Woman In Red*

★ 'Lady In Red' by Chris De Burgh – *Working Girl*

★ 'Call Me' by Blondie – *American Gigolo*

★ 'Under Pressure' by David Bowie and Queen – *Grosse Pointe Blank*

★ 'All Around The World' by Lisa Stansfield – *Fever Pitch*

★ 'Tainted Love' by Soft Cell – *Coneheads*

★ 'The One And Only' by Chesney Hawkes – *Buddy's Song*

★ 'Gangsta's Paradise' by Coolio featuring L.V. – *Dangerous Minds*

★ '(Everything I Do) I Do It For You' by Bryan Adams – *Robin Hood: Prince of Thieves*

★ 'I Will Always Love You' by Whitney Houston – *The Bodyguard*

★ 'Show Me Heaven' by Mariah McKee – *Days of Thunder*

★ 'Wannabe' by the Spice Girls – *Small Soldiers*

★ 'The Shoop Shoop Song (It's In His Kiss) by Cher – *Mermaids*

Forty Top-40 Hits from the Big Screen

Now that you've seen forty number ones, here's another forty well-known songs, all of which featured in the movies, and all of which made the British Top Forty. However, you'll notice that we haven't always gone for the obvious!

★ 'When I Fall In Love' by Nat King Cole – *Mona Lisa*

★ 'Tutti Frutti' by Little Richard – *Cocktail*

★ 'Return To Me' by Dean Martin – *Donnie Brasco*

★ 'Hound Dog' by Elvis Presley – *Forrest Gump*

★ 'Ain't No Mountain High Enough' by Marvin Gaye and Tammi Terrell – *Stepmom*

★ 'Dream A Little Dream Of Me' by Mama Cass – *French Kiss*

★ 'I'm Sorry' by Brenda Lee – *The Fisher King*

★ 'Big Spender' by Shirley Bassey – *Little Voice*

★ 'Green Onions' by Booker T and the MGs – *Get Shorty*

★ 'Mrs Robinson' by Simon and Garfunkel – *Forrest Gump*

★ 'Signed, Sealed, Delivered – I'm Yours' by Stevie Wonder – *You've Got Mail*

★ 'Is She Really Going Out With Him?' by Joe Jackson – *There's Something About Mary*

★ 'Hot Stuff' by Donna Summer – *The Full Monty*

★ 'Stuck In The Middle With You' by Stealer's Wheel – *Reservoir Dogs*

★ 'Eighteen With A Bullet' by Pete Wingfield – *Lock, Stock and Two Smoking Barrels*

★ 'Love Is In The Air' by John Paul Young – *Strictly Ballroom*

★ 'What a Fool Believes' by the Doobie Brothers – *Frankie and Johnny*

★ 'Didn't I (Blow Your Mind This Time)' by the Delfonics – *Jackie Brown*

★ 'London's Calling' by Clash – *Face*

★ 'Lady Marmalade (Voulez-Vous Coucher Avec Moi Ce Soir?)' by Labelle – *Carlito's Way*

★ 'Rock The Boat' by Hues Corporation – *Carlito's Way*

★ 'I Love Rock 'N' Roll' by Joan Jett and the Blackhearts – *Wayne's World*

★ 'Hold Me Now' by the Thompson Twins – *The Wedding Singer*

★ 'Waiting For A Star To Fall' by Boy Meets Girl – *Three Men and a Little Lady*

★ 'It Must Have Been Love' by Roxette – *Pretty Woman*

★ 'Everybody Wants To Rule The World' by Tears for Fears – *Peter's Friends*

★ 'Walking On Sunshine' by Katrina and the Waves – *Look Who's Talking*

★ 'I'm So Excited' by Pointer Sisters – *Working Girl*

★ 'Fashion' by David Bowie – *Clueless*

★ 'Good Thing' by Fine Young Cannibals – *Fever Pitch*

★ 'Let's Hear It For The Boy' by Deniece Williams – *Footloose*

★ 'Moving On Up' by M-People – *The First Wives Club*

★ 'Ocean Drive' by Lighthouse Family – *Jack and Sarah*

★ 'Why' by Annie Lennox – *Boys On The Side*

★ 'Female Of The Species' by Space – *Austin Powers: The Spy Who Shagged Me*

★ 'Fantasy' by Mariah Carey – *Rush Hour*

Chapter 8
A Star is Born

CHRISTINA RICCI – MERMAIDS (1990)

First Big-Screen Roles of 50 Actresses

★ **Anne Archer** – *Cancel My Reservation* (1972)

★ **Lauren Bacall** – Marie 'Slim' Browning in *To Have and Have Not* (1944)

★ **Anne Bancroft** – *Don't Bother to Knock* (1952)

★ **Drew Barrymore** – Margaret Jessup, daughter of William Hurt's character in *Altered States* (1980) at the age of five.

★ **Kim Basinger** – *Hard County* (1981)

★ **Sandra Bullock** – Lisa Edwards in *Hangmen* (1987)

★ **Neve Campbell** – Rose in *Ruskin* (1994)

★ **Claire Danes** – *Dreams of Love* (1990)

★ **Bette Davis** – *Bad Sister* (1931)

★ **Catherine Deneuve** (billed as Catherine Dorléac) – *Les Collégiennes* (1956) a.k.a. *The Twilight Girls*

★ **Bo Derek** (porn) – Anastasia in *Fantasies* (1973)

JIM CARREY & CAMERON DIAZ – THE MASK (1994)

★ **Cameron Diaz** – Tina Carlyle in *The Mask* (1994)

★ **Faye Dunaway** – *The Happening* (1966)

★ **Bridget Fonda** – *Partners* (1982)

★ **Jane Fonda** – *Tall Story* (1959)

★ **Jodie Foster** – Samantha in *Napoleon and Samantha* (1971)

★ **Greta Garbo** – a maid in *En Lyckoriddare* (1921)

★ **Judy Garland** – *Pigskin Parade* (1936)

★ **Pam Grier** – *Beyond the Valley of the Dolls* (1970)

★ **Goldie Hawn** – *The One and Only Genuine Original Family Band* (1968)

★ **Ann Heche** – Denise in *An Ambush of Ghosts* (1993)

★ **Holly Hunter** – a girl camper named Sophie in *The Burning* (1981); she had one line of dialogue

★ **Diane Keaton** – Joan in *Lovers and Other Strangers* (1970)

★ **Nicole Kidman** – Helen in *Prince and the Great Race* (1983)

★ **Shirley Maclaine** – Jennifer Rogers in *The Trouble with Harry* (1955)

★ **Andie MacDowell** – Jane Porter in *The Legend of Tarzan, Lord of the Apes* (1984)

★ **Madonna** (porn) – Bruna in *A Certain Sacrifice* (1979)

★ **Jayne Mansfield** – cigarette girl in *Pete Kelly's Blues* (1955)

★ **Liza Minnelli** – *The Good Old Summertime* (1949)

★ **Marilyn Monroe** – background shot of the 22-year-old in a rowing boat in *Scudda-Hoo! Scudda-Hay!* (1948).

★ **Demi Moore** – *Choices* (1981)

★ **Gwyneth Paltrow** – Rebecca in *Shout* (1991); she also appeared as the young Wendy in *Hook* (1991)

★ **Michelle Pfeiffer** – carhop in *Hollywood Knights* (1980)

★ **Vanessa Redgrave** – Pamela Gray in *Behind the Mask* (1958)

★ **Debbie Reynolds** – as Boo's girlfriend in *June Bride* (1948)

★ **Christina Ricci** – Kate Flax in *Mermaids* (1990)

★ **Julia Roberts** – *Satisfaction* (1987)

★ **Meg Ryan** – Young Debby in *Rich and Famous* (1981)

★ **Winona Ryder** – Rina in *Lucas* (1985)

★ **Susan Sarandon** – Melissa Compton in *Joe* (1970)

★ **Sharon Stone** – girl on train in *Stardust Memories* (1980)

★ **Meryl Streep** – Anne Marie Travers in *Julia* (1976)

★ **Elizabeth Taylor** – Gloria Twine in *There's One Born Every Minute* (1942)

★ **Uma Thurman** – Laura in *Kiss Daddy Goodnight* (1987)

★ **Kathleen Turner** – Matty Walker in *Body Heat* (1981)

★ **Liv Tyler** – Sylvie Warden in *Silent Fall* (1994)

★ **Sigourney Weaver** – Woody Allen's date in *Annie Hall* (1976), a role with zero dialogue.

★ **Raquel Welch** – hooker in *House Is Not a Home* (1964)

★ **Kate Winslet** – Juliet Hulme in *Heavenly Creatures* (1994)

★ **Natalie Wood** – *Happy Land* (1943)

First Big-Screen Roles of 50 Actors

★ **Ben Affleck** – Chesty Smith in *School Ties* (1992)

★ **Woody Allen** – *What's New Pussycat* (1964)

★ **Alec Baldwin** – *Forever Lulu* (1986)

★ **Antonio Banderas** – Sadec in *Labyrinth of Passion* (1982)

★ **Warren Beatty** – Bud Stamper in *Splendor in the Grass* (1961)

★ **Humphrey Bogart** – *A Devil With Women* (1930)

★ **Yul Brynner** – *Port of New York* (1949)

★ **Richard Burton** – *The Last Days of Dolwyn* (1948)

★ **Nicolas Cage** – as Brad's pal in *Fast Times* at Ridgemont High (1982) (billed as Nicolas Coppola)

★ **Jim Carrey** – as Tony Moroni in *Introducing … Janet* (1983) a.k.a. Rubberface (unusually apt!)

★ **Sean Connery** – 2nd Welder in *Time Lock* (1957)

★ **Kevin Costner** – *Sizzle Beach USA* (1978)

★ **Tom Cruise** – Billy in *Endless Love* (1981)

★ **John Cusack** – as Roscoe in *Class* (1983)

★ **Matt Damon** – Steamer in *Mystic Pizza* (1988)

★ **James Dean** – *Sailor Beware* (1951)

★ **Robert De Niro** – Cecil in *The Wedding Party* (1963); while this was De Niro's first part it was not actually released until 1969, one year after the release of *Greetings* (1968).

★ **Johnny Depp** – Glen Lantz in *A Nightmare on Elm Street* (1984)

★ **Leonardo DiCaprio** – as Josh in *Critters 3* (1991)

★ **Michael Douglas** – *Hail, Hero!* (1969)

★ **Harrison Ford** – Lieutenant Shaffer in *A Time for Killing* (1967)

★ **Mel Gibson** – Scollop in *Summer City* (1977)

★ **Jeff Goldblum** – as Lloyd Harris in *California Split* (1974); also appeared in *Death Wish* (1974)

★ **Tom Hanks** – *He Knows You're Alone* (1980)

★ **Charlton Heston** – *Peer Gynt* (1941)

★ **Dennis Hopper** – *The Jagged Edge* (1955); also as a goon in *Rebel Without a Cause* (1955)

★ **Val Kilmer** – *Top Secret* (1984)

★ **Steve Martin** – *Sergeant Pepper's Lonely Hearts Club Band* (1978)

★ **Ewan McGregor** – as Alvarez in *Being Human* (1993)

★ **Steve McQueen** – *Somebody Up There Likes Me* (1956)

★ **Robert Mitchum** – *Border Patrol* (1942)

★ **Paul Newman** – *The Silver Chalice* (1954)

★ **Jack Nicholson** – Jimmy in *The Cry Baby Killer* (1958)

★ **Gary Oldman** – as Daniel in *Remembrance* (1982)

★ **Al Pacino** – dance partner in *Me, Natalie* (1969)

★ **Sean Penn** – Alex Dwyer in *Taps* (1981)

★ **Joe Pesci** – *The Death Collector* (1975)

★ **Brad Pitt** – Brian in *Happy Together* (1989)

★ **Vincent Price** – *Service De Luxe* (1938)

★ **Ronald Reagan** – *Love Is on the Air* (1937)

★ **Keanu Reeves** – as Matt in *River's Edge* (1986)

★ **Arnold Schwarzenegger** – Arnold Strong/ Hercules in *Hercules in New York* (1969)

★ **Christian Slater** – *The Legend of Billie Jean* (1984)

★ **Sylvester Stallone** – Stud in *A Party at Kitty and Stud's* (1970); as a result of his limp performance Stallone subsequently became known as the Italian Stallion; he also had an unbilled role in Woody Allen's *Bananas* of the same year

★ **Kiefer Sutherland** – as Bill in *Max Dugan Returns* (1983)

★ **Patrick Swayze** – Ace in *Skatetown, U.S.A.* (1979)

★ **John Travolta** – Danny in *The Devil's Rain* (1975)

★ **Jean-Claude Van Damme** – *Rue Barbare* (1983)

★ **Bruce Willis** – as a man entering dinner as Delaney in *First Deadly Sin* (1980)

★ **James Woods** – *The Visitors* (1972)

20 Stars Who Started Their Careers as Extras

★ **Michael Caine** (1953)

★ **Gary Cooper** (1925)

★ **Marlene Dietrich** (1922)

★ **Clint Eastwood** (1954)

★ **Clark Gable** (1924)

★ **Stewart Granger** (1929)

★ **Melanie Griffith** (1973)

★ **Jean Harlow** (1927)

★ **Harold Lloyd** (1912)

★ **Sophia Loren** (1950)

★ **Peter Lorre** (1929)

★ **Fred MacMurray** (1930)

★ **Robert Mitchum** (1943)

★ **Marilyn Monroe** (1947)

★ **Roger Moore** (1945)

★ **David Niven** (1935)

★ **Ramon Novarro** (1917)

★ **Lana Turner** (1937)

★ **Rudolph Valentino** (1914)

★ **Loretta Young** (1927)

First Films of 100 Directors

★ **Woody Allen** – *Take the Money and Run* (1969)

★ **Robert Altman** – *The Delinquents* (1957); he also directed the TV features *Bonanza* and *Hitchcock Presents*

★ **Richard Attenborough** – *Oh! What a Lovely War* (1969)

★ **Warren Beatty** – *Heaven Can Wait* (1978)

★ **Luc Besson** – *L'Avant-dernier* (1981)

★ **Peter Bogdanovich** – *Targets* (1968)

★ **John Boorman** – *Catch Us If You Can* (1965), starring the Dave Clark Five

★ **Kenneth Branagh** – *Henry V* (1989)

★ **James L Brooks** – *Terms of Endearment* (1983)

★ **Mel Brooks** – *The Producers* (1968)

★ **Tim Burton** – *Pee-wee's Big Adventure* (1985): Burton also directed two shorts in 1982; *Frankenweenie*, and *Vincent*.

★ **Jane Campion** – *Sweetie* (1989)

★ **Joel Coen** – *Blood Simple* (1984)

★ **Chris Columbus** – *Adventures in Babysitting* (1987)

★ **Francis Ford Coppola** – *Tonight for Sure* (1961): a soft-porn feature.

★ **Kevin Costner** – *Dances With Wolves* (1990)

★ **Wes Craven** – *Last House on the Left* (1972)

★ **David Cronenberg** – *Shivers* (1975) a.k.a. *The Parasite Murders/They Came from Within*; also the short film *Stereo* (1969)

★ **George Cukor** – *Virtuous Sin* (1930)

★ **Michael Curtiz** – *Az Utolsó bohém* (1912) (as Mihály Kertész)

★ **Cecil B DeMille** – *The Squaw Man* (1914)

★ **Jonathan Demme** – *Caged Heat* (1974)

★ **Brian De Palma** – *Murder à la Mod* (1968)

★ **Danny DeVito** – *Throw Momma from the Train* (1987)

★ **Richard Donner** – *X-15* (1961)

★ **Clint Eastwood** – *High Plains Drifter* (1973); also *Play Misty For Me* (1971), originally a TV movie.

★ **Blake Edwards** – *Bring Your Smile Along* (1955)

★ **Peter Farrelly** – *Dumb & Dumber* (1994)

★ **Peter Fonda** – *The Hired Hand* (1971)

★ **Bryan Forbes** – *Whistle Down the Wind* (1961)

★ **John Ford** – *Trail of Hate* (1917)

★ **Bob Fosse** – *Sweet Charity* (1969)

★ **Jodie Foster** – *Little Man Tate* (1981)

★ **William Friedkin** – *Good Times* (1967)

★ **Terry Gilliam** – *And Now for Something Completely Different* (1971)

★ **Guy Hamilton** – *The Ringer* (1952)

★ **Howard Hawks** – *The Road to Glory* (1926)

★ **Brian Helgeland** – *Payback* (1999)

★ **Alfred Hitchcock** – *The Pleasure Garden* (1925)

★ **Tobe Hooper** – *The Texas Chainsaw Massacre* (1974); *Eggshells* (1974), though actually his first film, saw only limited distribution

★ **Anjelica Huston** – *Bastard Out of Carolina* (1996)

★ **John Huston** – *The Maltese Falcon* (1941)

★ **Derek Jarman** – *Jubilee* (1978), co-directed *Sebastiane* (1976) with Paul Humfress

★ **Norman Jewison** – *Forty Pounds of Trouble* (1963)

★ **Terry Jones** – *Monty Python and the Holy Grail* (1974)

★ **Neil Jordan** – *Angel* (1982)

★ **Stanley Kubrick** – *Fear and Desire* (1953)

★ **John Landis** – *Schlock* a.k.a. *The Banana Monster* (1971)

★ **Charles Laughton** – *The Man on the Eiffel Tower* (1949)

★ **David Lean** – *This Happy Breed* (1944); also co-directed (with Noel Coward) *In Which We Serve* (1942)

★ **Spike Lee** – *She's Gotta Have It* (1986); also the short films *Joe's Bed-Stuy Barber Shop: We Cut Heads* (1980)

★ **Mike Leigh** – *Bleak Moments* (1971)

★ **Richard Lester** – *It's Trad, Dad!* (1961); prior to this Lester made an eleven-minute short entitled *The Running Jumping & Standing Still Film* (1959)

★ **Barry Levinson** – *Diner* (1982)

★ **George Lucas** – *THX1138* (1971)

★ **Sidney Lumet** – *12 Angry Men* (1957)

★ **David Lynch** – *Eraserhead* (1977) (Prior to this Lynch made the four-minute moving painting *Alphabet* (1968), which he used to raise money from the American Film Institute in order to make the animation live action short *The Grandmother* (1970), about a bed-wetting boy who successfully grows the grandmother he always wanted from a seed!)

★ **Terrence Malick** – *Badlands* (1973)

★ **Joseph L Mankiewicz** – *Dragonwyck* (1946)

★ **Garry Marshall** – *Young Doctors in Love* (1982)

★ **John McTiernan** – *Nomads* (1986)

★ **Vincente Minnelli** – *I Dood It* (1943)

★ **Mike Newell** – *Bad Blood* (1983)

★ **Mike Nichols** – *Who's Afraid of Virginia Woolf?* (1966); the same Mike Nichols who was part of the Nichols and May comedy team, a huge Broadway success in the 1960s with 'An Evening with Mike Nichols and Elaine May'.

★ **Leonard Nimoy** – *Star Trek III: The Search for Spock* (1984)

★ **Laurence Olivier** – *Henry V* (1944)

★ **Alan J Pakula** – *The Sterile Cuckoo* (1969)

★ **Alan Parker** – *Bugsy Malone* (1976)

★ **Sam Peckinpah** – *The Deadly Companions; Trigger Happy* (1961)

★ **Roman Polanski** – *Noz w wodzie/ Knife in the Water* (1962); prior to this Polanski made several short films, including the award-winning *Mammals*

★ **Sydney Pollack** – *The Slender Thread* (1965)

★ **Otto Preminger** – *Die Große Liebe* (1931)

★ **Sam Raimi** – *The Evil Dead* (1980)

★ **Robert Redford** – *Ordinary People* (1980)

★ **Carol Reed** – *Midshipman Easy* (1935) as well as *It Happened in Paris* (1935), which he co-directed with Robert Wyler

★ **Mark Robson** – *The Seventh Victim* (1943)

EL MARIACHI (1992)

★ **Robert Rodriguez** – *El Mariachi* (1992); as well as the earlier short *Bedhead* (1991)

★ **George Romero** – *Night of the Living Dead* (1968)

★ **Herbert Ross** – *Goodbye, Mr. Chips* (1969)

★ **Ken Russell** – *Peepshow* (1956)

★ **John Schlesinger** – *Terminus* (1961)

★ **Joel Schumacher** – *The Incredible Shrinking Woman* (1981)

★ **Martin Scorsese** – *Who's That Knocking at My Door?* (1967); also the short film *What's a Nice Girl Like You Doing in a Place Like This?* (1963) as a student

★ **Ridley Scott** – *The Duellists* (1977)

★ **Tony Scott** – *The Hunger* (1983)

★ **Todd Solondz** – *Fear, Anxiety & Depression* (1989)

★ **Steven Spielberg** – *The Sugarland Express* (1974); also the TV movie *Duel* (1971); theatrical release 1983; also directed *Columbo* in 1971 and the 1990s

★ **Sylvester Stallone** – *Paradise Alley* (1978)

★ **Oliver Stone** – *Seizure* (1974)

★ **Barbra Streisand** – *Yentl* (1983)

★ **Gus Van Sant** – *Mala Noche/Bad Night* (1985)

★ **Paul Verhoeven** – *Een Hagedis teveel/ A Lizard Too Much* (1960)

★ **Raoul Walsh** – *Life of Villa* (1912) (co-directed with Christy Cabanne); *The Fencing Master* (1915)

★ **Peter Weir** – *Homesdale* (1971)

★ **Billy Wilder** – *Mauvaise Graine* (1933)

★ **Gene Wilder** – *The Adventure of Sherlock Holmes' Smarter Brother* (1975)

★ **Michael Winner** – *Climb Up the Wall* (1960)

★ **Franco Zeffirelli** – *Camping* (1957)

★ **Robert Zemeckis** – *The Lift* (1972)

★ **Fred Zinnemann** – *Menschen am Sonntag/People on Sunday* (1929)

From TV to Eternity

15 stars who successfully made the leap from TV to the movies

★ **Alan Alda** – *M*A*S*H*

★ **Alec Baldwin** – *The Doctors*

★ **Ted Danson** – *Cheers*

★ **Danny DeVito** – *Taxi*

★ **Clint Eastwood** – *Rawhide*

★ **Michael J Fox** – *Family Ties*

★ **John Goodman** – *Roseanne*

★ **Mark Hamill** – *The Texas Wheelers*

★ **Woody Harrelson** – *Cheers*

★ **Goldie Hawn** – *Rowan and Martin's Laugh-In*

★ **Steve McQueen** – *Wanted: Dead or Alive*

★ **Tom Selleck** – *Magnum*

★ **John Travolta** – *Welcome Back, Kotter*

★ **Robin Williams** – *Mork and Mindy*

★ **Bruce Willis** – *Moonlighting*

The Golden Oldies!

Veterans of the screen

★ **Don Ameche** – his first role was in *Clive of India* (1935); his last was *Corrina, Corrina* (1994). Ameche died in 1993.

★ **Milton Berle** – *Tillie's Punctured Romance* (1914); still going strong.

★ **Noah Beery Jr** – *The Mark of Zorro* (1920); died 1994.

★ **Claudette Colbert** – *For the Love of Mike* (1927); died 1996.

★ **Cyril Cusack** – *Knocknagow* (1918); *Far and Away* (1992); died 1993.

★ **Lillian Gish** – *An Unseen Enemy* (1912); *The Whales of August* (1987); died 1993.

★ **Sir John Gielgud** – *Who is the Man?* (1924); the voice of Merlin in *Quest for Camelot* (1998) and still with us.

★ **Helen Hayes** – *The Weavers of Life* (1917); played Miss Marple in the 1980s TV movies; died 1993.

★ **Brian Keith** – *Pied Piper Malone* (1924); *Follow Your Heart* (1998); died 1997.

★ **Bessie Love** – *The Birth of a Nation* (1915); *The Hunger* (1983); died 1986.

★ **Myrna Loy** – *Pretty Ladies* (1925); *Summer Solstice* (1981) (television); died 1993.

★ **Burgess Meredith** – *Winterset* (1936); played Mickey in the Rocky films; died 1997.

★ **Luise Rainer** – *Ja, der Himmel über Wien* (1930); *The Gambler* (1997); still going.

★ **Gilbert Roland** – *The Lost World* (1925); *Barbarosa* (1982); died 1994.

★ **Mickey Rooney** – *Not to be Trusted* (1926); *Babe: Pig in the City* (1998); still going.

★ **Sylvia Sidney** – *Broadway Nights* (1927); *Mars Attacks* (1996); still with us.

★ **Gloria Stuart** – *Street of Women* (1932); played Rose Dawson Calvert in *Titanic* (1997).

★ **Jessica Tandy** – *The Indiscretions of Eve* (1932); *An African Love Story* (1996); died 1994.

★ **Fay Wray** – *Gasoline Love* (1923); still living but no longer hanging out with overgrown apes. We hope!

★ **Billy Crystal** (1984–1985)

★ **Joan Cusack** (1985–1986)

★ **Robert Downey Jr** (1985–1986)

★ **Chris Farley** (1990–1995)

★ **Anthony Michael Hall** (1985–1986)

★ **Julia Louis-Dreyfus** (1982–1985)

★ **Eddie Murphy** (1981–1984)

★ **Bill Murray** (1977–1980)

★ **Mike Myers** (1989–1994)

★ **Randy Quaid** (1985–1986)

★ **Chris Rock** (1990–1993)

★ **Adam Sandler** (1991–1995)

★ **Martin Short** (1984–1985)

★ **Ben Stiller** (1989)

★ **Daman Wayans** (1985–1986)

Saturday Night Live Regulars

★ **Dan Aykroyd** (1975–1979)

★ **James Belushi** (1983–1985)

★ **John Belushi** (1975–1979)

★ **Dana Carvey** (1986–1993)

★ **Chevy Chase** (1975–1976)

Chapter 9
What's Up Doc?

WATERSHIP DOWN (1978)

Toons, Toons, Glorious Toons! Yes, this section of the book is devoted to nothing but the world of cartoons, or toons as they're more lovingly known.

First off, we take a look at the feature-length animated movie, beginning with one of the first, Disney's *Snow White and the Seven Dwarfs*, made way back in 1937. Since those pioneering days much has changed, not least of all the choice of subject matter. Back then we had cuddly little dwarfs; nowadays we have the likes of Beavis and Butt-head.

Mind you, today's toons are little short of a celebrity fest, with top stars featuring in almost as many toons as they do regular movies. Although a toon appearance means that they're heard rather than seen, modern toons increasingly caricature the celebrity in question. Anyway, we follow up our list of feature-length cartoons with a look at some of the more interesting stars to have lent their voices to animated characters.

However, no discussion of cartoons would be complete without some reference to the creations of Matt Groening, especially *The Simpsons*, and that's exactly where we finish up.

The Feature-Length Toon

The release of 1998's *The Prince of Egypt* sees the animated movie match some of the screen's biggest action films in terms of its dramatic content; with technology no longer a constraint anything is possible. How things have changed since 1937 when *Snow White and the Seven Dwarfs* created such a stir as the first feature-length animated movie to incorporate both sound and colour. The following list is a salute to the continuing efforts of the world's greatest cartoon creators.

★ **Snow White and the Seven Dwarfs** (1937)
A $1 million adaptation of Grimm's classic fairy story.

★ **Gulliver's Travels** (1939)
Jonathan Swift's tale of the (relatively) giant Gulliver and the inhabitants of Lilliput brought to life on the big screen.

★ **Pinocchio** (1939)
The animated adventures of the woodcarver Geppetto's puppet.

★ **Fantasia** (1940)
Well-known pieces by composers such as Bach, Tchaikovsky, Beethoven and Ponchielli are brought to life in this visual feast of animation.

★ **Dumbo** (1941)
Disney's rendering of Helen Aberson and Harold Pearl's tale 'Dumbo The Flying Elephant,' in which an elephant learns to makes the best of his big ears.

★ **Hoppity Goes to Town** (1941)
(a.k.a. *Mr. Bug Goes to Town*)
A group of developers put a community of insects in danger.

★ **Bambi** (1943)
Probably one of the most famous of Disney's films, telling the story of the deer Bambi and all his cuddly little friends.

★ **Make Mine Music** (1946)
A collection of Disney cartoon shorts including *Peter and the Wolf*, *Willie the Singing Whale* and *Johnny Fedora*.

★ **Cinderella** (1950)
Even in this classic cartoon version of the story Cinderella still gets to go to the ball. (Oops! Sorry if we've spoilt the plot for you.)

★ Alice in Wonderland (1952)
A modernised and as a result Americanised version of the famous Lewis Carroll story.

★ Peter Pan (1953)
Disney's tale of the magic flying boy who couldn't grow up and his trip with three London children to fairyland.

ANIMAL FARM (1954)

★ Animal Farm (1954)
Good old George Orwell tries to prove that 'all animals are equal but some animals are more equal than others'.

★ Lady and the Tramp (1956)
The adventures of Lady the Spaniel and her romance with the muttish Tramp.

★ Sleeping Beauty (1959)
A $6 million adaptation of the story of Princess Aurora and her unhappy encounter with the bad fairy Maleficent.

★ Arabian Nights (1942)
How to win back your throne with the help of an acrobat and a dancer.

★ One Hundred and One Dalmatians (1961)
Cruella De Ville's attempts to dog-nap young puppies are foiled by London's four-legged friends.

★ Alakazam the Great (1960)
Japanese-made cartoon concerning the adventures of a magical monkey.

★ The Sword in the Stone (1963)
Based on the novel *The Once and Future King* by TH White, about a youngster named Wart as he follows his destiny to become King Arthur.

★ Gay Purr-ee (1963)
Judy Garland, Robert Goulet and Red Buttons, among others, supply the voices to this tale of a country cat's trip to Paris.

★ Pinocchio in Outer Space (1964)
A US/French production following the little wooden fellow's journey to the heavens.

★ Hey There, It's Yogi Bear (1964)
Hanna-Barbera's first full-length animated feature, following Yogi's search for his beloved Cindy Bear, who he believes has been taken to San Diego Zoo.

★ The Man Called Flintstone (1966)
Fred gets involved in a spy ring headed by the mysterious Green Goose.

★ Gulliver's Travels Beyond the Moon (1966)
The gentle giant and his friends head for the skies.

★ The Jungle Book (1967)
Cartoon animal life in this classic Disney feature.

★ A Boy Named Charlie Brown (1969)
Charlie Brown and friends make their big-screen debut.

★ The Phantom Tollbooth (1969)
Adaptation of Norman Juster's novel about a boy who finds his way into the strange world of the Kingdom of Wisdom, where numbers and letters are at war with each other.

★ The Aristocats (1970)
An inheritance war between a cat, her kittens and a scheming butler.

★ Shinbone Alley (1971)
An adult feature telling the story of unrequited love between Archie the Cockroach and Mehitabel the Cat, with voices supplied by John Carradine and Carol Channing.

★ Fritz the Cat (1972)
Unusual in the fact that Ralph Bakshi's cartoon was X-rated for its graphic sexuality; it is based on the successful 'underground' comic strip by the satirist Robert Crumb, concerning an alley cat's adventures in New York.

★ Snoopy, Come Home (1972)
Snoopy the dog, fed up with the growing number of 'No Dogs Allowed' signs, runs away with his feathered friend Woodstock.

★ Robin Hood (1973)
The famous legend comes alive with all parts being played by animals, featuring Prince John as a thumb-sucking lion, Little John as a bear and Friar Tuck as a badger.

★ The Fantastic Planet (1973)
A tiny race of creatures battle it out with the mammoth Draggs.

★ Heavy Traffic (1973)
Another Ralph Bakshi animated X-rated movie, this time about a young New Yorker who relieves his sexual frustration through erotic drawings. Considered by many to be unnecessarily gross.

★ Journey Back to Oz (1974)
As the title suggests, Dorothy finds her way back to the Emerald City. Voices provided by Liza Minnelli, Mickey Rooney, Ethel Merman and Milton Berle.

★ The Nine Lives of Fritz the Cat (1975)
The older, married and now pot-smoking tabby fantasises about his former exploits. Not surprisingly, like the original it too is X-rated.

★ Hugo, the Hippo (1975)
Marie and Jimmy Osmond as you've never heard them before, alongside Robert Morley and Burl Ives, supplying the voices for this story of incompatibility between Hippos and Sharks on the Island of Zanzibar.

★ The Rescuers (1976)
Following the exploits of two mice, Bernard and Bianca, agents of the 'Mouse Rescue Aid Society', as they attempt to save a young girl named Penny from the evils of Madame Medusa.

★ Wizards (1977)
The creator of Fritz the Cat offers an animated view of Earth 3,000 years after a nuclear war, with a number of factions battling for control of the planet. Featuring the voice of Mark Hamill.

★ Raggedy Ann and Andy (1977)
Rag dolls go in search of adventure, rescuing a French doll from pirates along the way.

★ Watership Down (1978)
Featuring Art Garfunkel's number-one hit, 'Bright Eyes', a song about a rabbit, written by a bat (that's Mike Batt!). Based on the story of a colony of rabbits in search of a new home by Richard Adams. Voices are provided by John Hurt, Richard Briers, Denholm Elliott and Joss Ackland among others.

LORD OF THE RINGS (1978)

★ **The Lord of the Rings** (1978)
JRR Tolkien's story of the struggle
between good and bad for the control of
a magical ring.

★ **Animalympics** (1979)
The Olympic Games come to Toon Land,
with animals going for gold.

★ **Grendel, Grendel, Grendel** (1980)
The observations of a medieval monster
named Grendel about creatures known to
him as 'man', who commit heinous crimes.
Based on the novel by John Gardner.

★ **American Pop** (1981)
Charting the history of American pop music
from the turn of the century to New Wave.

★ **The Fox and the Hound** (1981)
A fox cub and hound pup put their friendship
to the test as they grow older together.

★ **Heavy Metal** (1981)
The work of many studios, writers and
directors bring about this anthology of sexy
sci-fi stories.

★ **Hey, Good Lookin'** (1982)
The antics of two young womanisers in
Brooklyn, based on the director and writer
Ralph Bakshi's own adolescence.

★ **Heidi's Song** (1982)
Based on Johanna Spyri's classic novel
Heidi, following the story of Heidi, separated
from her beloved grandfather and forced to
live in Frankfurt. Musical score by Sammy
Cahn and Burton Lane; voices provided by
Sammy Davis Jr, Lorne Greene and Margery
Grey as Heidi.

★ **The Secret of NIMH** (1982)
Produced by a forum of ex-Disney studio
staff, the story concerns the efforts of a
widowed mouse as she battles to save her
home and family from imps, with the help of
super-intelligent rats.

★ **The Plague Dogs** (1982)
Based on a Richard Adams novel, in which
an entire countryside is under threat from
a deadly virus carried by two dogs, who have
escaped from a research laboratory.

★ **The Last Unicorn** (1982)
The voices of Jeff Bridges, Angela Lansbury,
Mia Farrow, Alan Arkin and Christopher Lee
feature in this tale of a lonely unicorn who
goes in search of company.

★ **Fire and Ice** (1983)
A disappointing story from the director
Ralph Bakshi of good meeting evil is saved
by the design work of the acclaimed fantasy
illustrator Frank Frazetta.

★ **Rock & Rule** (1983)
Featuring the music of Lou Reed, Debbie
Harry, the bands Earth, Wind and Fire and
Cheap Trick and others in this animated story
of an evil plan to release a monster from
another dimension into a world of rock music.

★ **Lensman** (1984)
(a.k.a. *The Power of the Lens*)
A feeling of *Star Wars* permeates this
story about a young boy who is forced to
fight a number of hazards in his attempt to
neutralise the dangerous weapons of the
Boskone Empire.

★ **The Smurfs and the Magic Flute** (1984)
The little people discover a magic flute
which has the power to make anyone who
hears it dance uncontrollably.

★ **The Black Cauldron** (1985)
A young boy must beat the evil Horned King
in the race to find the magical black cauldron.

★ **The Cosmic Eye** (1985)
The story of the needs and struggles of men
and children around the world. Among others,
Dizzy Gillespie supplies both voice and music.

★ **The Care Bears Movie** (1985)
The lovable bears become good Samaritans
when they help children in need. Music by
Carole King and narration by Mickey Rooney.

★ **Starchaser: The Legend of Orin** (1985)
A 3-D animated movie following the efforts
of the galactic hero Orin as he attempts to aid
the Princess Aviana.

★ **Rainbow Brite and the Star Stealer** (1985)
The last star in the sky is in danger of being
extinguished. Can one little girl save the day?

★ **The Great Mouse Detective** (1986)
Based on the Eve Titus book, *Basil of Baker
Street*, about a mouse detective who must
pit his wits against the wretched Professor
Ratigan, voiced by Vincent Price.
Re-released in 1992 as *The Adventures of
the Great Mouse Detective*.

★ **Heathcliff: The Movie** (1986)
Feature-length outing for the feline hero,
in which he relates his many adventures to
his nephew.

★ **The Care Bears Movie 2:
A New Generation** (1986)
The sequel tells the story of the bears and
their adventures in the Kingdom of Caring.

★ **My Little Pony** (1986)
The good little ponies come head to head
with an evil witch, encountering a mass of
living lava on the way. Voices provided
by Danny DeVito, Madeline Kahn, Cloris
Leachman and Tony Randall.

★ **GoBots: Battle of the Rock Lords** (1986)
The good GoBots fight the evil Renegades;
featuring, among others, the voices of
Telly Savalas and Roddy McDowall.

★ **An American Tail** (1986)
In the late nineteenth century a young
Russian mouse gets separated from his family
on their journey to America. Incidentally,
the first animated movie to be produced by
Steven Spielberg.

★ **The Chipmunk Adventure** (1987)
As the Chipmunks sail around the world in
a balloon race, they find themselves entangled
in diamond smuggling.

★ **The Care Bears' Adventures
in Wonderland** (1987)
Adventures ensue when the bears follow
Alice through the looking glass.

★ **The Brave Little Toaster** (1987)
Following the adventures of five disillusioned
household appliances, who set off in search of
a little boy they once knew as 'Master'.

★ Pinocchio and the Emperor of the Night (1987)
While celebrating his first birthday, Pinocchio finds himself being led astray by an unscrupulous carnival owner.

★ Pound Puppies and the Legend of Big Paw (1988)
Adventures involving the puppies during their quest to recover a magic bone.

★ Oliver and Company (1988)
Bette Midler, Cheech Marin and Billy Joel head the list of stars who provide the voices for this animated version of Oliver Twist. Set in a modern-day New York with animals playing the characters.

★ Who Framed Roger Rabbit? (1988)
A mixture of live action and animation, starring Bob Hoskins as detective Eddie Valiant. Roger Rabbit, a major star at Maroon studios, becomes the prime suspect in a murder case.

★ The Land Before Time (1988)
An orphaned dinosaur and his tribe of friends have adventures on their way to a valley where they can all survive.

★ Light Years (1988)
Glenn Close and Christopher Plummer are among the stars providing the voices for this French-produced movie telling the story of a time-travelling princess.

★ All Dogs Go to Heaven (1989)
After a premature death, an ex-con mutt returns to Earth to repent for his life of crime by adopting an orphan.

★ The Little Mermaid (1989)
Adaptation of Hans Christian Andersen's fairy tale about a prince who is saved from drowning by a mermaid who wants to become human in order to be his girl.

★ Daffy Duck's Quackbusters (1989)
After inheriting a small fortune, Daffy sets up his own Ghostbuster agency employing his chums, Bugs Bunny and Porky Pig. The movie incorporates clips from many of the Warner Brothers' horror-movie spoofs.

★ Jetsons: The Movie (1990)
Based on the sixties TV cartoon series, following the exploits of a twenty-first-century family. George is given promotion by his boss and sent to a distant asteroid to take charge of an ore-extraction plant.

★ Duck Tales: The Movie – Treasure of the Lost Lamp (1990)
The Ali Baba story revisited with Scrooge McDuck and his nephews in pursuit of a magic lamp that once belonged to a notorious bandit.

★ The Rescuers Down Under (1990)
Following in the footsteps of *The Rescuers* Margery Sharp's heroic mice are summoned to Australia where they protect various creatures from a mean villain.

★ The Nutcracker Prince (1990)
Based on the book, *The Nutcracker and the Mouse King*, by ETA Hoffmann, this reworking of the classic story about a shrinking girl who enters the magical land of toys is accompanied by the music of Tchaikovsky and features the voices of Kiefer Sutherland and Peter O'Toole, to name but a few.

★ Happily Ever After (1990)
(a.k.a. *Snow White and the Land of Doom*) A star-studded cast, including Zsa Zsa Gabor, Tracey Ullman, Malcolm McDowell, Sally Kellerman, Michael Horton, Irene Cara, Carol Channing and Ed Asner provide the voices for this animated sequel to the story of Snow White.

★ **Rock-a-Doodle** (1991)
A star-struck cock finds fame and fortune as an Elvis Presley sound-alike in a Las Vegas nightclub.

★ **The Magic Riddle** (1991)
Blending several famous fairy stories together, not least of all 'Cinderella'. Here, Cindy is put to work by her ugly sisters and wicked stepmother and, as fate would have it, she gets to marry the handsome prince.

★ **Beauty and the Beast** (1991)
The Disney studio's thirteenth full-length cartoon movie was an adaptation of the famous classic *Beauty and the Beast*, in which the beautiful Belle is held prisoner in the Beast's castle during which time they fall in love.

★ **Rover Dangerfield** (1991)
The comedian Rodney Dangerfield lends his voice and career to the antics of a wisecracking cartoon dog who finds himself demoted from the bright lights of Las Vegas to darkest downtown nowhere.

★ **An American Tail: Fievel Goes West** (1991)
The sequel to *An American Tail* finds Fievel and family en route to the American West, with the voice of James Stewart adding additional value to the movie as Sheriff Wylie Burp.

★ **The Tune** (1992)
Created by Bill Plympton, the award winning director of animated shorts, and following a struggling songwriter in search of that number-one hit.

★ **FernGully ... The Last Rainforest** (1992)
When the rainforest comes under threat from the developer's bulldozers, a fairy with the assistance of a young lumberjack saves the day. An Australian production with an ecological message, featuring the voices of Tim Curry, Christian Slater, Robin Williams, Cheech Marin and Tommy Chong, among others.

★ **Bebe's Kids** (1992)
Taking a leaf out of the books of 'The Chipmunks' and 'The Simpsons', *Bebe's Kids* is based on the routines of the late black comedian Robin Harris, notably his first date, which turns into a nightmare when she insists upon bringing four mischievous children.

★ **Cool World** (1992)
Comic-strip characters come to life in this live-action/animated feature by Ralph Bakshi, featuring the voices of Gabriel Byrne, Brad Pitt, Kim Basinger and Frank Sinatra Jr.

★ **Little Nemo: Adventures in Slumberland** (1992)
The young Little Nemo finds his dreams lead him into Slumberland, where the Dream King plans for him to take over his throne.

★ **Freddie as F.R.O.7** (1992)
James Bond meets Kermit the Frog in this animated secret-agent spoof. Voices are provided by a star-studded cast, including Michael Hordern, Billie Whitelaw, Ben Kingsley, Jonathan Pryce, Brian Blessed, Jenny Agutter, Nigel Hawthorne, Phyllis Logan and Prunella Scales. The movie was later re-edited under the title, *Freddie the Frog*, with narration by James Earl Jones.

★ **Vampire Hunter D** (1992)
A Japanese-produced movie with vampires and demons freely roaming the world.

★ **Tom and Jerry: The Movie** (1992)
Heavens above, Tom and Jerry not only begin to speak but also become chums, as they join forces to help find a young girl's missing father.

★ **Aladdin** (1992)
Aladdin, a street urchin, helps to retrieve the magic lamp that has been lost in the desert cave. Featuring the hit song, 'A Whole New World', sung by Peabo Bryson and Regina Belle.

★ **The Princess and the Goblin** (1992)
Follows the adventures of Princess Irene and a miner's son, Curdi, in their attempts to ward off evil goblins. Based on the 1872 fairy tale by George MacDonald.

★ **A Troll in Central Park** (1993)
Banished from Troll Land, Stanley and his green thumb bring a ray of sunshine to New York City and the lives of two neglected youngsters.

★ **Once Upon a Forest** (1993)
A fairy's rainforest home is brought under threat due to the arrogance of the human race in this animated ecological commentary.

★ **Batman: The Animated Movie** (1993)
(a.k.a. *Mask of the Phantasm*)
Batman pursues his archenemy the Joker, as well as the Phantasm, in this animated adventure.

★ **The Nightmare Before Christmas** (1993)
Halloween town hero Jack Skellington puts all of his energy into trying to redefine Christmas in this Tim Burton marvel, which was years in the making.

★ **We're Back!**
(a.k.a. *We're Back! A Dinosaur's Story*) (1993)
Four dinosaurs have their brainpower increased and find themselves transported to modern-day New York to the amusement of the city's children.

★ **The Swan Princess** (1994)
Based on the legend of Swan Lake, the story tells of a princess who is turned into a swan by a banished magician.

★ **The Pagemaster** (1994)
A neurotic child, voiced by Macaulay Culkin, takes shelter from a storm in a huge library, only to find that the paintings on the ceiling splash on him, turning him and his surroundings into cartoons.

Other voices include those of Christopher Lloyd, Patrick Stewart, Leonard Nimoy and Whoopi Goldberg.

★ **Thumbelina** (1994)
Based on the fairy tale by Hans Christian Andersen, it relates the adventures of the thumb-sized heroine as she attempts to find her way home.

★ **The Land Before Time II: The Great Valley Adventure** (1994)
This sequel to *The Land Before Time* failed to get a cinema release and went straight to video. It tells the tale of Littlefoot, a young brontosaurus and his friends who meet up with baby Tyrannosaurus Rex, who wants to become part of their group.

★ **The Lion King** (1994)
Set in the African jungle, in which the Lion King Mufasa is planning for his son Simba to take over as King. Unfortunately, Uncle Scar, Mufasa's brother, has designs on the throne and plots to kill his young nephew. Contains the two Elton John songs, 'Can You Feel the Love Tonight' and 'Circle of Life'.

★ **A Goofy Movie** (1995)
An attempt at father-and-son bonding between Goofy and his teenage son Max, as they embark upon a road trip.

★ **Balto** (1995)
Loosely based on a true story from the 1920s, this tells of an outcast wolf-dog called Balto, who risks life and limb to retrieve life-saving medicines for a town of sick Alaskan children.

★ **Toy Story** (1995)
The story of the secret life of toys who come to life when humans aren't present. A cowboy called Woody, voiced by Tom Hanks, finds himself more than irritated by his spaceman buddy Buzz Lightyear, voiced by Tim Allen.

★ The Pebble and the Penguin (1995)
The likable penguin Hubie sets off with his sidekick Rocko in search of his true love.

★ Pocahontas (1995)
Against her will, Pocahontas's father wishes her to marry the tribe's bravest warrior but unfortunately she has other ideas, in the shape of a rugged, blond Englishman, Captain John Smith, voiced by the Australian actor Mel Gibson.

★ Arabian Knight (1995)
Princess Yum Yum falls for the humble young cobbler Tack, and together the two set out to save her father's kingdom, by trying to retrieve three gold balls that are believed to protect the city.

★ All Dogs Go to Heaven 2 (1996)
Canine Charlie Barkin and his friend Itchy return to Earth in an effort to stop the evil Red from turning Alcatraz into an eternal dog pound. Featuring the voices of Ernest Borgnine, Sheena Easton, Charlie Sheen and Dom DeLuise.

★ Beavis and Butt-head Do America (1996)
The MTV morons find themselves involved with the FBI when they try to retrieve their stolen television set.

★ The Hunchback of Notre Dame (1996)
Victor Hugo's classic brought to life by the Disney Studio.

★ Hercules (1997)
Hercules is forced to prove himself as a man, before being allowed to re-enter the home of the gods.

★ Anastasia (1997)
Anastasia beware! The evil Rasputin, having had his powers restored by his pet bat, could unleash his demons upon you.

★ Mulan (1998)
In this tale of Imperial China, a young woman disguises herself as a man in order to take her father's place on the battlefield, thereby bringing honour to her family.

★ Quest for Camelot (1998)
An evil knight's plot against King Arthur is thwarted by a young girl and a blind hermit.

★ The Prince of Egypt (1998)
A Dreamworks production that was four years in the making depicts various stories from the Bible, including the Burning Bush, the Parting of the Red Sea and the conflict between the Pharaoh and Ramses.

★ A Bug's Life (1998)
A bug called Flik goes in search of help to save the colony from tyrannical grasshoppers in this reworking of Kurosawa's *Seven Samurai*.

★ Antz (1998)
A wimpy worker ant named Z, forever complaining about life as the middle child in a family of five million, locks horns with the bullying General Mandible.

★ The Rugrats Movie (1999)
Based on the TV series; Tommy, Angelica, Chucky, Phil and Lil find themselves lost while taking a short vacation and have trouble finding their way home.

★ The King and I (1999)
Animated version of the 1956 Rodgers and Hammerstein hit musical reviving those well-loved songs, including 'Shall We Dance?', 'I Feel Pretty' and 'March of the Siamese Children'.

★ Toy Story 2 (1999)
Things get out of hand when Andy goes off to Summer Camp leaving the toys to their own devices. A toy-napper steals Woody and his pals go to his rescue.

★ South Park: Bigger, Longer and Uncut (1999)

The South Park kids are badly influenced while watching a movie containing foul language. Their parents are up in arms and declare war on anyone and everyone associated with the film.

★ Tarzan (1999)

An animated adaptation of the Edgar Rice Burroughs novel, this tells the story of a small orphan who was raised by an ape named Kala since he was a child. Featuring the voices of Brian Blessed, Nigel Hawthorne, Minnie Driver and Glenn Close.

Look Who's Talking!

Sometimes it can just be so frustrating watching animated movies. Take *Antz* (1998) for example. Did you find yourself asking some variation of the question, 'Where have I heard that ant before?' Yes, you recognise the voice but just can't seem to place the mandible. Well it's time to relax because we've done the hard work for you.

★ A Bug's Life (1998)
Francis (Denis Leary)
Hopper (Kevin Spacey)
Princess Atta (Julia Louis-Dreyfus)
PT Flea (John Ratzenberger)
Soil (Roddy McDowall)

★ A Goofy Movie (1995)
Bigfoot (Frank Welker)
Pete (Jim Cummings)
Principal Mazur (Wallace Shawn)

★ Aladdin (1992)
Abu (Frank Welker)
Genie (Robin Williams)
Iago (Gilbert Gottfried)
Jafar (Jonathan Freeman)

★ Anastasia (1997)
(Young) Anastasia (Kirsten Dunst)
Anastasia (Meg Ryan)
Dimitri (John Cusack)
Dowager Empress Marie (Angela Lansbury)
Rasputin (singing voice) (Jim Cummings)

★ Antz (1998)
Azteca (Jennifer Lopez)
Bala (Sharon Stone)
Barbados (Danny Glover)
Colonel Cutter (Christopher Walken)
General Mandible (Gene Hackman)
Muffy (Jane Curtin)
The psychologist (Paul Mazursky)
Weaver (Sylvester Stallone)
Z-4195 (Woody Allen)

★ Arabian Knight (1995)
Tack (Matthew Broderick)
Zigzag (Vincent Price)

★ Babe (1995) and
★ Babe: Pig in the City (1998)
Fly (Miriam Margoyles)

★ Balto (1995)
Balto (Kevin Bacon)
Boris (Bob Hoskins)
Jenna (Bridget Fonda)

★ Batman: The Animated Movie (1993)
The Joker (Mark Hamill)

★ Beauty and the Beast (1991)
Monsieur D'Arque (Tony Jay)

★ Beavis and Butt-head Do America (1996)
Motley Crue Roadie #1 (David Letterman)

★ Doctor Dolittle (1998)
Compulsive Dog (Gilbert Gottfried)
Raccoon (Paul Reubens)

★ FernGully … The Last Rainforest (1992)
Stump (Cheech Marin)
Batty Koda (Robin Williams)

★ Hercules (1997)
Hades (James Woods)
Hera (Samantha Eggar)
Nessus (Jim Cummings)
Phil (Danny DeVito)
The Fates (Amanda Plummer)
Zeus (Rip Torn)

★ Look Who's Talking (1989) and
★ Look Who's Talking Too (1990)
Mikey (Bruce Willis)

Look Who's Talking Too (1990)
Eddie (Damon Wayans)
Julie (Roseanne Barr)

★ Look Who's Talking Now (1993)
Mr Toilet Man (Mel Brooks)
Daphne the Poodle (Diane Keaton)
Rocks the Dog (Danny DeVito)

★ Mulan (1998)
Khan (Frank Welker)
First Ancestor (George Takei)
General Li (James Shigata)
Grandmother Fa (June Foray)
Mulan (Ming-Na Wen)
Mushu (Eddie Murphy)
Shang (BD Wong)
The Emperor (Pat Morita)
The Matchmaker (Miriam Margoyles)

★ My Favourite Martian (1999)
Zoot (Frank Welker)

★ Pocahontas (1995)
Ben (Billy Connolly)
Flit (Frank Welker)
Grandmother Willow (Linda Hunt)
John Smith (Mel Gibson)
Thomas (Christian Bale)

★ Quest for Camelot (1998)
Cornwall (Din Rickles)

★ Small Soldiers (1998)
Archer (Frank Langella)
Brick Bazooka (George Kennedy)
Butch Meathook (Jim Brown)
Chip Hazard (Tommy Lee Jones)
Gwendy Doll (Christina Ricci)
Gwendy Doll (Sarah Michelle Gellar)
Insaniac/Freakenstein (Michael McKean)
Kip Killagin (Ernest Borgnine)
Link Static (Bruce Dern)
Nick Nitro (Clint Walker)
Punch-It (Harry Shearer)
Slamfist/Scratch-It (Christopher Guest)

★ Space Jam (1996)
Charles the Dog (Frank Welker)
Swackhammer (Danny DeVito)

★ The Hunchback of Notre Dame (1996)
Baby Bird (Frank Welker)
Esmeralda (Demi Moore)
Frollo (Tony Jay)
Phoebus (Kevin Kline)
Quasimodo (Tom Hulce)

★ The Lion King (1994) and
★ The Lion King 2: Simba's Pride (1998)
(Adult) Simba (Matthew Broderick)

The Lion King (1994)
Banzai (Cheech Marin)
Ed the Laughing Hyena (Jim Cummings)
King Mufasa (James Earl Jones)
Queen Sarabi (Madge Sinclair)
Scar (Jeremy Irons)
Shenzi (Whoopi Goldberg)
Timon (Nathan Lane)
Zazu (Rowan Atkinson)

★ The Nightmare Before Christmas (1993)
Lock (Paul Reubens)

★ The Pagemaster (1994)
Adventure (Patrick Stewart)
Fantasy (Whoopi Goldberg)
Horror (Frank Welker)

★ The Pebble and the Penguin (1995)
Hubie (Martin Short)

★ The Plague Dogs (1982)
Major (Patrick Stewart)

★ The Prince of Egypt (1998)
Aaron (Jeff Goldblum)
Hotep (Steve Martin)
Huy (Martin Short)
Jethro (Danny Glover)
Miriam (Sandra Bullock)
Moses and God (Val Kilmer)
Pharaoh Seti (Patrick Stewart)
Ramses (Ralph Fiennes)
The Queen (Helen Mirren)
Tzipporah (Michelle Pfeiffer)

★ The Rescuers Down Under (1990)
Joanna (Frank Welker)

★ The Rugrats Movie (1998)
Ranger Margaret (Whoopi Goldberg)

★ Thumbelina (1994)
Mr Beetle (Gilbert Gottfried)

★ Tom & Jerry: The Movie (1992)
Lickboot (Tony Jay)

★ Toy Story (1995) and
★ Toy Story 2 (1999)
Bo Peep (Annie Potts)
Buzz Lightyear (Tim Allen)
Hamm (John Ratzenberger)
Mr Potato Head (Don Rickles)
Rex (Wallace Shawn)
Slinky Dog (Jim Varney)
Woody (Tom Hanks)

★ Were Back! A Dinosaur's Story (1993)
Stubbs the Clown (Martin Short)

★ Who Framed Roger Rabbit? (1988)
Jessica Rabbit (Kathleen Turner)
Singing Sword (Frank Sinatra)

The Simpsons

At this stage, you may well be asking yourself, exactly what TV's *The Simpsons* is doing in a book on movies. Well, since the creation of *The Simpsons* by Matt Groening back in 1987, and its undeniable rise to success, it has become a feature of the show for Hollywood's greatest, and perhaps not so great, to provide many of the characters' voices. Therefore, we provide for your edification a list of the more notable voices to be heard on the show.

The Cast:

★ Gillian Anderson
Dana Scully in 'The Springfield Files'

Anderson has achieved cult status as Agent Scully in TV's *The X Files*, and the resultant 1998 big-screen adaptation.

★ Alec Baldwin
As himself in 'When You Dish Upon A Star'

Baldwin recently appeared alongside Bruce Willis in *Mercury Rising* (1998).

★ Anne Bancroft
Dr Zweig in 'Fear of Flying'

Aside from playing Mrs Robinson in 1967's *The Graduate*, she can be heard providing the voice of the Queen in *Antz* (1998).

★ Kim Basinger
As herself in 'When You Dish Upon A Star'

★ Ernest Borgnine
As himself in 'Boy Scoutz N the Hood'

Borgnine gives a memorable performance as the taxi driver who assists Kurt Russell in *Escape from New York* (1981). He can also be heard providing the voice of Kip Killagin in *Small Soldiers* (1998).

★ Albert Brooks
Cowboy Bob in 'The Call of the Simpsons'

Not only does Brooks write and direct, but he's also a notable actor: he received an Oscar nomination for his performance as an aspiring news anchorman in *Broadcast News* (1987). More recently, Brooks provided the voice of the Tiger in the Eddie Murphy version of *Dr. Dolittle* (1998).

★ Glenn Close
Mother Simpson in 'Mother Simpson'

A five-times Oscar nominee, including her performance as the adulterous Alex Forrest in *Fatal Attraction* (1987).

★ Beverly D'Angelo
Lurleen Lumpkin in 'Colonel Homer'

Memorable for her performance as Chevy Chase's wife in *National Lampoon's Vacation* (1983) and the subsequent *National Lampoon's European Vacation* (1985).

★ Willem Dafoe
The Commandant in 'The Secret War of Lisa Simpson'

Oscar-nominated for his charged and engaging performance as Sergeant Elias in Oliver Stone's *Platoon* (1986). He can also be seen playing the character Gas in Cronenberg's *eXistenZ* (1999).

★ Rodney Dangerfield
Larry Burns in 'Burns Baby Burns'

The comedian can be seen in *Back to School* (1986).

★ William Daniels
K.I.T.T. in 'The Wizard of Evergreen Terrace'

Daniels makes a cameo appearance in 'The Simpsons', re-creating his role as the voice of K.I.T.T., David Hasselhoff's in-car computer, in the hit 80s TV series *Knight Rider*. Daniels can be seen playing Judge Harold Bedford in the romantic farce *Blind Date* (1987).

★ Ted Danson
Sam Malone in 'Fear of Flying'

Having achieved legendary status as the womanising Cheers barman Sam Malone, he has since played more serious roles, including that of Captain Hamill in *Saving Private Ryan* (1998).

★ Danny DeVito
Herbert Powell in 'Oh, Brother, Where Art Thou?'

The famously diminutive actor recently played a reporter, Sid Hudgeons, in the Oscar-winning *L.A. Confidential* (1997); in addition he provided the voice of Phil in *Hercules* (1997).

★ Kirk Douglas
Chester J Lapwick in 'The Day the Violence Died'

A most memorable performance as Spartacus in the 1960 film of the same name.

★ David Duchovny
Fox Mulder in 'The Springfield Files'

Aside from appearing in TV's *The X Files* and the 1998 movie, *The X Files*, Duchovny can also be seen playing Brian Kessler, alongside Brad Pitt, in *Kalifornia* (1993).

★ Robert Englund
Freddy Krueger in 'Treehouse of Horror IX'

Aside from achieving cult status as
the teen-slasher Freddy Krueger in the
Nightmare on Elm Street movies, Englund
acted as narrator in the 1978 surfer movie
Big Wednesday.

★ R(onald) Lee Ermey
Colonel Hapablap in 'Sideshow Bob's Last
Gleaming'

Having served in Vietnam, Ermey gives
a convincing performance as Gunnery Sergeant
Hartman in *Full Metal Jacket* (1987); he can be
heard providing the voice to Sergeant in both
Toy Story (1995) and *Toy Story 2* (1999).

★ Brendan Fraser
Brad in 'King of the Hill'

Fraser has gone from aping Tarzan in
George of the Jungle (1997) to thief of hearts
in *Gods and Monsters* (1998). Talking of
monsters, he can also be seen in 1999's
The Mummy.

★ Janeane Garofalo
As herself in 'The Last Temptation of Krusty'

Garofalo can be seen playing Deputy
Cindy Bretts in 1997's *Copland*.

★ Jeff Goldblum
MacArthur Parker in 'A Fish Called Selma'

Goldblum enjoyed success as Dr Ian Malcolm
in both *Jurassic Park* (1993) and its sequel.
He can be heard providing the voice of
Aaron in *The Prince of Egypt* (1998).

★ Kelsey Grammer
Sideshow Bob in 'Sideshow Bob's Last
Gleaming'

Grammer played Joe Cabot in Tarantino's
1992 cult classic *Reservoir Dogs*.

★ Mark Hamill
As himself in 'Mayored to the Mob'

Immortalised as the man who played Luke
Skywalker in the *Star Wars* trilogy, he can be
heard providing the voice of the Joker in
Batman: The Animated Series.

★ Woody Harrelson
Woody Boyd in 'Fear of Flying'

As the character Woody Boyd, he became a
regular of the hit American TV series *Cheers*;
he has since played Billy in 1992's *White
Men Can't Jump*, and more recently Ray in
EdTV (1999).

★ Dustin Hoffman
Mr Bergstrom in 'Lisa's Substitute'

Hoffman first earned the respect of
audiences with his performance as a young
man who is seduced by an older woman,
namely Mrs Robinson (Anne Bancroft),
in *The Graduate* (1967)

★ Helen Hunt
Renee in 'Dumbbell Indemnity'

Memorable for making Jack Nicholson
want to be a better person in *As Good As
It Gets* (1997).

★ James Earl Jones
The Narrator, Moving Man and Serak the
Preparer in 'The Tree House of Horrors'

More famously perhaps, James Earl Jones
provided the voice of Darth Vader, in the
Star Wars trilogy.

★ Lisa Kudrow
Alex Whitney in 'Lard of the Dance'

A successful graduate of TV's *Friends*,
she offers a notable performance as Lucia in
1998's *The Opposite of Sex*.

★ Jack Lemmon
Frank Ormand in 'The Twisted World of Marge'

A talented veteran of the screen, he gives a memorable performance, for the most part in drag, as a female musician playing opposite Tony Curtis and Marilyn Monroe, in the Billy Wilder classic *Some Like It Hot* (1959).

★ Joe Mantegna
Fat Tony in 'Bart the Murderer'

An apt choice for the part, having played Joey Zasa in *The Godfather, Part 3* (1990). More recently, he can be seen in Woody Allen's *Celebrity* (1998).

★ Steve Martin
Trash Commissioner in 'Trash of the Titans'

A former crazy guy of the American stand-up circuit, Martin gives an entertaining performance as Lucky Day in 1986's *Three Amigos*. Martin can also be heard providing the voice of Hotep in 1998's *The Prince of Egypt*.

★ Bette Midler
As herself in 'Krusty Gets Kancelled'

Midler can be seen playing Barbara Stone in the popular comedy *Ruthless People* (1986).

★ Sam Neill
Malloy in 'Homer the Vigilante'

Memorable as Dr Alan Grant in 1993's blockbuster, *Jurassic Park*.

★ Leonard Nimoy
As himself in 'Marge vs. the Monorail'

Famed for his performance as Mr Spock in the *Star Trek* TV series and subsequent movies.

★ Catherine O'Hara
Collette the Waitress in 'Flaming Moe's'

Memorable for her performance as the panic-stricken mother of the Macaulay Culkin character Kevin McCallister in *Home Alone* (1990).

★ Luke Perry
As himself in 'Krusty Gets Kancelled'

A Beverly Hills 90210 regular, he can also be seen in *Buffy the Vampire Slayer* (1992).

★ Michelle Pfeiffer
Mindy Simmons in 'The Last Temptation of Homer'

This beauty of the big screen can be seen playing Catwoman in *Batman Returns* (1992).

★ David Hyde Pierce
Cecil Terwilliger in 'Brother From Another Series'

Screen credits include his performance as Dennis Reed in the romantic comedy, *Sleepless in Seattle* (1993). More recently, he can be heard providing the voice of Slim in 1998's *A Bug's Life*.

★ John Ratzenberger
Cliff Clavin in 'Fear of Flying'

Playing Cliff Clavin, he became a regular prop at the Cheers bar. He also played Major Derlin in *The Empire Strikes Back* (1980), as well as providing the voices to PT Flea in *A Bug's Life* (1998) and Hamm in *Toy Story* (1995) and *Toy Story 2* (1999).

★ Christina Ricci
Erin in 'Summer of 4' 2"'

The diminutive nymph Ricci is still remembered for her role as the sombre Wednesday. More recently, she provided the voice of Gwendy Doll in *Small Soldiers* (1998).

★ **Kimmy Robertson**
Samantha Stanky in 'Bart's Friend Falls
in Love'

Not exactly well known, she can be seen
playing Liza the cruise director in *Speed 2:
Cruise Control* (1997).

★ **Mickey Rooney**
As himself in 'Radioactive Man'

This screen veteran can be seen playing the
grandfather of Erik in *Erik the Viking* (1989)
and heard as Fugly Floom in *Babe: Pig in
the City* (1998).

★ **Winona Ryder**
Alison Taylor in 'Lisa's Rival'

Memorable for her intelligent performance
in *Heathers* (1989) as Veronica Sawyer, she is
also set to appear in the forthcoming sequel.

★ **Susan Sarandon**
Bart's ballet teacher in 'Homer vs. Patty
and Selma'

A talented actress, she can be seen playing
Janet Weiss in *The Rocky Horror Picture Show*
(1975), and more recently opposite Sean Penn
in *Dead Man Walking* (1995).

★ **Martin Sheen**
Seymour Skinner in 'The Principal and
the Pauper'

Father of both Emilio Estevez and his
bad-boy brother Charlie Sheen, he truly gave
his all as Captain Benjamin L Willard in
1979's *Apocalypse Now*, so much so that he
suffered a heart attack during filming.

★ **Brooke Shields**
As herself in 'The Front'

Memorable for a particularly 'natural'
performance in *The Blue Lagoon* (1980).
Since 1997 she has been married to the
tennis player André Agassi.

★ **Rod Steiger**
Captain Tenille in 'Simpson Tide'

An Academy Award winner for *In the
Heat of the Night* (1967), more recently he
can be seen playing General Decker in
Mars Attacks! (1996).

★ **Patrick Stewart**
Number One in 'Homer the Great'

For many he is a cult figure on account of
his performance as Captain Jean-Luc Picard
in *Star Trek Generations* (1994) and the
subsequent movies.

★ **Meryl Streep**
Jessica Lovejoy in 'Bart's Girlfriend'

A two-times Oscar winner, one of which she
received for her role in *Sophie's Choice* (1982).

★ **Donald Sutherland**
Hollis Hurlbut in 'Lisa the Iconoclast'

Father of Kiefer, he gained stardom as
a result of his performance in Robert Altman's
M*A*S*H (1970). He can also be seen in
Outbreak (1995).

★ **George Takei**
Akira in 'One Fish, Two Fish, Blowfish,
Blue Fish'

George Takei is legendary for his role
as Lieutenant Sulu in the 1960s TV series
Star Trek and its subsequent dramatisation
on the big screen.

★ **Elizabeth Taylor**
Maggie Simpson in 'Lisa's First Word'

The former screen goddess is memorable
for her role as Cleopatra in the epic 1963
production of the same name. More recently
she can be seen playing Pearl Slyhoople in
1994's *The Flintstones*.

★ Kathleen Turner
Stacy Lavelle in 'Lisa vs. Malibu Stacy'

This screen siren also put her sultry tones to good effect when she provided the voice for Jessica Rabbit in *Who Framed Roger Rabbit?* (1988).

★ John Waters
John in 'Homer's Phobia'

The director of such cult classics as *Pink Flamingos* (1972), he was responsible for bringing the 300-pound female impersonator Divine to the big screen.

★ Steven Weber
Neil in 'King of the Hill'

Weber can be seen in *At First Sight* (1999) with Val Kilmer.

★ Adam West
'Mr Plow'

Famed for his performance as Bruce Wayne/ Batman in the 1960s TV series *Batman*, West is also set to feature in the forthcoming *Mr. Hughes* (2000), directed by Brian De Palma, and revolving around the life of the eccentric millionaire Howard Hughes.

★ James Woods
As himself in 'Homer and Apu'

Oscar-nominated for his performance as a journalist in Oliver Stone's *Salvador* (1986).

★ Steven Wright
As himself in 'The Last Temptation of Krusty'

Screen performances include Dr Emil Reingold in the controversial *Natural Born Killers* (1994), the voices of Bob in *Babe: Pig in the City* (1998) and of the DJ K-Billy in Tarantino's *Reservoir Dogs* (1992).

Chapter 10
Animal Crackers

BABE (1995)

100 Movies Featuring Animals

In 1951 the American Humane Association introduced the PATSY award (an acronym for Picture Animal Top Star of the Year), for the best animal performance in film; the award was extended to the world of television in 1958. The first winner of the award was Francis the Talking Mule, who subsequently went on to win it again in 1952, 1954, 1955, 1956 and 1957. Over the years all forms of animal life have been winners, including cats, dogs and fish.

This chapter lists one hundred movies that feature animals. We've chosen not to include the films of such well-known stars as Rin Tin Tin, Lassie, King Kong, Silver, Trigger, Cheetah etc. Oops! Looks like we've included them after all.

★ **Alligator**
Alligator (1980)

★ **Ant**
Ants! (1977)

★ **Ape**
Greystoke: The Legend of Tarzan, Lord of the Apes (1984)

★ **Bear**
The Life and Times of Grizzly Adams (1974)
Grizzly (1976)

★ **Bee**
The Savage Bees (1976)
The Swarm (1978)
The Bees (1978)

★ **Bigfoot**
Bigfoot (1971)
Bigfoot and the Hendersons (1987)

★ **Bird**
A Taste of Honey (1961) – budgie
Kes (1970) – kestrel
Jonathan Livingston Seagull (1973)

★ **Bull**
The Brave Bulls (1951)

★ **Camel**
Lawrence of Arabia (1962)
Conan the Destroyer (1984)

★ **Cat**
The Goldwyn Follies (1938) featuring hundreds of cats singing 'Hey Pussy, Pussy'
The Cat Creeps (1946)
Breakfast at Tiffany's (1961)
The Incredible Journey (1963)
From Russia With Love (1963)
The Three Lives of Thomasina (1964)
That Darn Cat (1965)
The Torture Garden (1968)
The Cat from Outer Space (1978)

★ **Chicken**
Freaks (1932) – Chicken-Woman
Bugsy Malone (1976)
Rocky 2 (1979)
Goin' South (1978)

★ **Chimpanzee**
The Barefoot Executive (1971)
Going Bananas (1987)
The 5th Monkey (1990)

★ **Deer**
The Yearling (1946)
The Deer Hunter (1978)

★ **Dog**
The Silent Call (1921)
The Man From Hell's River (1922) – the first appearance of Rin Tin Tin
After the Thin Man (1936)
The Awful Truth (1937)
Scott of the Antarctic (1948)
Old Yeller (1957)
The Incredible Journey (1963)
The Spy with the Cold Nose (1966) (a bulldog)
Benji (1974)
Digby, the Biggest Dog in the World (1974)
Cujo (1983)
Antarctic (1984)
K-9 (1989)
Turner and Hooch (1989)
Beethoven (1992)
The Mask (1994)
Fluke (1995)
As Good As It Gets (1997)

★ **Dolphin**
The Day of the Dolphin (1973)
Flipper (1963) and (1996)

★ Duck
Howard ... A New Breed of Hero (1986)

★ Eagle
Rescued From an Eagle's Nest (1907)

★ Fish
Piranha (1978)
A Fish Called Wanda (1988)

★ Fly
The Fly (1958 and 1986)

★ Horse
Black Beauty (1933, 1946, 1971 and 1994)
The Horseman (1970)
A Horse for Danny (1995)
The Horse Whisperer (1998)

★ Leopard
Bringing Up Baby (1938)
Leopard in the Snow (1977)

★ Fox
The Fox (1968)
The Belstone Fox (1973)

★ Goose
Oliver Twist (1948)
Fly Away Home (1996)

★ Gorilla
Gorillas in the Mist (1988)

★ Lion
Born Free (1966)

★ Lizard
The Freshman (1990)

★ Mule
A Romance of the Redwoods (1917)
Francis the Talking Mule (1950)

★ Mouse
Mouse Hunt (1997)

★ Orang-utan
Every Which Way But Loose (1978)
Any Which Way You Can (1980)

★ Otter
Ring of Bright Water (1969)
Tarka the Otter (1978)

★ Panther
Cat People (1942 and 1982)

★ Pig
A Private Function (1984)
Leon the Pig Farmer (1992)
Babe (1995)

★ Rabbit
Monty Python and the Holy Grail (1975)

★ Rat
Willard (1971)
Ben (1972)
The Rats (1982)
Rats: Night of Terror (1984)
Ratboy (1986)

★ Shark
Jaws (1975)

★ Shrew
The Killer Shrews (1959)

★ Snake
Cleopatra (1963)
Conan the Barbarian (1982)
Anaconda (1997)

★ Spider
The Incredible Shrinking Man (1957)
Arachnophobia (1990)

★ Whale
Moby Dick (1930 and 1956)
Orca (1977)
Free Willy (1993)

★ Wolf
The Flight of the Grey Wolf (1976)

★ Worm
Squirm (1976)

★ Zebra
Zebra in the Kitchen (1965)

Chapter 11
Child's Play

SHIRLEY TEMPLE

Acting? Child's play! Perhaps not as arrogant a statement as it might at first appear. Children, uninhibited by the insecurities that accompany age, are often more able to throw themselves into a role than adults. After all, childhood is the time of make-believe – and what is acting if not make-believe?

We take a look at ten of cinema's most popular child stars past and present, from the floppy-haired cheek of Jackie Coogan, to the boy destined for immortality as the young Darth Vader in 1999's continuation of the *Star Wars* legend, *Episode 1: The Phantom Menace*. Finally, we offer a list of notable performances by child actors.

10 Child Stars: Past and Present

★ Jackie Coogan (1914–84)

Jackie made his first appearance on screen at the tender age of one and a half in *Skinner's Baby*. His rise to stardom came several years later when Charlie Chaplin saw him performing in a revue and, impressed as he was, cast the young Coogan in the two-reel *A Day's Pleasure* (1919) and subsequently in his first feature film, *The Kid* (1921).

Coogan allegedly earned $4 million from his career as a child actor – although, as a result of a legal dispute with his mother and his stepfather, he ultimately received $125,000. To make matters worse his popularity decreased as his age increased.

During the 1960s he starred as Uncle Fester in TV's *The Addams Family*.

★ Macaulay Culkin (1980–)

The nephew of the actress Bonnie Bedelia, Macaulay made his stage debut at the age of four in *Bach's Babies* and his movie debut in 1988's *Rocket Gibraltar*. He subsequently hit the big time in 1990 with his performance as Kevin McCallister in *Home Alone*, and as a

result was paid $5,000,000 for his performance in the film's sequel, *Home Alone 2: Lost in New York*.

Since then he has slipped out of the limelight somewhat, his last film being *The Pagemaster* (1994). In 1998 he married the actress Rachel Miner.

★ Jodie Foster (1962–)

Following a succession of appearances in Disney TV productions during the late sixties and early seventies, Jodie gained her first feature appearance in 1972's *Napoleon and Samantha*. She subsequently made the headlines with her Oscar-nominated depiction of a teenage prostitute in Martin Scorsese's *Taxi Driver* (1976), at the tender age of twelve; the same year saw Jodie appear in Alan Parker's tongue-in-cheek gangster story, *Bugsy Malone*.

Since then Jodie's career has gone from strength to strength, seeing her gain Best Actress Oscars for her roles in both *The Accused* (1988) and *The Silence of the Lambs* (1991). She also made her debut as a director in 1991 with *Little Man Tate*.

JUDY GARLAND – THE WIZARD OF OZ (1939)

★ Judy Garland (1922–69)

Although best remembered for her portrayal of Dorothy in *The Wizard of Oz* (1939), Judy was by that stage something of a seasoned performer, having first appeared on stage at the age of three with her two older sisters, under the billing of the Gumm Sisters Kiddie Act (she was born as Frances Gumm). At the age of thirteen, having been auditioned by none other than Louis B Mayer, she accepted a contract with MGM. Her first screen appearance followed with the two-reel short, *Every Sunday*. Next came her feature debut in Fox's *Pigskin Parade* (1936). Several features followed, including *Thoroughbreds Don't Cry* (1937), where she appeared alongside Mickey Rooney, and the movie that would make her a star, *The Wizard of Oz*.

In 1939 she was awarded a Special Academy Award for 'her outstanding performance as a screen juvenile during the past year'.

However, the price of celebrity took its toll on Miss Garland, causing weight problems and as result nervous disorders. She began seeing a psychiatrist from the age of 21. Her success continued, though, and she starred in such films as *Meet Me in St. Louis* (1944), *A Star is Born* (1954) and *Judgment at Nuremberg* (1961).

Finally, Judy paid the ultimate price, when in 1968 she was found dead in her London apartment, as the result of an accidental sleeping-tablet overdose.

★ Jake Lloyd (1989–)

The release of the next episode in the *Star Wars* saga, *Episode 1: The Phantom Menace* (1999) sees ten-year-old Jake Lloyd play one of the most coveted roles in movie history, that of Anakin Skywalker, alias the young Darth Vader.

However *The Phantom Menace* is not the young Lloyd's first foray into the world of Hollywood. He previously played the Arnold Schwarzenegger character's son in *Jingle All the Way* (1996) and opposite Marisa Tomei in *Unhook the Stars* (1996).

The year 2000 should see the release of Lloyd's next feature, *Crown of Blood*, in which he plays the young Tsarevich Alexei Nicholaevich Romanov.

★ Tatum O'Neal (1963–)

The daughter of Ryan O'Neal and Joanna Moore, she made her screen debut in 1973's *Paper Moon*, in which she appeared alongside her father. For her performance she won Best Supporting Actress, becoming as yet the youngest person to do so. She did not make another feature until three years later, when she appeared in *Bad News Bears* (1976). For her part in the film she received $350,000 and a nine-per-cent cut of the net profit, making her the then highest-paid child star in history.

Lesser roles followed and she can most recently be seen in *Basquiat* (1996).

★ Anna Paquin (1982–)

Born in Wellington, New Zealand, Anna caused a stir at the 1993 Academy Awards when not only was she nominated for her first feature performance, as the daughter of Holly Hunter's character in Jane Campion's *The Piano*, but subsequently won the Award (Best Supporting Actress), becoming the seventh youngest person to win an Academy Award in the process.

Since her success with *The Piano*, Anna has featured in such films as *Amistad* (1997) and the romantic comedy *She's All That* (1999).

★ Mickey Rooney (1920–)

Mickey Rooney, born as Joe Yule, made his first appearance on screen at the age of six in *Not to be Trusted* (1926). He subsequently starred in fifty two-reel comedies in the series *Mickey McGuire*, from which he legally took the name Mickey McGuire, not becoming Mickey Rooney until 1932 when he began appearing more frequently in feature films.

In 1937 Rooney was cast as the son of a judge in the B-movie series, *A Family Affair*; the series boosted Rooney's popularity. Consequently, greater roles came his way, including what is probably his greatest achievement as a child actor, that of a little tough guy in the 1938 tearjerker *Boy's Town*.

In 1938 he received a Special Academy Award, along with Deanna Durbin, for 'significant contribution in bringing to the screen the spirit and personification of youth, and as juvenile players setting a high standard of ability and achievement'.

In spite of being America's most popular box-office draw during 1939, World War Two cut short his career, and saw him lean more and more towards television work and lesser features as a means of making ends meet.

Nevertheless, Rooney has remained active in the world of cinema, receiving an Honorary Academy Award for 'fifty years of versatility in a variety of memorable film performances'. Most recently he provided the voice of Fugly Floom in 1999's *Babe 2: Pig in the City*.

★ Shirley Temple (1928–)

Shirley made the break into cinema at the age of three when she appeared in a series of one-reel shorts entitled *Baby Burlesks*, imitating such stars as Marlene Dietrich. She became a household figure shortly after appearing in *Stand Up and Cheer* (1934), in which she performed 'Baby Take A Bow'. A contract with Fox followed, and most notably a Special Academy Award 'in grateful recognition of her outstanding contribution to screen entertainment during the year 1934'. By 1938 she had become the number-one draw at the box office.

However, the advent of adolescence marked the beginning of the end for Miss Temple, and by the close of the 40s her career was as good as over. She later attempted to revive her career by means of TV, hosting *The Shirley Temple Storybook* in 1958 and *The Shirley Temple Show* in 1960. Her attempts were unsuccessful, though, and she has subsequently pursued a career in politics. Since her marriage to the TV executive Charles Black in 1950 she has been known as Shirley Temple Black.

★ Natalie Wood (1938–81)

Natalie got her big break at the age of five when she made a brief appearance in 1943's *Happy Land*. As a result of her performance the film's director, Irving Pichel, cast her in *Tomorrow Is Forever* (1946), alongside such heavyweights of the screen as Orson Welles and Claudette Colbert. The following year she gave perhaps her greatest performance as a disbelieving child in the Oscar-winning *Miracle on 34th Street*.

Wood's success, unlike that of many other child stars, followed her into adulthood, during which time she gave notable performances in such films as *Rebel Without a Cause* (1955), *Splendor in the Grass* (1961), *Love With the Proper Stranger* (1963) (all three of which earned her an Oscar nomination!) and *Bob & Carol & Ted & Alice*. However, she is perhaps best remembered for her performance as Maria in *West Side Story* (1961).

Notable Performances by Child Actors

★ **Christian Bale** – *Empire of the Sun* (1987)

★ **Linda Blair** – *The Exorcist* (1973)

★ **Patty Duke** – *The Miracle Worker* (1962)

★ **Brigitte Fossey** – *Forbidden Games* (1951)

★ **Lukas Haas** – *Witness* (1985)

★ **Roddy McDowall** – *How Green Was My Valley* (1941)

★ **Eamonn Owens** – *The Butcher Boy* (1997)

★ **Ricky Schroeder** – *The Champ* (1979)

★ **Jean Simmons** – *Great Expectations* (1946)

★ **Brandon de Wilde** – *Shane* (1953)

Chapter 12
Talk of the Town

CASABLANCA (1942)

The Movie Fan's Essential List of Quotes

In the following section we offer a selection of classic one-liners and quotations from many of the great movies (and for that matter some of the not so great ones). Take the trouble to commit your favourites to memory and you'll always be the life and soul of parties.

Persuasion – The Gentle Art!

★ I'll make him an offer he can't refuse.
Al Pacino in *The Godfather* (1972)

★ If you get a customer, or an employee, who thinks he's Charles Bronson, take the butt of your gun and smash their nose in.
Harvey Keitel in *Reservoir Dogs* (1992)

★ I know what you're thinking: 'Did he fire six shots or only five?' Well, to tell you the truth, in all this excitement, I've kind of lost track myself. But, this being a forty-four Magnum, the most powerful handgun in the world, and would blow your head clean off, you've got to ask yourself one question: 'Do I feel lucky?'
Well, do ya, punk?
Clint Eastwood in *Dirty Harry* (1971)

DIRTY HARRY (1971)

★ When a man with a forty-five [gun] meets a man with a rifle, you said that a man with a pistol is a dead man. Let's see if that's true.
Clint Eastwood in *A Fistful of Dollars* (1964)

★ If you don't cooperate, you're gonna suffer from fistaphobia.
Robert De Niro in *Midnight Run* (1988)

Deep! Very Deep!

★ Let me tell you something my friend. Hope is a dangerous thing. Hope can drive a man insane.
Morgan Freeman to **Tim Robbins** in *The Shawshank Redemption* (1994)

★ Remember, Red, hope is a good thing, maybe the best of things. And no good thing ever dies.
Morgan Freeman subsequently reading a letter from **Tim Robbins** in *The Shawshank Redemption* (1994)

★ Intelligence. Nothing has caused the human race so much trouble as intelligence.
Thelma Ritter in *Rear Window* (1954)

★ We accept the reality with which we're presented.
Ed Harris in *The Truman Show* (1998)

★ You make me sick with your heroics. You and Colonel Nicholson, you're two of a kind, crazy with courage. For what? How to die like a gentleman? How to die by the rules? When the only important thing is how to live like a human being.
William Holden in *The Bridge on the River Kwai* (1957)

★ Stanley, see this? This is this. This ain't something else, this is this!
Robert De Niro in *The Deer Hunter* (1978)

★ It's when you start to really fear death that you start to appreciate life.
Gary Oldman in *Leon* (1994)

★ Men prefer sorrow over joy ... suffering over peace!
Ryu Daisuke in *Ran* (1985)

★ Real loss is only when you love something more than you love yourself.
Matt Damon in *Good Will Hunting* (1997)

★ Life is pain! Anyone who says differently is selling something.
Robin Wright in *The Princess Bride* (1987)

★ A world without string is chaos.
Nathan Lane in *Mousehunt* (1998)

★ In Italy for thirty years under the Borgias they had warfare, terror, murder, bloodshed. They produced Michelangelo, Leonardo da Vinci and the Renaissance. In Switzerland they had brotherly love, five hundred years of democracy and peace, and what did that produce? The cuckoo clock.
Orson Welles in *The Third Man* (1949)

Food and Drink!

★ Bring a pitcher of beer every seven minutes till somebody passes out, and then bring one every ten minutes.
Rodney Dangerfield in *Back to School* (1986)

★ We were young, gay, reckless! The night I drank champagne from your slipper – two quarts. It would have held more, but you were wearing innersoles.
Groucho Marx in *At the Circus* (1939)

★ A census taker once tried to test me ... I ate his liver with some fava beans and a nice chianti.
Anthony Hopkins in *The Silence of the Lambs* (1991)

★ The movie was shot in 3B ... three beers and it looks good, eh?
Rick Moranis in *Strange Brew* (1983)

★ I do wish we could chat longer, but I'm having an old friend for dinner.
Anthony Hopkins in *The Silence of the Lambs* (1991)

★ I always start [drinking] around noon – in case it gets dark early.
Peggy Lee in *Pete Kelly's Blues* (1955)

★ Awww ... this is one of those days that the pages of history teach us are best spent lying in bed.
Roland Young (hung over) in *The Philadelphia Story* (1940)

★ I was in love with a beautiful blonde once dear. She drove me to drink, that's the one thing I'm indebted to her for.
WC Fields in *Give a Sucker an Even Break* (1941)

Making an Exit to be Remembered by!

★ I'll be back!
Arnold Schwarzenegger in *The Terminator* (1984)

★ You tell him I'm coming! And hell's coming with me!
Kurt Russell in *Tombstone* (1994)

★ They may take our lives, but they'll never take our freedom!
Mel Gibson in *Braveheart* (1995)

★ Don't push it. Don't push it, or I'll give you a war you won't believe. Let it go. Let it go.
Sylvester Stallone in *First Blood* (1982)

BILL & TED'S EXCELLENT ADVENTURE (1989)

★ Be excellent to each other. Party on, dudes.
Keanu Reeves and **Alex Winter** in *Bill & Ted's Excellent Adventure* (1989)

Education

★ 'When Alexander saw the breadth of his domain, he wept for there were no more worlds to conquer.' The benefits of a classical education.
Alan Rickman in *Die Hard* (1988)

One Thing in Mind!

★ Don't know if I'm going to be able to sleep. Hint, hint.
Karen Black to **Jack Nicholson** in *Five Easy Pieces* (1970)

★ Why don't you come up sometime 'n' see me? I'm home every evening.
Mae West to **Cary Grant** in *She Done Him Wrong* (1933)

★ I always feel so selfish sleeping alone in a double bed, when there are people in China sleeping on the ground.
Barbra Streisand to **George Segal** in *The Owl and the Pussycat* (1970)

★ Would you like a leg or a breast?
Grace Kelly, offering some chicken to **Cary Grant**, in *To Catch a Thief* (1955)

★ It's been an evening of ups and downs, hasn't it? Care to continue the motion?
Maggie Smith to **Michael Caine** in *California Suite* (1978)

★ You're not too smart, are you? I like that in a man.
Kathleen Turner to **William Hurt** in *Body Heat* (1981)

★ Honey, the only question I ever ask any woman is, 'What time is your husband coming home?'
Paul Newman to **Patricia Neal** in *Hud* (1963)

★ How about coming up to my place for a spot of heavy breathing?
Walter Matthau to **Carol Burnett** in *Pete 'n' Tillie* (1972)

★ Why don't you slip out of these wet clothes and into a dry martini?
Robert Benchley to **Ginger Rogers** in *The Major and the Minor* (1942)

★ Cigarette me, big boy.
Ginger Rogers in *Young Man of Manhattan* (1930)

And (They Say) God Created Women!

★ Life's a bitch. Now so am I.
Michelle Pfeiffer in *Batman Returns* (1992)

★ There's a name for you ladies, but it isn't used in high society – outside of a kennel.
Joan Crawford in *The Women* (1939)

★ Little boy: Cream?
Little girl: No, thank you. I take it black – like my men.
Airplane! (1980)

★ Peel me a grape.
Mae West in *I'm No Angel* (1933)

★ That's OK, we can walk to the curb from here.
Woody Allen, getting out of **Diane Keaton's** car in *Annie Hall* (1977)

★ I was gonna go to UCLA, but I couldn't find a place to park.
Goldie Hawn in *Butterflies Are Free* (1972)

★ I have a head for business and a bod for sin. Is there anything wrong with that?
Melanie Griffith in *Working Girl* (1988)

★ In Sicily, women are more dangerous than shotguns.
Angelo Infanti in *The Godfather* (1972)

★ When I'm good I'm very very good but when I'm bad I'm better.
Mae West in *I'm No Angel* (1933)

Dressed to Kill

★ I remember every detail. The Germans wore grey. You wore blue.
Humphrey Bogart in *Casablanca* (1942)

★ That's quite a dress you almost have on.
Gene Kelly to **Nina Foch** in *An American in Paris* (1951)

★ I'll meet you tonight under the moon. Oh, I can see you now – you and the moon. You wear a necktie so I'll know you.
Groucho Marx to **Margaret Dumont** in *The Cocoanuts* (1929)

★ Look, Heather left behind one of her Swatches. She'd want you to have it, Veronica. She always said you couldn't accessorize for shit.
Lisanne Falk in *Heathers* (1989)

★ If I kept my hair 'natural' the way you do, I'd be bald.
Rosalind Russell to **Coral Browne** in *Auntie Mame* (1958)

★ Do you prefer 'fashion victim' or 'ensemble challenged'?
Alicia Silverstone, *Clueless* (1995)

Smokin'!

★ If she were a President, she'd be Babe-raham Lincoln.
Dana Carvey in *Wayne's World* (1992)

★ She came at me in sections. More curves than the scenic railway.
Fred Astaire talking about **Cyd Charisse** in *The Band Wagon* (1953)

★ With a binding like you've got, people are going to want to know what's in the book.
Gene Kelly to **Leslie Caron** in *An American in Paris* (1951)

★ Here's looking at you, kid.
Humphrey Bogart in *Casablanca* (1942)

★ It was nice to meet you. Surreal, but nice.
Hugh Grant to **Julia Roberts** in *Notting Hill* (1999)

★ I have this theory that you should be with another person who's just good-looking enough to turn you on. Any excess brings problems. She was much prettier than I needed.
Albert Brooks in *Defending Your Life* (1991)

★ You were cute. White, but cute.
Whoopi Goldberg to **Patrick Swayze** in *Ghost* (1990)

★ **Shandra Beri**: He's got a great ass.
Daryl Hannah: Too bad it's on his shoulders.
Roxanne (1987)

★ I've gone out with some bums in my day, but they were beautiful. That is the only reason to go out with a bum.
Mercedes Ruehl in *The Fisher King* (1991)

★ Michael was not a guy other guys would've made fun of in the locker room, OK?
Bette Midler in *Outrageous Fortune* (1987)

★ What God has not given to Antoinette Green, Antoinette Green has had done.
Liza Minnelli in *The Sterile Cuckoo* (1969)

Love Story a.k.a. Sex, Lies & Videotape

★ Was that canon fire, or is it my heart pounding?
Ingrid Bergman to **Humphrey Bogart** in *Casablanca* (1942)

★ I'd love to kiss yuh, but I just washed my hair.
Bette Davis in *Cabin in the Cotton* (1932)

★ **Jack Nicholson**: I like the lights on.
Shirley Maclaine: Then go home and turn them on.
Terms of Endearment (1983)

★ I can feel the hot blood pounding through your varicose veins.
Jimmy Durante to **Mary Wickes** in *The Man Who Came to Dinner* (1941)

★ Just remember that every relationship starts with a one-night stand.
Anthony Edwards in *The Sure Thing* (1985)

★ Oh, you men are all alike! Seven or eight quick ones and you're off with the boys, to boast and brag.
Madeline Kahn in *Young Frankenstein* (1974)

★ I never could understand why it has to be just even – male and female. They're invited for dinner, not for mating.
Louise Closser Hale in *Dinner at Eight* (1933)

★ Checking she's awake doesn't constitute foreplay.
Rhys Ifans to **Christopher Ecclestone** in *Heart* (1999)

★ It's the so-called normal guys who always let you down. Sickos never scare me. At least they're committed.
Michelle Pfeiffer in *Batman Returns* (1992)

★ **Martha Plimpton**: He told me he loved me.
Dianne Wiest: Aw, sweetie. They say that –
then they come.
Parenthood (1989)

★ I would never want to belong to any
club that would have someone like me for a
member. That's the key joke of my adult life,
in terms of relationships with women.
Woody Allen in *Annie Hall* (1977)

★ My relationship with Hal is totally honest.
He doesn't tell me he loves me, I don't tell him
he's fascinating. It's pure sex.
Kelly Bishop in *An Unmarried Woman* (1978)

★ **Humphrey Bogart**: If that plane leaves
the ground and you're not with him, you'll
regret it – maybe not today, maybe not
tomorrow, but soon, and for the rest of
your life.
Ingrid Bergman: But what about us?
Humphrey Bogart: We'll always have Paris.
Casablanca (1942)

★ Would you like me to seduce you?
Is that what you want?
Anne Bancroft in *The Graduate* (1967)

★ Hey, don't knock masturbation!
It's sex with someone I love.
Woody Allen in *Annie Hall* (1977)

★ I couldn't believe that she knew my name.
Some of my best friends didn't know my name.
Ben Stiller in *There's Something About Mary*
(1998)

★ Love means never having to say you're
sorry.
Ali MacGraw to **Ryan O'Neal** in *Love Story*
(1970)

★ It's as if I've taken love heroin – and I can
never have it again.
Hugh Grant describing his feelings for
Julia Roberts in *Notting Hill* (1999)

Married to the Mob

★ Marry me, and I'll never look at any
other horse.
Groucho Marx to **Margaret Dumont** in
A Day at the Races (1937)

★ Will you marry me? Did he leave you
any money? Answer the second question first.
Groucho Marx to **Margaret Dumont** in
Duck Soup (1933)

★ If you waited for a man to propose
to you from natural causes, you'd die of old
maidenhood.
Barbara Stanwyck in *The Lady Eve* (1941)

★ I want us to put our teeth in the same
glass at night.
Burt Reynolds to **Jill Clayburgh** in
Starting Over (1979)

★ Her father was very, very rich.
And very, very sick. The doctors assured
me he'd be dead any minute. There wasn't
a second to lose. I rushed out and married
the boss's daughter.
Danny DeVito in *Ruthless People* (1986)

★ I wanted to marry her when I saw
the moonlight shining on the barrel of her
father's shotgun.
Eddie Albert in *Oklahoma!* (1955)

★ Garth, marriage is punishment for
shoplifting, in some countries.
Mike Myers in *Wayne's World* (1992)

★ Marriage is like the Middle East.
There's no solution.
Pauline Collins in *Shirley Valentine* (1989)

★ Jerry should never have died.
I'd be better off. I could've divorced him.
Lily Tomlin in *Nine to Five*
(a.k.a. *9 to 5*) (1980)

★ The new Medusa – my good wife.
Peter O'Toole talking about
Katharine Hepburn in *The Lion in Winter*
(1968)

★ Why don't you get a divorce and
settle down?
Oscar Levant to **Joan Crawford** in
Humoresque (1946)

★ It's getting late. I was beginning to worry.
I was afraid you weren't in an accident.
Jill Clayburgh to **Burt Reynolds** in
Starting Over (1979)

★ Some people will pay a lot of money
for that information, but then your daughter
would lose a father, instead of gaining a
husband.
Al Pacino, in hiding from fellow gangsters,
ensures that the bride's father gives his consent
to the intended marriage in *The Godfather*
(1972)

★ Judah: If you were not a bride I would
kiss you good-bye.
Esther: If I were not a bride you would not
have to kiss me good-bye.
Charlton Heston to **Haya Harareet** in
Ben-Hur (1959)

★ By the authority vested in me by
Kaiser William II, I pronounce you husband
and wife. Proceed with the execution.
Peter Bull in *The African Queen* (1951)

Mommie Dearest

★ A boy's best friend is his mother.
Anthony Perkins in *Psycho* (1960)

★ Well, there won't never be no patter of
little feet in my house – unless I was to rent
some mice.
Peggy Lee in *Pete Kelly's Blues* (1955)

★ Sure, mom, I settle down with a
nice girl every night, then I'm free the
next morning.
Joe Pesci in *GoodFellas* (1990)

★ He's not the Messiah. He's a very
naughty boy!
Terry Jones in *The Life of Brian* (1979)

★ As for you, Mother, I love you very
much – but my address is Paris, France.
Audrey Dalton in *Titanic* (1953)

Hmmn!

★ Your idea of fidelity is not having more
than one man in the bed at the same time.
You're a whore, baby.
Dirk Bogarde to **Julie Christie** in
Darling (1965)

★ It's so great to wake up in the morning
with your rent paid.
Julie Christie in *Shampoo* (1975)

★ Coat check girl: Goodness, what a
beautiful diamond.
Mae West: Goodness had nothing to do
with it, dearie.
Night After Night (1932)

★ **Emma Walton** (anti-fur protester):
Do you know how many poor animals they
had to kill to make that coat?
Jobeth Williams: Do you know how many
rich animals I had to fuck to get this coat?
Switch (1991)

★ As long as they've got sidewalks,
you've got a job.
Joan Blondell to **Claire Dodd** in
Footlight Parade (1933)

Men

★ Bill's thirty-two. He looks thirty-two. He looked it five years ago, he'll look it twenty years from now. I hate them.
Bette Davis in *All About Eve* (1950)

★ **David Huddleston**: Isn't that what makes a man?
Jeff Bridges: That and a pair of testicles.
The Big Lebowski (1998)

★ Your eyes are full of hate, forty-one. That's good. Hate keeps a man alive.
Jack Hawkins to **Charlton Heston**, *Ben-Hur* (1959)

War... What is it Good For?

★ Somebody once wrote, 'Hell is the impossibility of reason.' That's what this place feels like. Hell.
Charlie Sheen referring to Vietnam in *Platoon* (1986)

★ I watched a snail crawl along the edge of a straight razor. That's my dream. That's my nightmare. Crawling, swiftly, along the edge of a straight ... razor ... and surviving.
Marlon Brando in *Apocalypse Now* (1979)

★ I love the smell of napalm in the morning.
Robert Duvall in *Apocalypse Now* (1979)

★ Let me see if I've got this straight: in order to be grounded, I've got to be crazy and I must be crazy to keep flying. But if I ask to be grounded, that means I'm not crazy any more and I have to keep flying.
Alan Arkin *Catch-22* (1970)

★ The dead only know one thing: it's better to be alive.
Matthew Modine in *Full Metal Jacket* (1987)

★ **Matthew Modine**: Are those ... live rounds?
Vincent D'Onofrio: Seven-six-two millimetre.
Full Metal Jacket.

★ O my God, I trust in thee: let me not be ashamed, let not mine enemies triumph over me.
Barry Pepper in *Saving Private Ryan* (1998)

★ What's the use in risking the lives of the eight of us to save one guy?
Edward Burns in *Saving Private Ryan* (1998)

Of God Above!

★ The path of the righteous man is beset on all sides by the inequities of the selfish and the tyranny of evil men. Blessed is he, who in the name of charity and good will, shepherds the weak through the valley of darkness, for he is truly his brother's keeper and the finder of lost children. And I will strike down upon thee with great vengeance and furious anger those who would attempt to poison and destroy my brothers. And you will know my name is the Lord when I lay my vengeance upon thee.
Samuel L Jackson in *Pulp Fiction* (1994)

Classic Quotes

★ I want to be alone.
Greta Garbo in *Grand Hotel* (1932)

★ **Vivien Leigh**: Rhett, if you go, where shall I go? What shall I do?
Clark Gable: Frankly, my dear, I don't give a damn.
Gone With the Wind (1939)

★ Toto, I've a feeling we're not in Kansas any more.
Judy Garland in *The Wizard of Oz* (1939)

★ Of all the gin joints in all the towns in all the world, she walks into mine.
Humphrey Bogart in *Casablanca* (1942)

★ Play it, Sam. Play 'As Time Goes by'.
Ingrid Bergman to **Dooley Wilson** in *Casablanca* (1942)

★ **William Holden**: You're Norma Desmond! You used to be in silent pictures. Used to be big.
Gloria Swanson: I am big. It's the pictures that got small.
Sunset Boulevard (1950)

★ No one ever leaves a star. That's what makes one a star.
Gloria Swanson in *Sunset Boulevard* (1950)

★ You don't understand. I coulda had class. I coulda been a contender. I coulda been somebody, instead of a bum, which is what I am, let's face it. It was you, Charlie.
Marlon Brando in *On The Waterfront* (1954)

★ You're tearing me apart!
James Dean in *Rebel Without a Cause* (1955)

★ **Paul Newman**: Wait a minute – you didn't see La Force out there did you?
Robert Redford: La Force? No, why?
Paul Newman: Thank God for that. For a moment there I thought we were in trouble.
Butch Cassidy and the Sundance Kid (1969)

★ Forget it, Jake. It's Chinatown.
Joe Mantell to **Jack Nicholson**
Chinatown (1974)

★ You talkin' to me? You talkin' to me? You talkin' to me? Then who the hell else are you talkin' to? You talkin' to me? Well I'm the only one here. Who do you think you're talking to? Oh yeah? Huh? OK.
Robert De Niro in *Taxi Driver* (1976)

★ ... , Ash and Captain Dallas are dead. Cargo and ship destroyed. I should reach the frontier in about 6 weeks. With a little luck, the network will pick me up. This is Ripley – last survivor of the Nostromo – signing off.
Sigourney Weaver in *Alien* (1979)

★ Here's Johnny... ?
Jack Nicholson in *The Shining* (1980)

★ **Robert Hays**: Surely you can't be serious.
Leslie Nielsen: I am serious, and don't call me Shirley.
Airplane (1980)

★ I've seen things you people wouldn't believe. Attack ships on fire off the shoulder of Orion. I watched C-beams glitter in the dark near the Tannhauser gate. All those moments will be lost in time, like tears in rain. Time to die.
Rutger Hauer in *Blade Runner* (1982)

★ **Tom Cruise**: I feel the need ...
Tom Cruise and **Anthony Edwards**: ... the need for speed!
Top Gun (1986)

★ Ha ha ha. That's not a knife. That's a knife.
Paul Hogan in *Crocodile Dundee* (1986)

★ The point is, ladies and gentlemen, that greed, for lack of a better word, is good. Greed is right. Greed works.
Michael Douglas in *Wall Street* (1987)

★ Show me the money!
Tom Cruise in *Jerry Maguire* (1996)

★ Choose life. Choose a job. Choose a career. Choose a family. Choose a fucking big television. Choose washing machines, cars, compact-disc players and electrical tin openers. Choose good health, low cholesterol, and dental insurance. Choose fixed-interest mortgage repayments. Choose a starter home. Choose your friends. Choose leisurewear and matching fabrics. Choose DIY and wondering who the fuck you are on a Sunday morning. Choose sitting on that couch watching mind-numbing, spirit-crushing game shows, stuffing junk food into your mouth. Choose rotting away at the end of it all, pissing your last in a miserable home, nothing more than an embarrassment to the selfish, fucked-up brats you spawned to replace yourself. Choose a future. Choose life …
But why would I want to do a thing like that?
Ewan McGregor in *Trainspotting* (1996)

★ **Geoffrey Rush**: The show must …
Joseph Fiennes (prompting him): Go on!
Shakespeare in Love (1988)

★ Wait a minute; wait a minute. You ain't heard nothing yet.
Al Jolson in *The Jazz Singer* (1927)

In the Words of…

★ **Julie Andrews** in the words of **Christopher Plummer**
'Working with her is like being hit over the head with a Valentine card.'

★ **Diana Barrymore** … **John Barrymore** (her father)
'Diana is a horse's arse, quite a pretty one, but still a horse's arse.'

★ **Warren Beatty** … **Mamie Van Doren**
'He's in danger of waking up one morning in his own arms.'

★ **Warren Beatty** … **Leslie Caron** (an ex-girlfriend)
'Warren has an interesting psychology, he has always fallen in love with girls who have just won or been nominated for an Academy Award.'

★ **Humphrey Bogart** … **William Holden**
'[I] hated that bastard.'

★ **Marlon Brando** … **Lee Marvin**
'Brando is not exactly a generous actor, he doesn't give. But he does make demands on you, and if you don't come through then he'll run right over the top of you.'

★ **Charles Bronson** … **Jill Ireland** (his wife)
'I think I'm in so many of his pictures because no other actress would work with him.'

★ **Yul Brynner** … **Jeffrey Bernard**
'One of the biggest shits I've ever come across in show business. He was just a pig.'

★ **Richard Burton** … **John Boorman**
'He's like all these drunks. Impossible when he's drunk and only half there when he's sober. Wooden as a board with his body, relies on doing all his acting with his voice.'

★ **Michael Caine** … **Richard Harris**
'Michael Caine? An overfat, flatulent, 62-year-old windbag. A master of inconsequence now masquerading as a guru, passing off his vast limitations as pious virtues.'

★ **Richard Chamberlain** … **Sir Cedric Hardwicke**
'You're doing it the wrong way round, my boy. You're a star and you don't know how to act.'

★ **Charlie Chaplin** … **Herman J Mankiewicz**
'If people don't sit at Chaplin's feet, he goes out and stands where they're sitting.'

★ Michael Cimino ... Ralph Novak
'A movie [*Year of the Dragon*] that is often so inept it's funny. Mike, have you thought of driving a bus or becoming a piano tuner or otherwise doing something useful!'

★ Francis Ford Coppola ... George Lucas
'Whatever Francis does for you always ends up benefiting Francis the most.'

★ Gary Cooper ... King Vidor
'He got a reputation as a great actor just by thinking hard about the next line.'

★ Joan Crawford ... Bette Davis
'The best time I ever had with Joan Crawford was when I pushed her down the stairs in *What Ever Happened to Baby Jane?*'

★ Timothy Dalton ... Sean Connery
'I hope he's got a good lawyer.'

★ Doris Day ... Oscar Levant
'I knew Doris Day before she was a virgin.'

★ James Dean ... Rock Hudson
'I don't mean to speak ill of the dead, but he was a prick. Pardon my French. He was selfish and petulant, and believed his own press releases. On the set, he'd upstage an actor and step on his lines. Arrogant. But let him alone and he was brilliant. Nobody could touch him.'

★ Robert De Niro ... Liza Minnelli
'Sure, a class-A bastard. After the sneak preview in San Francisco, Bobby said to me in the car, "I don't mind being a bastard, as long as I'm an interesting bastard." '

★ Brian De Palma ... Andrew Rissik
'De Palma can't make movies about sex or ones that tackle "serious" issues or themes because narrative trickery and manipulative dexterity are his almost exclusive concerns.

As with much of the work of Steven Spielberg, his movies come at you on the surface and they tend to resonate there as well.'

★ Kirk Douglas ... Burt Lancaster
'Kirk would be the first to tell you he's a difficult man. I would be the second.'

★ Faye Dunaway ... Roman Polanski
'She was a gigantic pain in the ass. She demonstrated certifiable proof of insanity.'

★ Blake Edwards ... Leslie Halliwell
'A man of many talents, all of them minor.'

★ Mia Farrow ... Ava Gardner
'Hah! I always knew Frank [Sinatra] would wind up in bed with a boy.'

★ Eddie Fisher ... Dean Martin
'The reason I drink is because when I'm sober I think I'm Eddie Fisher.'

★ Errol Flynn ... Leslie Mallory
'A fifty-year trespass against good taste.'

★ Peter Fonda ... Bruce Dern
'In *The Trip* I started to get fed up. I was fed up because Peter Fonda was a star and I wasn't. And Peter couldn't act. I'm sorry, man, he just can't act. He never bothered to sit and learn. He never studied. And he just kind of larked out. Now I don't begrudge the fact that he has talent. But he's not an actor, by any stretch of the imagination.'

★ Judy Garland ... Joe Pasternak
'An angel, with spurs.'

★ Richard Gere ... Debra Winger
'I'm always trying to find diplomatic ways to talk about Richard and the movie *An Officer and a Gentleman*. I liked him before we started but that is the last time I can remember talking to him.'

★ Cary Grant … Zsa Zsa Gabor
'They are trying to show he's a great lover, but they'll never prove it to me.'

★ Alec Guinness … Bette Davis
'He cut my part [in *The Scapegoat*] into such shreds that my appearance in the final product made no sense at all. This is an actor who plays by himself, unto himself. In this particular picture he plays a dual role, so at least he was able to play with himself.'

★ Rex Harrison … Christopher Cazenove
'The bastard of all time if he wants to be.'

★ Laurence Harvey … Jane Fonda
'Acting with Harvey is like acting by yourself – only worse.'

★ Goldie Hawn … Donald Zec
'She was landed with an idiot giggle, a remorseless inclination to squeak, and if a brain hummed behind those dumbfounded eyes the secret never leaked out.'

★ Paul Henreid … Richard Winnington
'He looks as though his idea of fun would be to find a nice cold damp grave and sit in it.'

★ Charlton Heston … Richard Harris
'Heston's the only man who could drop out of a cubic moon, he's so square. We never got on. The trouble is with him he doesn't think he's just a hired actor, like the rest of us. He thinks he's the entire production. He used to sit there in the mornings and clock us in with a stopwatch.'

★ Dustin Hoffman … Robert Mitchum
'I don't understand this Method stuff. I remember Laurence Olivier asking Dustin Hoffman why he stayed up all night. Dustin, looking really beat, really bad, said it was to get into the scene being filmed that day, in which he was supposed to have been up all night. Olivier said, "My boy, if you'd learn how to act you wouldn't have to stay up all night." '

★ Dennis Hopper … John Hargreaves
'A madman! Great performance. But a total madman! Incredibly unpredictable. You just never knew what he was going to say. It certainly wasn't going to be the script. It never was! Sometimes, it bore no relationship to the script at all and you were left there thinking of something to say as you couldn't use your own lines any more …'

★ Rock Hudson … Doris Day
'I call him Ernie because he's certainly no Rock.'

★ William Hurt … Ken Russell
'I hired William Hurt for Altered States, and found I was his analyst for six months … It wasn't the part he talked about, never that, but how it was such a terrible thing being a billionaire after being born in abject poverty. I was quite deferential to him, but [my wife] listened to the crap he was talking and said, "OK, preppy, let's cut the shit." He was stunned and amazed but he was quite human after that.'

★ Glenda Jackson … John Simon
'Quite aside from her age, Miss Jackson is not appealing in any part – face, body, or limbs … yet all this could, perhaps, be overlooked if she were an artist. But nothing she says or does stems from genuine feeling, displays an atom of spontaneity, leaves any room for the unexpected. It is all technique – and not the most intricate technique at that – about as good as computer poetry.'

★ Don Johnson … Mickey Rourke
'This man is unbearable.'

★ Klaus Kinski … Werner Herzog
'He's not ageing well. The best thing to happen to his career is for him to die immediately.'

★ Jessica Lange … Jack Nicholson
'She is like a delicate fawn, but crossed with a Buick.'

★ Rob Lowe ... Brian Dennehy
'If Rob Lowe can get somebody to give
him ten million dollars to hire seventy-five or
a hundred people to make a picture, he's aces
by me. They need the jobs.'

★ Madonna ... Alan Frank
'Who's that girl? Who cares?'

★ Madonna ... Rosanna Arquette
'She's jumped right into the movie game ...
but I think people should learn to act first,
you know what I mean?'

★ Jayne Mansfield ... Bette Davis
'Dramatic art in her opinion is knowing
how to fill a sweater.'

★ Lee Marvin ... Joshua Logan
'Not since Attila the Hun swept across
Europe leaving five hundred years of total
blackness has there been a man like
Lee Marvin.'

★ Steve McQueen ... Robert Mitchum
'A Steve McQueen performance just
naturally lends itself to monotony:
Steve doesn't bring much to the party.'

★ Bette Midler ... Ken Wahl
'In one scene [of *Jinxed*] I have to hit her
in the face, and I thought we could save some
money on sound effects here.'

★ Marilyn Monroe ... Otto Preminger
'Directing her was like directing Lassie.
You needed fourteen takes to get each one
of them right.'

★ Marilyn Monroe ... Tony Curtis
'It's like kissing Hitler.'

★ Marilyn Monroe ... Otto Preminger
'A vacuum with nipples.'

★ Eddie Murphy ... Walter Hill
'Eddie can hear the rustle of nylon stockings
at fifty yards.'

★ Kim Novak ... Robert Aldrich
'Is Kim Novak a joke in her own time?'

★ Rosie Perez ... Charlie Sheen
'Rosie Perez? I don't think I could spend
eight or ten weeks on a movie set with her.
Her voice would drive me back to heroin.'

★ Peter O'Toole ... Noël Coward
'If you had been any prettier, it would have
been Florence of Arabia.'

★ Dennis Quaid ... Jim McBride
(director of *Great Balls of Fire* (1989))
'A giant pain in the ass.'

★ Ronald Reagan ... Gloria Grahame
'I can't stand the sight of Ronnie Reagan.
I'd like to stick my Oscar up his arse.'

★ Eric Roberts ... Julia Roberts (his sister)
'For as many people I meet who love
Eric Roberts, I meet just as many who think
he's a jerk.'

★ Ken Russell ... Bob Guccione
'An arrogant, self-centred, petulant individual.
I don't say this in any demeaning way.'

★ Steven Seagal ... Henry Rollins
'I think I would rather drink latex paint than
be in a movie with Steven Seagal.'

★ Peter Sellers ... Billy Wilder
'Talk about unprofessional rat finks.'

Chapter 13
History of The World

KING KONG (1933)

Much water has passed under the bridge since those pioneering days of film making in the latter half of the nineteenth century – days when the very idea of capturing a moving image on film seemed somehow miraculous. What kind of heretic would have then dared to imagine the special effects that are nowadays commonplace?

In this chapter we chart the key developments in cinema from its humble beginnings in the nineteenth century through to the present day, during the course of which we examine the key moments in the development of special effects.

Making Movie History, Part 1

1870s

In 1872, under the sponsorship of Governor Leland Stanford of California, and using a technique known as 'series photography', Eadweard Muybridge (1830–1904) succeeds in recording the motion of horses, through an arrangement of 24 still cameras, placed in a row, along the racetrack. As a result, the governor wins a bet, that all four hooves of a horse are off the ground simultaneously, at one point in the cycle of movement. Muybridge, on the other hand, became the first person in history to record continuous live action.

Muybridge published his results, *Animal Locomotion: An Electro-photographic Investigation of Consecutive Phases of Animal Movements*, in 1887.
The accompanying photographic plates can be seen at London's Victoria and Albert Museum.

1880s

In 1882, Etienne-Jules Marey, a French physician and physiologist, inspired by the work of Muybridge, invents the 'chronophotographic gun', a single camera

capable of taking twelve pictures a second. A significant step on the way to true motion pictures.

In 1886, Mrs Harvey Henderson, wife of one of the area's first real-estate developers, christens her Cahuenga Valley ranch 'Hollywood'. She had taken the idea from a friend who lived near Chicago in a house named 'Hollywood'.

In 1887, Marey designs paper-roll film, thereby doing away with glass plates. However, by 1888 Marey had begun experimenting with celluloid film.

In 1889, George Eastman invents perforated celluloid film with dramatic consequences. As a result of his efforts, WKL Dickson and Thomas Alva Edison develop that same year a motion-picture camera called the 'Kinetograph', which uses Eastman's perforated film in 35mm format (the industry standard even today). The pair also invent a means of projecting their film, the 'Kinetoscope'.

In 1889, WKL Dickson experiments with sound, by seeking to synchronise the lip movements on film with a phonograph record. He christens his apparatus the 'Kinetophonograph'; it is essentially a Kinetoscope linked with a gramophone.

1890s

In 1894, brothers Louis and Auguste Lumière combine the innovations of Muybridge, Marey and Edison, to invent the 'Cinématographe', an apparatus able to both take and project motion pictures. On 22 March 1895 the brothers make the first projection of a motion picture; the film, their first, is called *La Sortie des Ouvriers de l'Usine Lumière* (*Workers Leaving the Lumière Factory*) (1894). Other short film clips are also shown. Later that year, 28 December to be exact, the brothers open the first ever pay-to-view movie theatre.

In 1895, a real-estate agent and inventor, Thomas Armat, develops the first true motion-picture projection machine, which he calls the 'Phantoscope'. The machine incorporates a loop-forming device and an intermittent motion mechanism.

Edison, disillusioned with his own attempts, subsequently buys the Phantoscope, marketing it as the 'Vitascope'. The Vitascope makes its debut, before a paying audience, on 23 April 1896 at a New York music hall. The projectionist is none other than Thomas Armat.

In 1896, the first primitive examples of colour movies appear. To achieve colour, each frame is painted by hand, using a magnifying glass. The technique is known as 'hand-tinting'.

Also in 1896, the French inventor Raoul Grimoin-Sanson utilises ten projectors to show a panoramic picture on a large circular screen. He calls the process 'Cineorama' and it is the first multiscreen system. Unfortunately, it proves such a hit with the crowds that it is closed down after three performances, for reasons of public safety.

In 1897, the Frenchman Georges Méliès builds Europe's first film studio at Montreuil. He subsequently makes probably his best film, *Le Voyage dans la Lune* (*A Trip to the Moon*) (1902) – a thirty-scene film, often referred to as marking the beginning of special effects.

1900s

In 1903, the village of 'Hollywood' is incorporated as a municipality.

In 1904, Edwin Stanton Porter releases a six-minute film entitled *The Life of a Fireman*. The film, which utilises the editing of staged footage with library stock, paves the way for narrative film and is the first known instance of intercutting in American cinema.

In June 1905 the first nickelodeon (a nickel a movie) opens in Pittsburgh. The films are usually accompanied by a live piano or organ; however, with time the nickelodeons employ live actors and sound-effect experts to provide sound from behind the screen.

Pathé Frères develop Pathé-Color around 1905. The process involves the cutting by hand of up to six stencils, one for each colour to be used, and the subsequent layering of the stencils on the selected areas of the frame.

In 1906, George Albert Smith patents the first commercially viable colour system, 'Kinemacolor', which utilises red-orange and blue-green filters during filming, and upon projection produces a wide range of colours. Smith, along with Charles Urban, subsequently markets Kinemacolor through their Natural Colour Kinematograph Company. However, the system is far from perfect: problems include the drifting of colours from one part of the frame to another, eye strain and increased film wear.

By 1908, the company of Pathé Frères (brothers Charles, Émile, Jacques and Théophile), established in 1896, distributes twice as many films in the US as those produced by all of the American companies together.

In 1908, the companies of Edison, Vitagraph, Biograph, Kalem, Lubin, Selig, Essanay, Pathé Exchange, Méliès and Gaumont join together to create the 'Motion Picture Patents Company', in an attempt to control the production and distribution of motion pictures. The MPCC is subsequently disbanded in 1917, having been ruled an illegal trust, following legal action by independent companies, including Fox, Universal and Paramount.

1910s

In 1910, 'Hollywood', following a citizens' vote, becomes a district of Los Angeles in order to secure water supplies.

In the same year, Eugene Augustin Lauste, a former assistant of WKL Dickson, effectively constructs a means of recording both sound and image on the same film strip, thereby synchronising them.

George Albert Smith and Charles Urban release their first major colour film, made using Kinemacolor, *The Durbar at Delhi* (1911).

In 1915, two Americans, Herbert T Kalmus and Daniel F Comstock, experiment with an additive two-colour process, which they christen 'Technicolor'. The technique utilises a special camera, equipped with two apertures, one covered with a red filter, the other with a green filter. While better than the competition, the technique still produces unwanted colour fringes and halos upon projection.

1920s

At the beginning of the decade, the Technicolor Company refine their process, and come up with a two-colour subtractive process. The process utilises two films, each developed and then dyed, one red-orange, one blue-green. The films are then cemented together, resulting in colour upon projection. The results are still not perfect.

The year 1921 marks the advent of postsynchronisation or dubbing, as it is more commonly known. As a result, both synchronous and asynchronous sound (that which is not synchronised with the action on film, e.g. the sound of a doorbell) can be edited into the same scene.

In 1922, the major Hollywood studios create the Motion Picture Producers and Distributors of America, in an attempt to rid their industry of scandal, and in response to requests for some form of film censorship.

The noted director Cecil B DeMille makes use of Technicolor film while shooting his biblical epic, *The Ten Commandments* (1923).

In 1926, Warner Brothers, in partnership with Western Electric, begin developing a sound system for motion pictures. The result of their efforts is the 'Vitaphone'. The company subsequently releases *Don Juan* (1926), featuring John Barrymore, and using the Vitaphone system.

One year later, in 1927, Warner Brothers releases *The Jazz Singer*, starring Al Jolson, which is received with critical acclaim, and wins a Special Award for pioneering talking picture, at the 1927–8 Academy Awards.

In 1927, the Fox film company, building on the work of the Tri-Ergon process for the direct recording of sound on film, and utilising the talents of Theodore W Case and Earl I Sponable, release a series of short sound films under the name 'Movietone'.

The director Abel Gance uses a triple-screen system to show his latest film, *Napoléon* (1927). He refers to the system as 'Polyvision'.

In 1928, Warner Brothers release the first all-talking feature, *Lights of New York*. Although a financial success, the film is afflicted by the problems associated with simultaneous sound recording, namely zero editing and contrived acting.

In 1928, the Walt Disney company release *Steamboat Willie*, a pioneering fusion of animation and melody synchronisation, paving the way for the 'musical' in the process.

Professor Henri Chrétien demonstrates his anamorphic system, which utilises special lenses to compress and distort the image during filming, yet subsequently allows the image to be projected undistorted, and on to a wider screen than the regular motion-picture one.

In 1929, the Fox company release the first all-talking sound-on-film feature, *In Old Arizona*; an overwhelming success, it signals the end of the Warners' Vitaphone system.

The advances in sound recording, in particular the process of postsynchronisation, allow film making to ascend a new plateau, with such films as King Vidor's *Hallelujah!* (1929), Hitchcock's *Blackmail* (1929) and Milestone's *All Quiet on the Western Front* (1930).

1930s

In 1930 a code of movie ethics, the 'Production Code', is established by the Motion Picture Producers and Distributors of America, under Will Hayes, and with effect from 1 July 1934. Its aim is to moderate what can and can't be shown in accordance with the rules of 'good taste'.

In 1932, the Technicolor Company take the quest for colour to new levels, with their invention of a three-colour process. Crucial to this process is the use of two 45-degree prisms, which split the incoming light, causing it to be absorbed by one of three negatives, each sensitive to green, blue or red, the three primary photographic colours. The negatives are then printed as a positive relief image (a matrix), from which the final print is made.

Walt Disney release the first three-colour Technicolor film, the animated *Flowers and Trees* (1932).

The musical choreographer and director Busby Berkeley signs for Warner Brothers, where he not only creates visually stunning dance scenes but also introduces innovative and liberating camera techniques, in particular the use of the 'Berkeley top shot', whereby the action can be shot from directly above, using a boom crane. As a result of this the picture and melody can be edited together more smoothly. Examples of his work are *Gold Diggers of 1935* (1935) and *Babes in Arms* (1939).

The year 1935 sees the release of the first feature made entirely in three-colour Technicolor, *Becky Sharp*. Classics of all genres follow in its wake, including the animated movies *Snow White and the Seven Dwarfs* (1937) and *Fantasia* (1940) – both made by Disney – *The Adventures of Robin Hood* (1938), *The Wizard of Oz* and *Gone With the Wind* (both 1939).

1940s

The Technicolor Company introduce the monopack system, which requires only one roll of film. Consequently, Technicolor films can be used in regular motion-picture cameras.

1950s

Twentieth Century Fox, in an attempt to combat the threat posed by television, invest in Henri Chrétien's anamorphic-lens system, christening it 'CinemaScope'. The new CinemaScope constitutes a considerable improvement, with an aspect ratio (width to height) of 2.35:1, compared with the 1.33:1 of the conventional screen. Fox subsequently release their first wide-screen movie, *The Robe*, in September 1953.

Another wide-screen process, the Paramount-designed, 35mm 'VistaVision', makes an entrance; Hitchcock uses it to great effect in *To Catch a Thief* (1955), *The Man Who Knew Too Much* (1956) and *Vertigo* (1958). VistaVision's success is short-lived as a result of economics.

VistaVision resurfaces in the 1970s when George Lucas's Industrial Light and Magic company, having bought the previously discarded equipment at knock-down prices, use it to make *Star Wars* (1977), and for all subsequent effects work.

At the same time 'stereoscopic 3-D' and 'Cinerama' (a refinement of the earlier Polyvision) arrive on the scene. The '3-D' films require the audience to wear special glasses in order to create an impression of depth. Cinerama, on the other hand, makes use of three cameras during filming, a multiple projector and a semicircular screen. The result is an image three times as wide as the traditional format. One of the last films to be made using this process is *How the West Was Won* (1962). Shortly afterwards Cinerama is abandoned owing to its high cost.

In direct competition with Cinemascope and Cinerama is the use of wide-screen stock. Michael Todd develops a 65mm stock and subsequently forms the Magna Corporation with the movie mogul Joseph M Schenck, in order to exploit this new format.

Their first production is *Oklahoma!* (1955); it utilises the process to stunning effect, creating breathtakingly sharp vistas on screen. It is a smash hit!

Also of note are the 'Panavision' wide-screen processes: Panavision, using 35mm film and an anamorphic lens; 'Super Panavision' (also known as 'Panavision 70'), using 65mm film stock and without distortion (subsequently used to great effect in *Ben-Hur* (1959)); and finally 'Ultra Panavision', using 65mm film and an anamorphic lens.

1960s

In 1965 the Dolby noise-reduction system is developed by Ray Dolby and his San Francisco-based Dolby Laboratories Inc. Primarily developed for use in the recording industry, it is soon adopted by the movie industry for use both during and after production.

1970s

The year 1970 sees the release of *Quiet Revolution*, the first film to be recorded using Dolby's patented noise-reduction system. Dolby also release their stereo sound system, which is capable of recording and subsequently reproducing four-channel sound, by means of a special optical soundtrack on 35mm film.

The hit motion picture *Star Wars* (1977) is subsequently released; the release prints feature Dolby stereo sound and as a result generate much interest in the work of Dolby. Before long it becomes the industry standard.

The 'Imax' wide-screen camera projection, designed in Canada by William C Shaw and PRW Jones, premieres at Expo 70 in Japan. The system uses 70mm film to provide an image of exceptional height and depth.

1980s

In 1983 the final film in the *Star Wars* trilogy, *Return of the Jedi*, is released. However, prior to its release, four American cinemas, including the Avco in Westwood, install a new sound system at a cost of about $15,000 each. The system has been designed under the guidance of George Lucas and is called 'THX Sound' (once more a reference to his earlier film, *THX 1138* (1971)). The resulting sound is of high clarity and low distortion.

Towards the end of the 80s, film makers come to rely more and more upon computers during the production process.

TITANIC (1997)

1990s

The year 1997 sees the release of James Cameron's epic disaster/love movie, *Titanic* (1997). The movie, building upon the advances of the 80s and early 90s, sets new standards for CGI (computer-generated imaging) and digital effects, obscuring the line between real and computer-generated effects. It can be only a matter of time before movies become entirely digital. More worryingly, though: how long before 'synthespians', i.e. computer generated actors, are upon us en masse?

Making Movie History, Part 2

Key moments in the development of special effects

★ A Trip to the Moon (1902)

Made in 1902 by the French magician Georges Méliès, *A Trip to the Moon* constitutes a milestone in the history of special effects. Rather than choosing to merely record reality as the camera sees it, Méliès uses the camera as a means of realising his imagination on film. An imagination that is not curtailed by reality.

Méliès's eyes were first opened to the possibilities of film while he was out shooting on the streets of Paris. Apparently his camera jammed, and, by the time he'd managed to release it, a few seconds had elapsed, during which time the view before the camera had changed. Upon viewing the affected film, Méliès was excited by what he saw: images merged into one another, or suddenly appeared, only to disappear as quickly, all as if by magic.

As a result Méliès begins to exploit the optical possibilities of the camera, introducing such techniques as multiple exposure, slow motion, time-lapse photography, dissolves and hand tinting of the film.

★ King Kong (1933)

King Kong is perhaps best remembered for its use of stop-motion, a technique pioneered by the special-effects expert Willis H O'Brien.

O'Brien uses a combination of front and rear projection, live action and stop-motion techniques to bring the puppet of King Kong to life, with startling results. Even today, the film is regarded by many as one of the finest displays of stop-motion.

Some sixteen years after making *King Kong*, O'Brien's talents were finally recognised, when he won an Oscar for his work on *Mighty Joe Young* (1949).

★ The Seventh Voyage of Sinbad (1958) and Jason and the Argonauts (1963)

Featuring the effects work of the legendary Ray Harryhausen, a former assistant to Willis H O'Brien on *Mighty Joe Young* (1949), both films are distinguished by the use of 'Dynamation'. This is a technique devised by Harryhausen, who, continuing the stop-motion advances of O'Brien, developed a means of enabling live actors and animated models to convincingly interact, as in the battle with the skeletons.

★ 2001: A Space Odyssey (1968)

Under the supervision of the special-effects maestro Douglas Trumbull, *2001: A Space Odyssey* remains to this day a convincing piece of work, even in the light of digital effects.

Trumbull, brings to the director Stanley Kubrick's sci-fi epic a documentary feel, thereby diminishing our focus upon the fictional aspect of the story, and consequently heightening the sense that what we are viewing is real.

For the record Kubrick took slightly over two years to complete *2001: A Space Odyssey*, shooting, according to Trumbull, more than 200 times the film's final length in the process.

★ Star Wars (1977)

Perhaps the one man who contributed the most to the special effects of George Lucas's *Star Wars* is John Dykstra. Dykstra is ultimately responsible for the 'Dykstraflex', a highly innovative camera system that made possible the trademark dogfight scenes between the ships of the Rebels and the Imperial TIE fighters.

In 1973, Dykstra, a former colleague of Doug Trumbull on *Silent Running* (1972), along with Al Miller and Jeffrey Jeffress, took the innovative step of using a computer (PDP II) to control a camera's shutter, along with a dolly mover to control the motions of the camera, thereby creating the first advanced, electronically operated motion-control camera system, with the ability to precisely repeat its movements as often as required by the film makers.

The Dykstraflex system, as used for the filming of *Star Wars*, allowed a camera unit consisting of boom arm with a mechanised camera attached to the end to be programmed to move down a steel track, performing the desired pans, tilts or rolls of the camera as it went. Gone were the days of flying wire-controlled models past the camera. It was now the camera that flew past the models.

A further innovation of *Star Wars* is the extensive use of 'storyboards' during the initial stages of the film's development. Thus, all creatures, spaceships and so on are sketched following consultation with the film's script, and directly with George Lucas himself. Additional details, such as the number of photographic elements and type of photography (animation, model or motion control), are also recorded on the storyboards.

Once the sketches are produced, small-scale models (five to seven feet) are sculpted; then, following selection or rejection by Lucas, filming can begin.

Thus storyboards, in spite of the time involved (some one thousand pages of storyboards were used for *Return of the Jedi*), provide an invaluable means of establishing exactly what is needed to re-create a specific scene on film, consequently saving time in the long run.

★ Dragonslayer (1981)

With the release of *Dragonslayer* we reach another stage in the evolution of special effects, with the introduction of 'Go-Motion' – the technique responsible for giving life to the film's dragon.

Go-Motion is achieved by attaching control rods to a puppet. The rods are subsequently connected via motors to a computer. As the puppeteer, by means of the rods, operates the puppet, the computer records the movements.

The scene can now be filmed, but this time it is the computer that controls the movements of the puppet. Consequently, the shutter can be left open during filming, thereby allowing the camera to record the natural blur of the object as it moves, achieving a greater degree of fluidity and thus realism than previously possible with stop-motion, which by its very nature results in a jerky portrayal of movement.

★ Young Sherlock Holmes (1985)

Motion-picture history in the making! *Young Sherlock Holmes* features the first 3-D digital character to appear in a motion picture, with its depiction of a sword-wielding knight who leaps from a stained-glass window.

'Stained-glass man' (as he came to be known) was achieved by first producing a matt painting of the subject, which is subsequently scanned into a computer, using an early Pixar laser-based scanner. The scanned image can now be digitally manipulated by the computer, adding motion blur and depth of field, thereby creating a convincingly lifelike image in as complex an environment as the scene dictates.

The next step is to bring the image to life: this is achieved by using a computer, specially programmed to mimic the movements of a human being, for example the motions of the hand as it wields a sword.

Consequently, after no fewer than four months of work, we are able to watch an entirely computer-generated character engage in realistic swordplay with a human actor.

★ Luxo Jr. (1986)

This Oscar-nominated short, although only two minutes long, is the first fully computer-animated film to be made, and with it the origin of such films as *Toy Story* (1995) and *A Bug's Life* (1998).

★ The Abyss (1989)

The director James Cameron's *The Abyss* (1989) represents another giant leap for computer-generated effects, with its depiction of a living, moving creature, composed entirely of sea water – the 'pseudopod'.

In order to create the pseudopod, the designers at George Lucas's Industrial Light and Magic first had to carry out an investigation into the properties of water. Hours were spent studying the characteristics of water, examining its motion using a wave machine, and not forgetting water's ability to both refract and reflect light. Models were also built in order to aid visualisation. Finally, the designers were ready to feed the data into the computers and enter the digital realm.

However, after twenty separate shots and 75 seconds of 3-D imagery, Cameron had his pseudopod.

★ Terminator 2: Judgment Day (1991)

The special effects of *Terminator 2* are largely dependent upon the idea of 'morphing', a technique first exploited in *Willow* (1988) – in particular, the scene where the character Willow transforms a bewitched possum back into the human shape of the sorceress Fin Raziel, changing from goat to ostrich to turtle to tiger in between. The effects for *Willow* were achieved by first photographing live-action animals or puppets, digitising the elements, and then distorting the images, one into the other by means of the 'morphing software', as developed by ILM's Doug Smythe.

To create the illusion of a chrome man, as seen in *Terminator 2*, the designers first had to grid up the body of the actor, Robert Patrick. Once gridded up, Patrick was filmed, the grid acting as a reference point, by which the computer could track the various elements of his body while he was still or in motion. The resulting images were then scanned into the computer.

Using a further piece of breakthrough software, called 'Make Sticky', the designers were now able to map the 2-D image from a live-action plate on to a 3-D computer model. Consequently, when the model moves, the mapped live-action image 'sticks' with it.

Thus, to achieve the scene of Robert Patrick as the metallic T-1000, rising out of the chequerboard floor of the hospital, while an unsuspecting security guard grabs a coffee, designers first had to scan in live-action footage of the floor. The 2-D image was then mapped on to the 3-D computer-generated image of the T-1000, producing the effects that we see in the film. The same technique was subsequently used for the scene of Patrick passing through the metal bars of the security door.

By the time ILM had finished their work for *Terminator 2* they had produced 7,695 frames of 3-D imaging.

JURASSIC PARK (1993)

★ Jurassic Park (1993)

With the release of 1993's *Jurassic Park*, the team at ILM realised the next stage in the evolution of digital effects: the creation of lifelike, fully animated, digitally 3-D creatures, capable of being digitally composited with live-action plates.

The first stage was to produce a wire-framed, 3-D model – but, unfortunately, dinosaurs have been extinct for several thousand years. So the designers had to turn to the research of palaeontologists in order to build up a picture of how the creatures lived and moved. The next stage was to build sculpted models, which were subsequently measured by lasers, in order to provide an exact digital representation of the models, which could now be animated. In order to achieve maximum realism the designers now utilised various software packages to give the models skin, muscle movement, texture and other characteristics. Finally, optical effects such as camera bounce and blurring were added.

The end result: approximately six minutes of film and the most convincingly lifelike man-made representations of dinosaurs to date.

★ Forrest Gump (1994)

Forrest Gump abounds with effects: the removal of the legs of the Vietnam veteran Lieutenant Dan, so as to create the illusion of a double amputee; the footage of Forrest Gump in such distinguished company as that of President Kennedy and John Lennon; the crowd (apart from those in the foreground) that listens to Gump speak at the Lincoln memorial; the ping-pong ball during Forrest's match against the Chinese; and even the feather that glides down through the air, before coming to rest on Gump's foot.

In order to create the feather scene, 25 different feathers were filmed against a blue screen. These shots were then digitally blended together, the blue screen removed and the background inserted. To facilitate the final shot of Forrest picking the fallen feather from atop his shoe, a real feather was attached during the live-action footage and erased later.

★ Matrix (1999)

The kung-fu sci-fi *Matrix* (1999), starring Keanu Reeves and Laurence Fishburne, achieves spectacular visuals, with the use of an effect known as 'flo-mo', or ' bullet time', as it has been christened by the directors of *Matrix*, Andy and Larry Wachowski.

Bullet time, a development of an effect previously seen in television adverts such as those for The Gap, enables the onscreen action to be seemingly held in time, while the camera continues to move around the subject. Thus, building upon the principles first exploited by stop-motion, the moviegoer is made to feel, somewhat paradoxically, as though the camera were still moving, while the subject remains strangely frozen.

In filming *The Matrix*, the effects supremo John Gaeta utilises 120 still cameras mounted on a 360-degree rig to circle the action; to achieve the illusion of movement, each camera is set to shoot a fraction of a second after the previous one, thereby providing a succession of near-continuous stills. Finally, by means of computer manipulation, each frame is made to run seamlessly into the next. Consequently all 120 frames appear as one continuous sweep of the camera upon projection.

★ Star Wars: Episode 1: The Phantom Menace (1999)

The next stage in special effects, *Phantom Menace* has two thousand effects shots compared with *Titanic's* (1997) five hundred or so. It features over sixty creatures, five of which have speaking parts. Digital highlights of the film include the exhilarating pod race, the floating senate meetings, the battle sequence between the Gungan and the Trade Federation battle droids, and the light-sabre duelling between Obi-Wan and Qui-Gon Jinn.

Well, where next? An all-talking, all-walking, all-directing, computer-generated George Lucas!

Chapter 14
They Call Me Mr Tibbs

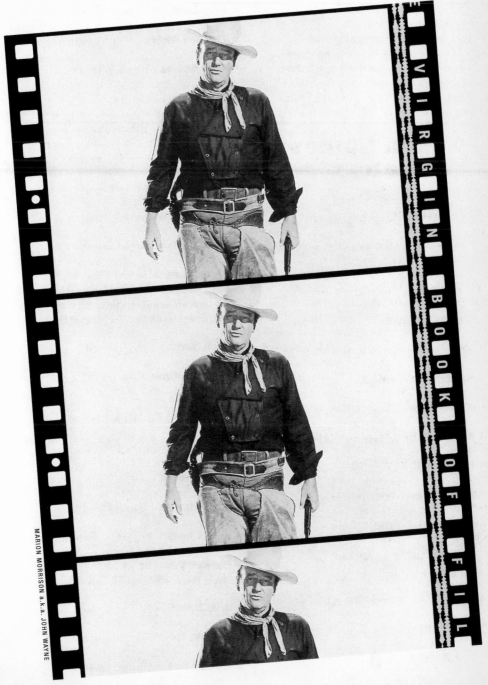

MARION MORRISON a.k.a. JOHN WAYNE

What's in a name? Well, if you're a budding Hollywood star, potentially everything. Somehow, we don't think 1971's tale of an avenging gangster, *Get Carter*, would have made quite the same impact had its leading man been billed under his original name of Maurice Micklewhite Jr. However, as we reveal, Michael Caine isn't alone in changing his name for the sake of his acting career.

As you've probably guessed by now this section of the book is all about names. Not only do we expose the original names of some of Hollywood's smoothest stars, but we also reveal some of their nicknames.

Original Names of 40 Actors

★ **Dan Aykroyd** – Daniel Agraluscarsacra

★ **Robert Alda** – Alphonso Giuseppe Giovanni Roberto D'Abruzzo

★ **Fred Astaire** – Frederick Austerlitz

★ **Charles Bronson** – Charles Buchinski

★ **Mel Brooks** – Melvin Kaminsky

★ **Red Buttons** – Aaron Chwatt

★ **Nicolas Cage** – Nicholas Coppola

★ **Michael Caine** – Maurice Micklewhite Jr

★ **Chevy Chase** – Cornelius Chase

★ **Sean Connery** – Thomas Connery

★ **Gary Cooper** – Frank Cooper

★ **Michael Crawford** – Michael Dumble-Smith

★ **Tom Cruise** – Thomas Mapother IV

★ **Tony Curtis** – Bernard Schwartz

★ **Troy Donahue** – Merle Johnson Jr

★ **Kirk Douglas** – Issur Danielovitch

★ **Adam Faith** – Terence Nelhams

★ **John Garfield** – Julius Garfinkle

★ **Stewart Granger** – James Stewart

★ **Cary Grant** – Archibald Leach

★ **Charlton Heston** – Charles Carter

★ **Rock Hudson** – Roy Scherer

★ **Howard Keel** – Harry Leek

★ **Boris Karloff** – William Pratt

★ **Danny Kaye** – David D Kaminsky

★ **Ben Kingsley** – Krishna Banji

★ **Stan Laurel** – Arthur S Jefferson

★ **Jerry Lewis** – Joseph Levitch

★ **Herbert Lom** – Herbert Charles Angelo Kuchacevich ze Schluderpacheru (with such an unforgettable name why on Earth did he bother to change it?)

★ **Dean Martin** – Dino Crocetti

★ **Walter Matthau** – Walter Matuschanskayasky

★ **Luke Perry** – Coy Luther Perry III

★ **Omar Sharif** – Michael Shalhoub

★ **Charlie Sheen** – Carlos Irwin Estevez

★ **Craig Stevens** – Gail Shikles Jr

★ **Robert Taylor** – Spangle Arlington Brough

★ **Rudolph Valentino** – Rodolfo Alfonzo Raffaele Pierre Philibert Guglielmi

★ **John Wayne** – Marion Morrison

★ **Gene Wilder** – Jerry Silberman

★ **Michael York** – Michael Johnson

Original Names of 40 Actresses

★ **June Allyson** – Ella Geisman

★ **Mary Astor** – Lucille Langhanke

★ **Lauren Bacall** – Betty Joan Perske

★ **Anne Bancroft** – Anna Maria Lousie Italiano

★ **Dyan Cannon** – Samille Friesen

★ **Cyd Charisse** – Tula Finklea

★ **Claudette Colbert** – Lilly Chauchoin

★ **Joan Crawford** – Lucille Le Sueur

★ **Bette Davis** – Ruth Davis

★ **Doris Day** – Doris von Kappelhoff

★ **Yvonne DeCarlo** – Peggy Yvonne Middleton

★ **Sandra Dee** – Alexandra Zuck

★ **Bo Derek** – Mary Cathleen Collins

★ **Diana Dors** – Diana Fluck

★ **Judy Garland** – Frances Gumm

★ **Whoopi Goldberg** – Caryn Johnson

★ **Kathryn Grayson** – Zelma Hedrick

★ **Jean Harlow** – Harlean Carpentier

★ **Goldie Hawn** – Goldie Studlenghawn

★ **Suzy Kendall** – Frieda Harrison

★ **Dorothy Lamour** – Mary Kaumayer

★ **Jennifer Jason Leigh** – Jennifer Morrow

★ **Carole Lombard** – Jane Peters

★ **Sophia Loren** – Sofia Scicolone

★ **Shirley MacLaine** – Shirley Mclean Beaty (sister of Warren Beatty)

★ **Jayne Mansfield** – Vera Jane Palmer

★ **Helen Mirren** – Ilyena Mironoff

★ **Demi Moore** – Demi Guynes

★ **Stefanie Powers** – Stefania Federkiewicz

★ **Winona Ryder** – Winona Horowitz

★ **Susan Sarandon** – Susan Tomalin

★ **Jane Seymour** – Joyce Frankenberger

★ **Stella Stevens** – Estelle Eggleton

★ **Sigourney Weaver** – Susan Weaver

★ **Raquel Welch** – Raquel Tejada

★ **Barbara Windsor** – Barbara Deeks

★ **Shelley Winters** – Shirley Schrift

★ **Natalie Wood** – Natasha Virapaeff

★ **Jane Wyman** – Sarah Jane Fulks

★ **Susannah York** – Susannah Yolande Fletcher

Call Me...

20 Movieland Nicknames

★ Look –
Lauren Bacall

★ The Sex Kitten –
Brigitte Bardot

★ The It Girl –
Clara Bow

★ The Clothes Horse –
Joan Crawford

★ The Professional / The Virgin –
Doris Day

★ Little Bastard –
James Dean (the words were painted on
the back of his Porsche)

★ The Girl With the Million-Dollar Legs –
Betty Grable

★ The Platinum Blonde –
Jean Harlow

★ The Horizontal Champ –
Richard Harris

★ The Peekaboo Girl –
Veronica Lake

★ La Guitarra –
Jennifer Lopez
(because her body curves like a guitar)

★ The Brazilian Bombshell –
Carmen Miranda

★ Gimmee Moore –
Demi Moore

★ The Sex Thimble –
Dudley Moore

★ Tinkerbell –
Julia Roberts
(given to her by the crew of *Hook* (1991)

★ The Oomph Girl –
Ann Sheridan

★ The Italian Stallion –
Sylvester Stallone

★ The Sweater Girl –
Lana Turner

★ The Muscles from Brussels –
Jean Claude Van Damme

★ The Duke –
John Wayne

Chapter 15
Scream!

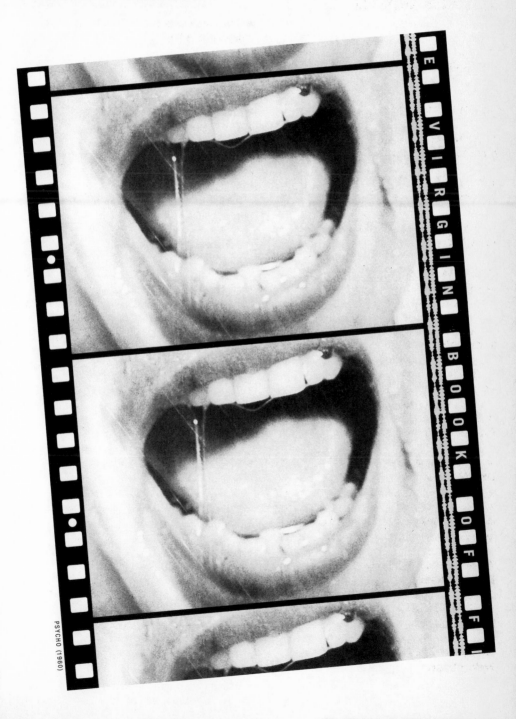

PSYCHO (1960)

Vampires drink it and psychos usually end up covered in it. What are we talking about? Well, what else could it be but blood? And by the bucketful. In this chapter we take a look at the knife-wielding, the blood-sucking, the skull-crushing and the generally depraved charmers to have graced the big screen over the years. Count Dracula, Hannibal the Cannibal and even Jack the Ripper are all here. So sit back, relax, put your feet up and enjoy a nice, warming glass of the red, red stuff. Cheers!

Guess Who's (Not) Coming to Dinner

★ **Horatio Alger** (Martin Sheen)
Badlands (1973)

★ **Clyde Barrow** (Warren Beatty)
Bonnie and Clyde (1967)

★ **Patrick Bateman** (Christian Bale)
American Psycho (1999)

★ **Norman Bates** (Anthony Perkins)
Psycho (1960)

★ **Travis Bickle** (Robert De Niro)
Taxi Driver (1976)

★ **Jerry Blake** (Terry O'Quinn)
The Stepfather (1987)

★ **Mr Blonde** (Michael Madsen)
Reservoir Dogs (1992)

★ **Danielle Breton** (Margot Kidder)
Sisters (1973)

★ **Martin Burney** (Patrick Bergin)
Sleeping With the Enemy (1991)

★ **Max Cady** (Robert De Niro)
Cape Fear (1991)

★ **Candyman** (Tony Todd)
Candyman (1992)

★ **Hedra Carlson** (Jennifer Jason Leigh)
Single White Female (1992)

★ **John Reginald Christie** (Richard Attenborough)
10 Rillington Place (1971)

★ **Vincenzo Coccotti** (Christopher Walken)
True Romance (1993)

★ **Matt Cordell** (Robert Z'Dar)
Maniac Cop (1988)

★ **Bud Corliss** (Robert Wagner)
A Kiss Before Dying (1956)

★ **Daryll Lee Cullum** (Harry Connick Jr)
Copycat (1995)

★ **Norma Desmond** (Gloria Swanson)
Sunset Boulevard (1950)

★ **D-Fens** (Michael Douglas)
Falling Down (1993)

★ **Evelyn Draper** (Jessica Walter)
Play Misty for Me (1971)

★ **Dr Robert Elliott** (Michael Caine)
Dressed to Kill (1980)

★ **Eric** (Jean-Hugues Anglade)
Killing Zoe (1994)

★ **Alex Forrest** (Glenn Close)
Fatal Attraction (1987)

★ **Professor Henry Jarrod** (Vincent Price)
House of Wax (1953)

★ **Early Grace** (Brad Pitt)
Kalifornia (1993)

★ **Lucy Harbin** (Joan Crawford)
Strait-jacket (1963)

★ **Henry** (Michael Rooker)
Henry Portrait of a Serial Killer (1989)

★ **Jack the Ripper** (James Spader)
Jack's Back (1988)

★ **Jason** (Warrington Gillette)
Friday the 13th Part 2 (1981)

★ **Mallory Wilson Knox** (Julliette Lewis)
Natural Born Killers (1994)

★ **Mickey Knox** (Woody Harrelson)
Natural Born Killers (1994)

★ **Freddy Krueger** (Robert Englund)
A Nightmare on Elm Street (1984)

★ **Leatherface** (Gunnar Hansen)
The Texas Chainsaw Massacre (1974)

★ **Hannibal 'The Cannibal' Lecter**
(Anthony Hopkins)
The Silence of the Lambs (1991)

★ **Carol Ledoux** (Catherine Deneuve)
Repulsion (1965)

★ **Beverly and Elliot Mantle** (Jeremy Irons)
Dead Ringers (1988)

★ **Dr Moreau** (Charles Laughton)
Island of Lost Souls (1933)

★ **Michael Myers a.k.a. The Shape**
(Nick Castle)
Halloween (1978)

★ **Bonnie Parker** (Faye Dunaway)
Bonnie and Clyde (1967)

★ **Peyon** (Rebecca DeMornay)
The Hand that Rocks the Cradle (1992)

★ **Horace Pinker** (Mitch Pileggi)
Shocker (1989)

★ **Pluto** (Michael Berryman)
The Hills Have Eyes (1978)

★ **Preacher Harry Powell** (Robert Mitchum)
The Night of the Hunter (1955)

★ **Reno a.k.a. Jimmy Laine** (Abel Ferrara)
Driller Killer (1979)

★ **Jack Torrance** (Jack Nicholson)
The Shining (1980)

★ **Mrs Trefoile** (Tallulah Bankhead)
Die! Die! My Darling! (1965)

★ **Victor the Cleaner** (Jean Reno)
Nikita (a.k.a. *La Femme Nikita*) (1990)

★ **Hughie Warriner** (Billy Zane)
Dead Calm (1989)

★ **Annie Wilkes** (Cathy Bates)
Misery (1990)

★ **Benjamin Willis a.k.a. The Fisherman**
(Muse Watson)
I Still Know What You Did Last Summer
(1997)

The Many Faces of Count Dracula

The films and all who've donned
the false teeth

★ *Nosferatu* (1922)
Max Schreck

★ *Spanish Dracula* (1931)
Carlos Villarias

★ *Dracula Istanbulda* (1953)
Atif Kaptan

★ *Curse of Dracula*
(a.k.a. *Return of Dracula;*
The Fantastic Disappearing Man) (1958)
Francis Lederer

★ *Billy the Kid vs. Dracula* (1965)
John Carradine

★ *Count Dracula* (1971)
Christopher Lee

★ *Dracula vs. Frankenstein*
(a.k.a. *Blood of Frankenstein*) (1972)
Zandor Vorkov

★ *Blacula* (1972)
Charles Macaulay

★ *Dracula's Great Love*
(a.k.a. *El Grande Amore del
Conde Dracula*) (1972)
Paul Naschy

★ *Lake of Dracula*
(a.k.a. *Choisu Me*) (1972)
Mori Kishida

★ *Lady Dracula*
(a.k.a. *Legendary Curse of Lemora;
Lemora, the Lady Dracula*) (1973)
Leslie Gibb

★ *Blood for Dracula*
(a.k.a. *Andy Warhol's Dracula*) (1974)
Udo Kier

★ *Vampira*
(a.k.a. *Old Dracula*) (1975)
David Niven

★ *Dracula and Son* (1976)
Christopher Lee

★ *Nocturna* (1978)
John Carradine

★ *Nosferatu* (1978)
Klaus Kinski

★ *Dracula* (1979)
Frank Langella

★ *The True Life of Dracula* (1979)
Stefan Sileanu

★ *Dracula's Last Rites* (1980)
Gerald Fielding

★ *The Monster Club* (1987)
Duncan Regehr

★ *Dracula*
(a.k.a. *Bram Stoker's Dracula*) (1992)
Gary Oldman

★ *Dracula Rising* (1993)
Christopher Atkins

★ *Dracula: Dead and Loving It* (1995)
Leslie Nielsen

★ *The Creeps* (1997)
Phil Fondacaro

Any list of Dracula films would be
incomplete without special mentions for
Universal and Hammer, both of whom made
the legend of Dracula their own.

Universal

★ *Dracula* (1931)
Bela Lugosi

★ *Dracula's Daughter* (1936)
Gloria Holden

★ *Son of Dracula* (1943)
Lon Chaney Jr

★ *House of Frankenstein* (1944)
John Carradine

★ *House of Dracula* (1945)
John Carradine

★ *Abbott and Costello Meet
Frankenstein* (1948)
Bela Lugosi

Hammer

★ *Dracula* (1958)
Christopher Lee

★ *Brides of Dracula* (1960)
the Count does not feature;
probably down the pub!

★ *Dracula, Prince of Darkness* (1964)
Christopher Lee

★ *Dracula Has Risen from the Grave* (1968)
Christopher Lee

★ *Taste the Blood of Dracula* (1970)
Christopher Lee

★ *Scars of Dracula* (1970)
Christopher Lee

★ *Dracula A.D. 1972*
(a.k.a. *Dracula Today*) (1972)
Christopher Lee

★ *The Satanic Rites of Dracula*
(a.k.a. *Count Dracula and His Vampire
Bride; Count Dracula Is Alive and
Well and Living in London*) (1973)
Christopher Lee

★ *The Legend of the Seven Golden
Vampires* (a.k.a. *The Seven Brothers Meet
Dracula*) (1974)
John Forbes Robertson

Mr Lee could well have been afflicted
with multiple-personality disorder as a result
of his numerous portrayals of the Count!

Dracula's Friends
and Neighbours

Films about vampires to get your teeth
stuck into!

★ *Vampyr*
(a.k.a. *The Strange Adventure of
David Gray*) (1932)

★ *The Return of the Vampire* (1943)

★ *The Vampire's Ghost* (1943)

★ *Dead Men Walk* (1943)

★ *My Son, the Vampire*
(a.k.a. *Old Mother Riley Meets the
Vampire; Vampires Over London*) (1952)

★ *Mark of the Vampire*
(a.k.a. *The Vampire*) (1957)

★ *Blood of Dracula* (1957)

★ *The Vampire*
(a.k.a. *El Vampiro*) (1957)

★ *The Vampire's Coffin*
(a.k.a. *El Ataud del Coffin*) (1958)

★ *Blood of the Vampire* (1958)

★ *Uncle Was a Vampire* (1959)

★ *Curse of the Undead* (1959)

★ *The World of Vampires*
(a.k.a. *El Mundo de los Vampiros*) (1960)

★ *Blood and Roses* (1960)

★ *The Vampire and the Ballerina* (1960)

★ *Slaughter of the Vampire*
(a.k.a. *Curse of the Blood Ghouls*) (1961)

★ *Kiss of the Vampire*
(a.k.a. *Kiss of Evil*) (1963)

★ *The Last Man on Earth* (1964)

★ *Goliath and the Vampires*
(a.k.a. *The Vampires*) (1964)

★ *Planet of the Vampires*
(a.k.a. *The Demon Planet*) (1965)

★ *Munster, Go Home!* (1966)

★ *Planet of Blood*
(a.k.a. *Queen of Blood*) (1966)

★ *Track of the Vampire*
(a.k.a. *Blood Bath*) (1966)

★ *The Fearless Vampire Killers;*
a.k.a. *Pardon Me, but Your Teeth Are in
My Neck* (1967)

★ *House of Dark Shadows* (1970)

★ *Vampire Men of the Lost Planet* (1970)

★ *The House that Dripped Blood* (1970)

★ *Count Yorga, Vampire* (1971)

★ *The Velvet Vampire*
(a.k.a. *Cemetery Girls*) (1971)

★ *The Return of Count Yorga* (1971)

★ *The Bloodsuckers*
(a.k.a. *Incense for the Damned*) (1971)

★ *Daughters of Darkness* (1971)

★ *Vampire Circus* (1971)

★ *Blacula* (1972)

★ *The Bloody Vampire* (1972)

★ *The Deathmaster* (1972)

★ *Scream, Blacula, Scream* (1973)

★ *Captain Kronos: Vampire Hunter*
(a.k.a. *Kronos*) (1974)

★ *Spermula* (1975)

★ *Martin* (1978)

★ *Love at First Bite* (1979)

★ *Vampire Hookers* (1979)

★ *Last Rites*
(a.k.a. *Dracula's Last Rites*) (1980)

★ *The Hunger* (1983)

★ *Fright Night* (1985)

★ *Lifeforce* (1985)

★ *Once Bitten* (1985)

★ *Vamp* (1986)

★ *Near Dark* (1987)

★ *The Lost Boys* (1987)

★ *Graveyard Shift* (1987)

★ *Dance of the Damned* (1988)

★ *The Vampire at Midnight* (1988)

★ *The Understudy: Graveyard Shift II* (1988)

★ *My Best Friend Is A Vampire* (1988)

★ *Fright Night Part 2* (1989)

★ *Vampire's Kiss* (1989)

★ *Thirst* (1989)

★ *Beverly Hills Vamp* (1989)

★ *Dracula's Widow* (1989)
(directed by none other than Christopher
Coppola, nephew of Francis Ford Coppola,
the man who brought us *Dracula*
(a.k.a. *Bram Stoker's Dracula*) (1992))

★ *Transylvania Twist* (1989)

★ *To Die For* (1989)

★ *I Bought A Vampire Motorcycle* (1990)

★ *Sundown: The Vampire in Retreat*
(a.k.a. *Sundown*) (1990)

★ *Subspecies* (1990)

★ *Pale Blood* (1990)

★ *Son of Darkness: To Die For II* (1991)

★ *Howling IV: The Freaks* (1991)

★ *Buffy the Vampire Slayer* (1992)

★ *Vampire Hunter D* (1992)

★ *Innocent Blood* (1992)

★ *A Vampire in Paradise*
(a.k.a. *Un Vampire au Paradis*) (1992)

★ *To Sleep with a Vampire* (1992)

★ *Tale of a Vampire* (1993)

★ *Blood in the Night* (1993)

★ *Knights* (1993)

★ *Love Bites* (1993) – with Adam Ant

★ *Bloodstone: Subspecies II* (1993)

★ *Bloodlust: Subspecies III* (1994)

★ *Embrace of the Vampire* (1994) – this one stars Martin Kemp, of Spandau Ballet fame

★ *Interview with the Vampire* (1994)

★ *Jugular Wine: A Vampire Odyssey* (1994) – with music muscle man Henry Rollins

★ *Nadja* (1994)

★ *Twisted Tales* (1994)

★ *Voodoo Soup* (1994)

★ *The Girl With Hungry Eyes* (1995)

★ *Night Hunter* (1995)

★ *Vampire Conspiracy* (1995)

★ *Vampire in Brooklyn* (1995)

★ *Vampire Vixens from Venus* (1995)

★ *The Addiction* (1995)

★ *Blood & Donuts* (1995) – look out for a Mr D Cronenberg in this one

★ *Bordello of Blood* (1996)

★ *Burnin' Love* (1996)

★ *From Dusk Till Dawn* (1996)

★ *Habit* (1997)

★ *Night Shade* (1997)

★ *Sleep When You're Dead* (1997)

★ *Man Into Vampire!* (1997)

★ *Night Flier* (1997)

★ *Friday Night* (1998)

★ *Victoria's Shadow* (1998)

★ *Tainted* (1998)

★ *Vampirates* (1998)

★ *Blood Kiss* (1998)

★ *The Wisdom of Crocodiles* (1998)

★ *Blade* (1998)

★ *Vampires* (1998)

Chapter 16
Screwballs

INDIANA JONES AND THE TEMPLE OF DOOM (1984)

Somehow there's nothing more satisfying than seeing Hollywood spend millions of dollars making a movie only to incorporate a cinematic cock-up or goof as they're commonly referred to in the final product.

Goofs can appear in many guises, they can be subtle or inexcusably obvious. For example the boom mike that just can't seem to stay out of shot or the camera crew that would rather be seen in front of the camera than behind it.

Anyway, so as to maximise your viewing pleasure, while simultaneously demonstrating that movie makers are only human after all, we've selected one hundred of the best bloopers, cock-ups, goofs and flaws.

100 of the Best Bloopers, Cock-Ups, Goofs and Flaws!

ARMAGEDDON (1998)

★ Above the Law (1988)

Pay attention to Mr Seagal's feet towards the end of *Above the Law* and you'll see him make an exceptionally quick change of footwear. Seagal, locked in combat in a grocery store, decides to make his escape by jumping through the store's window, using one of his attackers as a shield. Take a look at his feet though, as he jumps through the window: he's wearing leather boots, yet he lands on the pavement wearing trainers. Oh dear, the obligations of product placement!

★ Alien (1979)

Playing footsy. Who's fooling whom? When the alien's tail moves between the feet of Lambert, whose feet are we looking at? The feet shown are sporting trainers, yet Lambert wore cowboy boots while Kane wore trainers.

★ Armageddon (1998)

Movie makers discover grass in space! Look out for grass at the edge of the cliff, when the Armadillo comes to a stop, having just jumped over the canyon.

One more thing: what happened to the time zones? Towards the end of the film we see footage of people the world over simultaneously reacting to events, and all in glorious daylight.

★ Batman (1989)

So, the Batmobile can start up and drive itself. Not so, my friends! Look out for a helping hand steering the Batmobile during one of the scenes where Michael Keaton starts it automatically from outside.

★ The Birds (1963)

Try this for a teaser. See if you can spot the shadows of the birds as they swoop down upon the children playing on a particularly sunny day. No doubt, you'll spot the shadows of the children, yet the birds cast none. A small oversight by the FX crew perhaps?

★ Blade (1998)

As Blade and Karen escape from the hospital, watch as they take cover behind a rooftop metal door. The police subsequently fire at the door, which splinters like wood with each hit. In fact it is wood. However, once Blade and Karen have moved away from the door, we see that it is made of metal after all.

★ Blade Runner (1982)

The job of the stuntman or -woman is to make us believe what we see is real, yet at the same time minimise any possible danger to themselves. In light of this, watch closely as Zhora, played by Joanna Cassidy, launches herself through a plate-glass window. Underneath her futuristic outfit (styled on a see-through bin liner) you'll see a protective bodysuit – the sleeves of which are visible briefly as the stuntwoman breaks through the window.

★ Body Double (1984)

As the porn movie is being filmed, look for the reflection of the crew in the mirror on the door of Melanie Griffith's room.

★ Born on the Fourth of July (1989)

During the scene at the Chicago Democratic Convention, one of the Vietnam veterans sports a pair of Reebok trainers. He was truly a trendsetter – Reebok wasn't founded until 1978.

★ A Bridge Too Far (1977)

During the rooftop battle scene, look out for all the TV aerials. Remember, it's World War Two!

★ Bullitt (1968)

What a car chase!
What kind of car was Steve McQueen chasing? A six-wheeler? Must have been. Not only does it lose three hub caps during the chase, but a further three launch into the air when it crashes into a wall at the end of the chase. Finally, keep an eye out for the Volkswagen Beetle that keeps popping up during the chase. Strangely coincidental – or, there again, perhaps not!

★ Butch Cassidy and the Sundance Kid (1969)

Katherine Ross proves quite a performer as she rides pillion with Paul Newman during the 'Raindrops Are Falling On My Head' sequence. She begins by sitting on the handlebars, then as they ride around the orchard she is on the crossbar, but by the time they leave the orchard she is back on the handlebars.

★ Carrie (1976)

Front to back!
To achieve the footage of Carrie's final dream the film had to be played in reverse. Apparently the director, Brian De Palma, considered it a little too drastic to actually run Sissy Spacek down. All this sounds good in practice, until you look at the background wherein another car can be seen speeding past – backwards!

★ Casablanca (1942)

We see a soaked Rick, played by Humphrey Bogart, standing in the rain reading a note from Ilsa. Moments later Sam gets him on to a train; he must have given him a towel as well, for Rick is now completely dry.

★ Chariots of Fire (1981)

Keep an eye on the piece of paper with the Bible quote that Jackson Schultz gives to Eric Liddell prior to the start of the 400-metre race. Liddell starts the race note in hand and its still with him at 100 metres; however, at 200 metres his hand is outstretched and empty. Then, as if by magic, movie magic that is, Liddell is reunited with the note as he crosses the finish line.

★ City Slickers (1991)

Just what happens to the flowers on Curly's grave? Immediately after his burial flowers can be seen lying on top of his grave, but, only moments later, as Billy Crystal and the other 'cowboys' depart, the flowers have vanished!

★ Cleopatra (1963)

As Elizabeth Taylor, playing Cleo, enters Rome amid a spectacular procession, she passes under a triumphal arch – an arch that wasn't built until after Cleopatra's death.

★ Cocktail (1988)

Now showing ... if you're quick!
When Tom Cruise accompanies Lisa Banes to an art show, take a look at the advertising board of the adjacent theatre. As they enter it reads *Barfly*, yet when Tom Cruise leaves alone, only minutes later, it reads *Casablanca*.

★ The Color Purple (1985)

Watch as an unconscious Oprah Winfrey, having been knocked out with a pistol, reaches down to adjust her windblown skirt and preserve her modesty.

★ Congo (1995)

Take a look at the rocks falling down while the group are in the cave. The rocks that land in the river float. As rocks do – not!

★ Days of Thunder (1990)

Having been hurt in a crash, Mr Cruise, we notice, sports an injury to his right eye. Luckily for Tom the wound quickly heals and his right eye is fine. Unfortunately, it seems the wound has now moved to his left eye!

★ Diamonds Are Forever (1971)

Nifty Driving, Part 1.
In order to escape their pursuers Sean Connery and Jill St John take their car on to two wheels and drive through a narrow alleyway. The car enters the alleyway on its left wheels only to emerge from the alley on its right wheels. Now that's what we call advanced driving!

★ Die Hard (1988)

That groundhog moment!
The terrorists briefly enter a time loop when they fire a missile through an office window at the APC, shattering the window in the process. The terrorist boss, played by Alan Rickman, subsequently orders them to fire again – and they do exactly that, firing through, and shattering once more, the same window.

While we're on the subject, what happens to John McClane's (Bruce Willis's) tattoo during the fight sequence with Karl? Emergency laser removal or could it be a stunt double?

★ Die Hard 2: Die Harder (1990)

Make-up your mind!
Watch as Bruce Willis and John Amos slug it out on the wing of the aeroplane. Amos seems to be suffering from vanishing 'bloody wound' syndrome. One moment, he has blood all over his mouth, then suddenly the blood has vanished.

★ Double Indemnity (1944)

Fred MacMurray isn't the bachelor he seems in this Billy Wilder classic, for throughout the movie he sports a gold wedding band, and, worse still, makes no attempt to conceal it!

★ Easy Rider (1969)

Hippy materialism.
Check out Peter Fonda's wristwatch when he places rolled-up dollar bills into a tube in the petrol tank of his Harley, prior to setting off on the road to New Orleans with his

buddy Dennis Hopper – yes, it's a Rolex. Cut to the next scene and we see Fonda adopt the attitude of the times and, in eschewing the burden of time, symbolically cast his watch to the ground. Wait a minute, where's the Rolex gone? Fonda, the fool that he isn't, has had us on: on the ground lies not the Rolex but a considerably cheaper Timex. He must have valued time after all – well, Rolex time.

★ The Empire Strikes Back (1980)

Keep an eye out for the reflection of the crew as C3PO's head travels along the conveyor belt in Cloud City.

★ Eraser (1996)

It seems Arnie's credit is good for nothing round here. Pay attention when Arnie's credit card is used: the card is swiped but the magnetic strip is facing the wrong way.

★ Excalibur (1981)

Look for the reflection of a cameraman in the metal of Merlin's helmet towards the end of the film.

★ Face / Off (1997)

During the final boat scene, as Nicolas Cage's character hangs from the side of the speedboat, keep an eye out for his stunt double. He's the one with the long sideburns unlike Mr Cage, whose cropped hair is clearly shown in the close-up shots.

★ Flatliners (1990)

During the film we see the medical student played by Kiefer Sutherland stitch up a cut to his own right cheek. However, subsequent shots show the wound to be on his left cheek. Now that's just plain cheeky!

★ The Fly (1988)

Getting in the picture.
When Jeff Goldblum crouches in his teleport pod, look for the reflection of the crew in the glass door.

★ Forrest Gump (1994)

Here's one for the eagle-eyed among you. Watch the feather scene at the beginning of the film very, very carefully; if you can see double then your eyes aren't deceiving you. At one point during the scene, when the camera is about three metres away from Forrest, the feather can be seen both falling through the air and resting on his right shoe. To achieve the effect of a feather falling to his shoe, both live-action and digital effects were used; in particular, a real feather was attached to his shoe – thus as a result of an editing goof we see the real and digital feathers simultaneously.

★ Ghost (1990)

There are more ghosts than initially meet the eye in this romantic fantasy. When the bad guy Rick Aviles is hit and as a result killed by a car, we see the spirit emerge from his body, which lies motionless in the street; however, when the spirit looks back, the body is no longer in the street but on top of the car bonnet.

Oh, and one more thing: following the particularly messy scene at the potter's wheel wherein Demi Moore and Patrick Swayze show us just how stimulating pottery can be, what happens to all of the clay that once oozed and squelched from the lovers' hands once they can no longer contain their desires. Lubricant? Surely not!

★ The Godfather (1972)

When Al Pacino shoots the chief of police in the neck, we see the chief, played by Sterling Hayden, grab his neck in agony; however, when the camera draws back and in the subsequent scene, Hayden is bleeding not from the neck, but from his forehead.

★ Grease (1978)

A flirting Dinah Manoff, playing Marty Maraschino, reveals something very close to her heart, just after she says, 'Maraschino, like in cherries', her strapless dress slips down uncovering … well you'll just have to rent the movie!

★ The Great Outdoors (1988)

Watch for the yellow stick of the trainer poking at the bear, which crashes through the door and falls on top of John Candy.

★ The Hunt for Red October (1990)

During the opening scene, with Ramius and Borodin, the bottom of the fake submarine can be seen.

★ Independence Day (1996)

Keep an eye on the fridge as Levinson and Connie argue while in Area 51: the shelves are full one moment, empty the next, and so on.

Another continuity error occurs when Levinson, having poured himself a whisky, slams the bottle down, only to then take the bottle cap off.

★ Indiana Jones and the Temple of Doom (1984)

Look out for a flash of light when Indy comes eye to eye with a hooded cobra – it's light reflecting on the glass safety screen that separates Harrison Ford from the snake.

★ Indiana Jones and the Last Crusade (1989)

During the movie, set in 1938, we see Indy crossing the Atlantic by airliner, a year before the first transatlantic passenger service began; he subsequently starts back by airship a year after transatlantic airship services ceased!

★ Interview with the Vampire (1994)

Observe as Louis, having encountered Santiago in Paris, seeks to impress by walking up the sides of a tunnel. However, his cape rather than complying with the laws of gravity, hangs, quite normally, at his feet.

★ The Invisible Man (1933)

Boots are made for walking!
Towards the end of the film, Claude Rains, seeking to avoid capture by the police, strips naked, thereby becoming invisible, and sets off on foot through the snow. Strange then that Rains leaves shoeprints rather than mere footprints.

★ Jagged Edge (1985)

Quick-change chameleon.
When Glenn Close first enters the courtroom she is wearing a grey suit; as she makes her opening statement she is wearing a dark-blue suit and white blouse; she subsequently questions a witness wearing a brown suit and blouse.

★ Jaws (1975)

They must have been short of extras when they filmed this, the ultimate in killer-shark movies. Watch as the fishermen prepare to go after the $3,000 bounty, particularly the scene where Hooper tells some men not to overload their boat. One of the men, wearing a blue windbreaker, goes down the ladder to the boat three times.

★ Jaws: The Revenge (1987)

Water off Michael's back.
Having swum to the rescue of Lorraine Gary and climbed aboard, Michael Caine, in the blink of an eye, is as dry as the proverbial desert and sporting that freshly-starched-shirt look.

★ Jurassic Park (1993)

Here we witness what constitutes a sacking offence by the continuity editor. As the raptor egg begins to hatch in the lab, a robotic arm grabs and stabilises the egg. Watch closely, though: the arm subsequently disappears completely.

Later in the film, when Tim and Lex are hiding from the raptors in the kitchen, look out for the shadow of a crew member's finger helping one of the ladles fall to the ground.

★ Kelly's Heroes (1970)

Twenty minutes into the movie and we see Clint Eastwood in a jeep, surrounded by soldiers; not to mention two embarrassed studio technicians wearing striped shirts, who creep stealthily out of shot.

★ The King and I (1956)

Has anyone seen my earring?
Observe the case of the illusive earring as Yul Brynner sings 'Puzzlement' – it's a case of 'now you see it, now you don't, now you see it …'!

★ The Last Temptation of Christ (1988)

He buys his clothes from Marks & Spencer!
Look at Willem Dafoe's robe carefully and

you'll see the stitching where the label is sewn in the back of his garment. A bespoke tailor, no doubt.

★ Lethal Weapon (1987)

Early in the film we see Mel Gibson handcuff himself to a suicidal man on a rooftop. The man proceeds to jump, taking the handcuffed Mel with him; however, the rubber stunt cuffs break. As a result, we see the pair complete the fall with hands linked, so as not to give the game away.

★ Little Man Tate (1991)

Keep an eye on the hands of young Adam Hann-Byrd as he gives Dianne Wiest a virtuoso performance at the piano. One moment they are the small hands of a child, and the next, as the camera focuses on the keyboard, those of a somewhat more mature pianist, with long and graceful fingers.

★ The Lodger (1944)

Shape of things to come.
Hitchcock's *The Lodger* features shots of London's Tower Bridge, yet the film was set ten years prior to its being built. Presumably Hitchcock had a premonition.

★ Men in Black (1997)

Boom in black.
As Agents K and J interview the farmer's wife, watch out for a boom mike getting in on the scene.

★ Mission: Impossible (1996)

When Ethan Hunt, played by Tom Cruise, uses the magnetic screwdriver to remove the vent cover, for a split second we see the device that is really turning the screw.

★ The Naked Prey (1966)

Look out for a car passing by in the background, as the hunted Cornel Wilde looks for food in nineteenth-century tribal Africa.

★ The Prisoner of Zenda (1979)

Or, as they say in Ruritania,
Vorsprung Dürch ...
Watch the horizon during the Graustarkian chase, just as Peter Sellers approaches the city, and you'll see a pair of Volkswagens and a tank truck 'discreetly' driving past.

★ Quadrophenia (1979)

Tomorrow's movies today!
A cinema can be seen showing Warren Beatty in *Heaven Can Wait*, which was made in 1978. Correct us if we're wrong, but weren't the Mods a sixties phenomenon?

★ Rambo III (1988)

News scoop: arms-for-Russia exposé!
Look for the little American flag on the rotor housing of the supposedly Russian helicopter that Stallone steals, after he's released Richard Crenna and some Afghans from their cells.

★ Rear Window (1954)

The Case of the Phantom Plastercast.
Pay attention during the scene when James Stewart is arguing with Grace Kelly, and you'll see the wheelchair-bound Stewart's plastercast switch momentarily, from his left leg to his right one.

★ Return of the Jedi (1983)

The aerial on Boba Fett's helmet just can't seem to stay still. It moves from one side of his helmet to the other throughout the movie.

Look out for the reflection of Han Solo in the glass that protects the actors, during the scene where the shield generator bunker is blown up.

★ Risky Business (1983)

Near the end we see a removal van outside the house, loaded with furniture; however, as the van drives away, we see that it is in fact empty. Truly removed!

★ Robin Hood: Prince of Thieves (1991)

Azeem, played by Morgan Fairchild, is a man ahead of his times as he accompanies Kevin Costner around twelfth-century England. Not only does he have gunpowder, which wasn't brought from China to the West until the late thirteenth century, but he also uses a primitive telescope. The inventor of the telescope, very probably the Dutch spectacle-maker Hans Lippershey, wasn't born until about 1570.

★ The Silence of the Lambs (1991)

When Clarice (Jodie Foster) examines the room of the first murder victim, the girl's father tells her that the room has been left as it was when she died, including her poster for Debbie Harry's Def, Dumb & Blonde – an album that wasn't released until 1989, approximately three years after the girl's death!

★ Smokey and the Bandit (1977)

Burt Reynolds certainly clocks up a lot of miles in this comical chase movie, as he drives his Trans-Am from Texas to Georgia; strange, then, that the car's mileage reads the same throughout the movie!

★ The Sound of Music (1965)

During the scene where Miss Andrews and the children visit the market a crate stamped 'Jaffa Oranges – Product of Israel' can be seen. Yet The Sound of Music is set in the 1930s and the state of Israel wasn't founded until 1948. Food for thought?

★ Spartacus (1960)

Look out for Peter Ustinov's jockey shorts as he dismounts his horse, while out scouting for fresh gladiator fodder.

★ Speed (1994)

Which leg was Harry shot in? We thought it was the left leg. However, if you watch him at the subsequent awards ceremony, he uses the crutch as though he'd been shot in the right leg!

Later in the film Payne, played by Dennis Hopper, performs a neat trick, he clicks his fingers – without a thumb.

★ Star Trek – The Motion Picture (1979)

Watch closely as Kirk, having discovered that Spock is gone, exits the ship by means of an airlock. In the next shot, a close-up, we see Kirk floating away from the ship; however, as the camera pulls back, perhaps just a little too far, we see the walls and ceiling of the sound stage where the scene was filmed.

★ Star Trek VI (1991)

During an attack scene we see Sulu's cup of tea smash into pieces, as both he and the cup and saucer fall to the floor; however when Sulu stands up the pieces of the cup and saucer have vanished.

★ Star Wars (1977)

Keep an eye on the dent to C3PO's head: following his run-in with the sand people, it changes position, disappears and reappears throughout the movie.

Things also go amiss(ing) when Ben first gives Luke the light sabre; as Luke turns the light sabre on, the cape hanging on the wall behind him vanishes, only to reappear when he turns the weapon off.

This goof isn't really funny, but who cares? Pay attention when the stormtroopers break into the control room. A trooper in the second row on the right hits his head on the door frame as he comes in. Oww!

Spoiler Alert: Chewbacca is actually a man in a suit. If you don't believe us look out for an exposed rubber sole as he follows Han Solo in the Death Star.

During the final scene of the movie, when the medals are given out, look closely at the sides of the screen and you'll see that the victorious rebel forces in the foreground are no more than cardboard cutouts!

★ Superman (1978)

Marlon Brando certainly earns his stratospheric fee when he gives a flawless performance as Superman's father. Look out for his Rolex wristwatch as he places the baby into the space capsule.

★ The Ten Commandments (1956)

Keeping an eye on the time.
Look for the blind man sporting a wristwatch in this biblical epic.

★ Terminator (1984)

Emergency calls, as is the case in Britain, are free of charge in America. So why does Linda Hamilton insert a quarter, prior to dialling 911, when she suspects that she's being followed?

★ Terminator II: Judgment Day (1991)

Listen to the sound of Linda Hamilton's 'bare' feet as she runs down the hospital corridor, and you'll swear that you can hear the sound of feet wearing shoes.

Also, pay attention to the windscreen of the truck that Robert Patrick drives from the bridge. As the truck crashes down on to the drainage channel the glass pops out, yet when the chase proceeds the glass, though cracked, is back in place.

Finally look out for an extra hand sneaking into the picture while Robert Patrick uses both hands to load his gun, while flying the helicopter towards the end of the movie.

★ Titanic (1997)

The best goof from this $200 million epic occurs while the ship is moored at Southampton and a strip of the Mexican desert, where *Titanic* was filmed, can be seen between the ship and the dock.

The reflection of the crew can also be seen several times throughout the movie: on the screen of Rose's television set; in the glass of the door as Jack enters the dining room; and in a brass panel of the Renault that Jack and Rose find in the cargo hold.

★ Tomorrow Never Dies (1997)

Watch closely when Bond test-drives his new BMW by remote, and you'll see a member of the film crew driving the car from beneath a black cloth.

Not only does Bond's BMW have self-repairing tyres, it also has a self-repairing rear windscreen. As can be seen when it mends itself, immediately after a missile flies through the hole in it.

★ Top Gun (1986)

Exactly which plane was Tom Cruise flying during the final scenes of *Top Gun*? Several, judging by the number of times his tail number changes – and all this while midair.

Also, if the final battle occurs miles out at sea, why do we see a mountain in the corner of one shot?

★ True Lies (1994)

Watch the tyre tracks as the terrorist leader, Aziz, rides the motorbike through the hotel. They can be seen on the carpet before the motorbike reaches them.

★ The Untouchables (1987)

A slight oversight occurs during the set design of this hit movie. The crates of alcohol shown during the warehouse raid proudly display Canada's maple-leaf emblem. Yet *The Untouchables* was set during the era of prohibition, i.e. the 1930s, and Canada didn't adopt the maple leaf until 1965! The power of foresight.

Later in the film, during the baby's-pram-down-the-stairs scene, things really do occur in slow motion. The scene begins, according to the station clock, at 5 o'clock and ends three minutes later, when the station clock reads 6 o'clock!

★ Wall Street (1987)

Wall Street, we are told, begins in the winter of 1985. Shortly into the film, though, we hear a stockbroker telling another broker that Gordon Gekko is so sharp he was selling NASA shares ten minutes after the Challenger disaster – which for the record occurred in January 1986.

★ War and Peace (1956)

Stay alert during King Vidor's epic three-and-a-half-hour take on the Napoleonic Wars and you'll be rewarded with the sight of a crew member directing the action – from a jeep!

★ Waterworld (1995)

When Mariner, played by Kevin Costner, is teaching the girl to swim, telltale bubbles from the crew's breathing apparatus can be seen.

Chapter 17
The Producers

ALFRED HITCHCOCK

In this chapter we take a look at some of the creative forces behind the movies, in particular the great directors. In our whistle-stop tour we not only expose the in-jokes of the directors but also identify their stylistic traits. We reveal the cameo appearances of directors, not only in their own movies but also in those of fellow directors. We also take a look at the one-hit wonders, as well as at the special releases or directors' cuts.

Screenwriters!

Writers and the films they've appeared in

★ **Maya Angelou**
How to Make an American Quilt (1995)

★ **Clive Barker**
Sleepwalkers (1992)

★ **Saul Bellow** (and **Susan Sontag**)
Zelig (1983)

★ **Peter Benchley**
Jaws (1975)

★ **Truman Capote**
Murder by Death (1976)

★ **GK Chesterton** (and **George Bernard Shaw**)
Rosy Rapture – The Pride of the Beauty Chorus (1914)

★ **Sir Arthur Conan Doyle**
The $5,000,000 Counterfeiting Plot (1914)

★ **Graham Greene**
Day for Night (1973)

★ **Thomas Keneally**
The Devil's Playground (1976)

★ **Jerzy Kosinski**
Reds (1981)

★ **Norman Mailer**
Ragtime (1981)

★ **John Sayles**
Eight Men Out (1988)

★ **Mickey Spillane**
The Girl Hunters (1963); as Mike Hammer

★ **Jacqueline Susann**
Valley of the Dolls (1967)

★ **Mark Twain**
A Curious Dream (1907)

★ **Gore Vidal**
Bob Roberts (1992)

Sneaky Little So and Sos!

Directors who have made uncredited appearances in their own movies

★ **James Cameron**
Cameron makes a brief appearance during the steerage dance scene in *Titanic* (1997).

★ **Francis Ford Coppola**
Mr Coppola plays the director of a TV crew in *Apocalypse Now* (1979).

★ **Wes Craven**
Horrormeister Wes can be see playing Fred the janitor in *Scream* (1996).

★ **Rob Reiner**
Reiner appears as a helicopter pilot in *Misery* (1990).

★ **Steven Spielberg**
Spielberg, or rather his reflection, can be seen eating popcorn and sitting next to Jeff Goldblum, during the CNN television story about dinosaurs, in *The Lost World: Jurassic Park* (1997).

★ **Oliver Stone**
Stone, who actually served in Vietnam, makes a cameo appearance in his 1986 masterpiece *Platoon*. He plays an army officer in the bunker that's destroyed by the suicide bomber's attack.

★ **Quentin Tarantino**
Tarantino, not normally one to avoid the spotlight, makes an uncredited contribution

to *Jackie Brown* (1997). His is the voice we hear on Jackie's (Pam Grier's) answering machine.

The Kindest Cut of All

A number of classic movies have been made available after their original release, in order that the public might see the picture as the director originally intended. Such a release is known as the 'director's cut' (original-version release dates shown):

★ *The Alamo*
Director's Cut (1960) – **John Wayne**

★ *Attack of the Killer Tomatoes*
Director's Cut (1979) – **John De Bello**

★ *Blade Runner*
Director's Cut (1982) – **Ridley Scott**

★ *Basic Instinct*
Original Director's Cut (1992) – **Paul Verhoeven**

★ *The Blue Angel*
Original Director's Cut (1930) – **Josef von Sternberg**

★ *Das Boot*
Director's Cut (1982) – **Wolfgang Petersen**

★ *Dawn of the Dead*
Collector's Edition Director's Cut (1978) – **George A Romero**

★ *Highlander*
10th Anniversary Director's Cut (1986) – **Russell Mulcahy**

★ *Highlander 2 – The Quickening*
Director's Cut (1991) – **Russell Mulcahy**

★ *Jail Bait*
Director's Cut (1954) – **Edward D Wood Jr**

★ *JFK*
Director's Cut (1991) – **Oliver Stone**

★ *The Last Emperor* (1987) – **Bernardo Bertolucci**

★ *Lethal Weapon*
Director's Cut (1987) – **Richard Donner**

★ *Lethal Weapon 2*
Director's Cut (1989) – **Richard Donner**

★ *Lethal Weapon 3*
Director's Cut (1992) – **Richard Donner**

★ *Natural Born Killers*
Director's Cut (1994) – **Oliver Stone**

★ *Shivers*
Director's Cut (1975) – **David Cronenberg**

★ *Toxic Avenger Part II*
Director's Cut (1989) – **Lloyd Kaufman**

★ *True Romance*
Director's Cut (1993) – **Tony Scott**

★ *The Wild Bunch*
Restored Director's Cut (1969) – **Sam Peckinpah**

★ *Woodstock: Three Days of Peace & Music*
Director's Cut (1970) – **Michael Wadleigh**

Directors Directed!

Appearances by directors in other people's movies

★ **Woody Allen** – *The Front* (1976) – Martin Ritt

★ **Paul Bartel** – *Rock 'n' Roll High School* (1979) – Allan Arkush

★ **Tim Burton** – *Singles* (1992) – Cameron Crowe

★ **John Cromwell** – *A Wedding* (1978) – Robert Altman

★ **David Cronenberg** – *Escape from New York* (1981) – John Carpenter

★ **Jonathan Demme** – *That Thing You Do*
(1996) – Tom Hanks

★ **Jan De Bont** – *Lethal Weapon*
(1992) – Richard Donner

★ **Cecil B DeMille** – *Sunset Boulevard*
(1950) – Billy Wilder

★ **Vittoria De Sica** – *The Earrings of
Madame De …*
(1953) – Max Ophuls

★ **John Ford** – *Big Time*
(1929) – Kenneth Hawks

★ **Samuel Fuller** – *Pierrot le Fou*
(1965) – Jean-Luc Godard

★ **John Huston** – *Chinatown*
(1974) – Roman Polanski

★ **Elia Kazan** – *City for Conquest*
(1940) – Anatole Litvak

★ **Fritz Lang** – *Contempt*
(1963) – Jean-Luc Godard

★ **Sydney Pollack** – *Husbands and Wives*
(1992) – Woody Allen

★ **Otto Preminger** – *Stalag 17*
(1953) – Billy Wilder

★ **Leni Riefenstahl** – *The Wonderful,
Horrible Life of Leni Riefenstahl*
(1993) – Ray Muller

★ **George A Romero** – *Escape from New York*
(1981) – John Carpenter

★ **Mark Rydell** – *The Long Goodbye*
(1973) – Robert Altman

★ **Martin Scorsese** – *Dreams*
(1990) – Akira Kurosawa

★ **Victor Sjöström** – *Wild Strawberries*
(1957) – Ingmar Bergman

★ **Steven Spielberg** – *Gremlins*
(1984) – Joe Dante

★ **Lee Strasberg** – *The Godfather, Part 2*
(1974) – Francis Ford Coppola

★ **François Truffaut** – *Close Encounters of
the Third Kind*
(1977) – Steven Spielberg

★ **Orson Welles** – *The Third Man*
(1949) – Carol Reed

The Rise and Fall of the Hollywood Director

In this section we highlight the follow-ups of
the then director of the moment – follow-ups
that ultimately fell flatter than the proverbial
pancake!

★ **Emile Ariolino** from *Dirty Dancing* to
Chances Are

★ **Clive Barker** from *Hellraiser* to *Nightbreed*

Barker's 'dive' is significant because of
the success of *Hellraiser*, in what is typically
a low-buck genre; *Nightbreed* subsequently
failed to match Barker's supposed bankability.

★ **Paul Brickman** from *Risky Business* to
Men Don't Leave

★ **Amy Heckerling** from *Fast Times at
Ridgemont High* to *Johnny Dangerously*

★ **Dennis Hopper** from *Easy Rider* to
The Last Movie

★ **Michael Lehmann** from *Heathers* to
Meet the Applegates to *Hudson Hawk*

Lehmann's efforts are notable for three
reasons: it was his first film; it also made
a profit; and, above all, it launched the
careers of two of Hollywood's hottest stars,
Christian Slater and Winona Ryder.
Unfortunately, Lehmann went on to achieve
a double whammy with *Meet the Applegates*
and the forgettable Bruce Willis vehicle
Hudson Hawk.

★ **George A Romero** from *Night of the Living Dead* to *Season of the Witch*

★ **Ron Shelton** from *Bull Durham* to *Blaze*

★ **Shelton** realised the error of his ways and remixed the ingredients of *Bull Durham*, namely sport, comedy and sex, into the highly enjoyable *White Men Can't Jump*.

★ **John Singleton** from *Boyz 'n the Hood* to *Poetic Justice*

★ **Steven Soderbergh** from *sex, lies & videotape* to *Kafka*

Soderbergh's *sex, lies & videotape* is not as its name suggests a Whitehouse docudrama but rather an exploration of one man's penchant for home video and the subsequent ramifications upon family life.

Dial C for Cameo!

Alfred Hitchcock is remembered not only for his ability to leave us in 'suspenders', but also for the varied and imaginative cameo appearances he makes in his own films.

★ **The Lodger** (1926)
Hitchcock appears twice: on the first occasion he is seen sitting at a desk in the newsroom scene; he subsequently appears in the crowd scene towards the end of the film.

★ **Easy Virtue** (1927)
Hitchcock is seen walking past a tennis court carrying a walking stick.

★ **Murder** (1930)
The trial is over. However, Sir John (Herbert Marshall), unconvinced of Diana's guilt, returns to the scene of the crime with Ted (Edward Chapman) and Dulcie (Phyllis Konstam). As the three of them leave the house, Hitchcock walks past.

★ **The 39 Steps** (1935)
Following the gunshots, Annabella (Lucie Mannheim) and Richard (Robert Donat) leave the show; as they cross the street to board a bus, Hitchcock walks by tossing litter.

★ **Sabotage** (1936)
The film is nearing its end; the bomb maker is at the theatre. As the police inspector gets out of his car, we see Hitchcock outside the theatre.

★ **Young and Innocent** (1937)
As Robert Tisdall (Derrick de Marney) slips away from the courthouse, Hitchcock appears as a bumbling photographer among the crowd by the front door.

★ **The Lady Vanishes** (1938)
Gilbert Redman (Michael Redgrave) and Iris Henderson (Margaret Lockwood) are getting ready to leave the train. The scene changes to Victoria Station where Hitchcock walks by, wearing a black coat and smoking a cigarette.

★ **Jamaica Inn** (1939)
Hitchcock is seen wearing a waistcoat and top hat.

★ **Foreign Correspondent** (1940)
Johnny Jones (Joel McCrea), having left his hotel, walks by a newsstand; Hitchcock, reading a newspaper, passes him.

★ **Rebecca** (1940)
While Jack Favell (George Sanders) makes a phone call, Hitchcock is seen waiting outside the phone booth.

★ **Mr. and Mrs. Smith** (1941)
Having discovered Mrs Smith (Carole Lombard) together with his friend Jeff (Gene Raymond), Mr Smith (Robert Montgomery) leaves his wife's apartment. Hitchcock crosses in front of the building, from left to right, smoking and wearing a hat.

★ **Suspicion** (1941)
Following the marriage celebrations and near choking of Beaky (Nigel Bruce) on his celebratory drink, the scene changes to the village; Hitchcock is seen putting something in the postbox.

★ **Saboteur** (1942)
As the saboteur's car stops in front of Cut Rate Drugs, Hitchcock is seen standing on the sidewalk looking in the window.

★ **Shadow of a Doubt** (1943)
Hitchcock is seen on the train to Santa Rosa, playing cards with his back to the camera – he is holding all the spades.

★ **Lifeboat** (1944)
One of Hitchcock's more cunning cameos – as Gus (William Bendix) reads the newspaper, Hitchcock appears in the 'before' and 'after' pictures of the Reduco Obesity Slayer advert.

★ **Spellbound** (1945)
While Constance (Ingrid Bergman) stakes out the lobby of the Empire State Hotel, Hitchcock gets off the elevator carrying a violin case and smoking a cigarette.

★ **Notorious** (1946)
Hitchcock is seen sipping champagne at a party at the mansion of Alex Sebastian (Claude Raines).

★ **The Paradine Case** (1948)
Hitchcock is seen leaving the Cumberland Station, behind Keene (Gregory Peck), smoking a cigarette and carrying a cello.

★ **Rope** (1948)
Hitchcock appears twice: crossing the street after the opening credits; subsequently as a silhouette on a neon sign over the shoulder of Janet (Joan Chandler) as she is talking to Kenneth (Douglas Dick).

★ **Under Capricorn** (1949)
Hitchcock is seen in the town square, during a parade. He is wearing a blue coat and brown hat. He also appears as one of three men on the stairs of Government House.

★ **Stage Fright** (1950)
Hitchcock is seen casting a backward glance at Eve Gill (Jane Wyman), who is disguised as Charlotte Inwood's (Marlene Dietrich's) maid.

★ **Strangers on a Train** (1951)
As Guy Hainest (Farley Granger) gets off the train, we see Hitchcock boarding, this time carrying a double bass.

★ **I Confess** (1953)
Immediately after the opening credits, Hitchcock appears in silhouette, walking across the top of some steps.

★ **Dial M for Murder** (1954)
Tony (Ray Milland) shows Captain Swan Lesgate (Anthony Dawson) a photo, in which we see Hitchcock, seated with others at a school reunion.

★ **Rear Window** (1954)
Hitchcock is seen winding a clock in the screenwriter's apartment.

★ **The Trouble with Harry** (1955)
Hitchcock, wearing a trench coat, passes behind the car of a man who is examining the paintings of Sam Marlowe (John Forsythe).

★ **To Catch a Thief** (1955)
At the beginning of the film we see John Robbie (Cary Grant) catch a bus, and among his fellow passengers is our Alfred.

★ **The Man Who Knew Too Much** (1956)
Hitchcock, his back to the camera, joins Dr and Mrs Ben McKenna (James Stewart and Doris Day) in watching the acrobats at the Moroccan marketplace.

★ **The Wrong Man** (1957)
Hitchcock narrates the prologue; this is
the only time he speaks during any of his films.

★ **Vertigo** (1958)
As Scottie Ferguson (James Stewart) leaves
for an appointment, we see Hitchcock walking
down the street, wearing a grey suit and
carrying a black case.

★ **North by Northwest** (1959)
Hitchcock is shown missing a bus at the end
of the opening credits.

★ **Psycho** (1960)
As Marion Crane (Janet Leigh) returns
to work, we see Hitchcock standing on the
street outside her office window, wearing
a cowboy hat. (Gus Van Sant reproduces this
cameo in his 1998 remake. We see Van Sant
outside Marion Crane's office talking to
someone who looks remarkably like
Mr Hitchcock.)

★ **The Birds** (1963)
Hitchcock walks a pair of dogs, his own
Sealyham terriers, named Geoffrey and Stanley,
out of Davidson's Pet Shop, moments before
Melanie Daniels (Tippi Hedren) enters.

★ **Marnie** (1964)
Hitchcock steps into the hallway, from
the left, shortly after Mr Strutt's secretary
(Tippi Hedren) passes along the hotel corridor.

★ **Torn Curtain** (1966)
Hitchcock is seen sitting in the lobby of the
hotel in Copenhagen. He is holding a baby,
who has a little accident! His TV theme music
can also be heard in the background.

★ **Topaz** (1969)
We see Hitchcock at the airport, being
pushed in a wheelchair. He subsequently
stands, shakes hands with a man in a dark suit
and walks away.

★ **Frenzy** (1972)
Hitchcock is seen among the crowd
listening to the politician's speech; when the
Necktie Murder victim is sighted, we see
Hitchcock straining to see the body.

★ **Family Plot** (1976)
Hitchcock is seen in silhouette, through
the office window of the Registrar of Births
and Deaths. He is obtaining copies of death
certificates.

Inside Moves!

The inside jokes and sneaky references
exposed for all to see

★ **Alien** (1979) – Ridley Scott
If you've ever wondered where the ship
Nostromo takes its name from, then
wonder no more: *Nostromo* is the title of a
Joseph Conrad novel written at the beginning
of the twentieth century. The Conrad
connection continues with the name of
Ripley's escape shuttle, *Narcissus*, which
is taken from *The Nigger of the Narcissus*,
written by Conrad in 1897.

★ **Back to the Future Part II** (1989) –
Robert Zemeckis
It is now the year 2015. In an antique shop,
we see a Roger Rabbit doll. Zemeckis also
directed *Who Framed Roger Rabbit?* (1988).

★ **Blade Runner** (1982) – Ridley Scott
If you look closely, really closely, you'll
see the *Millennium Falcon* tattooed on the
forehead of the snake seller in the street scene.

★ **Blown Away** (1994) – Stephen Hopkins
During the arrests, a police radio can be heard
announcing the capture of Dr Richard Kimble,
the man Tommy Lee Jones sought in
The Fugitive (1993).

★ The Bodyguard (1992) – Mick Jackson
The film that Rachel (Whitney Houston) and
Frank (Kevin Costner) go to see, Kurosawa's
Yojimbo (1961), was released in America as
The Bodyguard.

★ Cape Fear (1991) – Martin Scorsese
With more than a hint of irony Scorsese casts
Robert Mitchum as Lieutenant Elgart in his
remake of J Lee Thompson's 1962 shocker.
In the original Mitchum played a bad boy from
hell, Max Cady. Scorsese doesn't fail us though,
casting De Niro as Cady in the remake.

Scorsese casts two further members of the
original cast in his remake: Gregory Peck and
Martin Balsam.

★ Christine (1983) – John Carpenter
The book that Dennis (John Stockwell) takes
from the bookshelf prior to asking Leigh
(Alexandra Paul) out is *Christine* – the book
by Stephen King, from which the film is
adapted.

★ A Clockwork Orange (1971) –
Stanley Kubrick
Should you have been afforded the freedom
to see Kubrick's long unavailable look at a
world of anarchic ultraviolence, you may have
spotted among the items on sale in the record
shop a copy of the soundtrack for *2001:
A Space Odyssey* (1968), which quite
coincidentally was also directed by Kubrick.

★ Close Encounters of the Third Kind
(1977) – Steven Spielberg
An inverted R2D2 can be seen in part of
the spacecraft that flies over Devil's Mountain;
it is visible at the point when Jillian
(Melinda Dillon) sees the mother ship close
up for the first time.

★ Contact (1997) – Robert Zemeckis
If the satellite dish looks familiar, but you just
can't place it, that's because it was used in the
final scenes of *GoldenEye* (1995).

★ Dark Star (1974) – John Carpenter
After the ship blows up we see, among the
debris, a THX 1138 Toilet Tank. *THX 1138*
(1971) is the feature-length version of
George Lucas's student film about the
quest for freedom in a futuristic world of
programmed determinism.

Carpenter also gives us an indication of
his respect for the film's co-producer and
distributor Jack H Harris. At one stage in
the film we see 'Fuck You, Harris' appear on
the computer screen.

★ Deep Impact (1998) – Mimi Leder
When Marcus Wolf (Charles Martin Smith)
spots the comet he is eating pizza and watching
a ball game; exactly as his character in *Starman*
(1984) when notified of the alien ship's landing.

★ Die Hard with a Vengeance (1995) –
John McTiernan
In a conversation between Samuel L Jackson
and Bruce Willis, we hear Willis tell Jackson
about getting used to his day job and 'smoking
cigarettes and watching *Captain Kangaroo*'.
The same line features in the song 'Flowers on
the Wall' by the Statler brothers, as included in
the *Pulp Fiction* (1994) soundtrack. Willis,
along with Jackson, starred in *Pulp Fiction*.

★ The Empire Strikes Back (1980) –
George Lucas
According to rumour one of the asteroids
that the *Millennium Falcon* avoids collision
with is a shoe. Yes that's right, a shoe
(state-of-the-art effects even then)!

★ Enemy of the State (1998) – Tony Scott
Enemy of the State is directly influenced
by *The Conversation* (1974); among the
borrowings is the photo of Brill (Gabriel
Byrne) twenty years before – it is actually
a photo of Harry Caul (Gene Hackman)
from *The Conversation*.

★ E.T. – The Extra-Terrestrial (1980) –
Steven Spielberg
Among E.T.'s plant collection can be seen
a triffid from *The Day of the Triffids* (1962).

★ A Few Good Men (1992) – Rob Reiner
As Danny (Tom Cruise) watches the ball game, two copies of *Misery* by Stephen King can be seen next to his typewriter. Rob Reiner directed both *A Few Good Men* and *Misery* (1990).

★ The Fisher King (1991) – Terry Gilliam
A video store in *The Fisher King* has a poster for *The Adventures of Baron Munchausen* (1989) in the window, and on the wall of the store is a poster for *Brazil* (1985). All three films were, of course, directed by Gilliam.

★ GoldenEye (1995) – Martin Campbell
The title for this Bond movie was taken from Ian Fleming's Jamaican beach-front retreat where many of the Bond novels were written.

★ Godzilla (1998) – Roland Emmerich
A statue of one of the aliens from *Independence Day* (1995) can be seen in the broadcast booth at Madison Square Garden. Emmerich also directed *Independence Day*.

★ Gremlins (1984) – Joe Dante
If you look closely, you'll see the time machine from, strangely enough, *The Time Machine* (1960), appear during the inventor's convention.

★ Gremlins 2: The New Batch (1990) – Joe Dante
Anyone seen *Invasion of the Body Snatchers* (1956)? If so you may recognise the pod that Dr Catheter (Christopher Lee) carries in *Gremlins 2*, for that's where it came from – not outer space as some of you might believe!

★ Home Alone (1990) – Chris Columbus
Home Alone was inspired by the filming of *Uncle Buck* (1989), which also starred Macaulay Culkin, in particular the scene where Kevin (Culkin) interrogates a potential babysitter through the letterbox.

★ Independence Day (1996) – Roland Emmerich
Jeff Goldblum, as the character Levinson, repeats a line he first used in *Jurassic Park* (1993) while fleeing from the T. rex; 'Faster, must go faster.' Only this time he's fleeing from the alien mother ship.

★ Indiana Jones and the Temple of Doom (1984) – Steven Spielberg
Spielberg makes two references to the earlier *Star Wars* (1977 – George Lucas): first, a scene takes place in the Club Obi-Wan; secondly the plane that plucks Indy (Harrison Ford) from the hands of the natives has OBI-CPO as its licence letters.

★ Indiana Jones and the Last Crusade (1989) – Steven Spielberg
Indiana was the name of Spielberg's dog at the time of the making of *Star Wars* (1977). The same breed of dog, an Alaskan Malamute, can be seen barking when the young Indy passes with the cross in his hand.

★ Jurassic Park (1993) – Steven Spielberg
Jeff Goldblum, as Dr Malcolm, experiences déjà vu when Ellie Satler (Laura Dern) observes, 'something went wrong'. Goldblum first heard the line as Seth Brundle in *The Fly* (1986).

★ Last Action Hero (1993) – John McTiernan
When the teacher (Joan Plowright) praises the work of Sir Laurence Olivier there is more than a little underlying bias: Plowright, was previously married to him.

★ The Last Boy Scout (1991) – Tony Scott
Darian (Danielle Harris) is watching *Lethal Weapon* (1987) on TV. Shane Black was the screenwriter for both films.

★ Lethal Weapon 2 (1989) – Richard Donner
Before the 'condom' commercial, we see the Murtaghs watching *Tales from the Crypt*; that particular episode stars Mary Ellen Trainer,

who also plays the police psychiatrist in, yes, you guessed it, *Lethal Weapon 2*.

★ **The Lost World: Jurassic Park** (1997) – Steven Spielberg
The ship that carries the T. rex to San Diego is called the Venture: this is also the name of the ship that brought the giant ape to America in *King Kong* (1933).

★ **Men in Black** (1997) – Barry Sonnenfeld
If the punchline to Kay's (Tommy Lee Jones's) joke at the restaurant: '… yeah, but this one's eatin' my popcorn!' sounds familiar, that's because the same gag was told by the comedian at the burlesque show in *The Sting* (1973).

★ **The Mighty Ducks** (1992) – Stephen Herek
The name of the rival team's number ten is Herek.

★ **Misery** (1990) – Rob Reiner
The general store in *Misery* displays a copy of *When Harry Met Sally* (1989). This was Reiner's previous directorial work.

★ **A Perfect World** (1993) – Clint Eastwood
A department store that Butch (Kevin Costner) and Phillip (TJ Lowther) visit displays a poster for *Bull Durham* (1988), which also starred Costner.

★ **Pleasantville** (1998) – Gary Ross
The scene with Big Bob (JT Walsh) in front of the bowling-alley scorecard mimics the American-flag speech from *Patton* (1970), in which George C Scott plays the general.

★ **Psycho** (1998) – Gus Van Sant
On her approach to the car dealership, Marion Crane (Anne Heche) passes a bus stop displaying a poster for *Six Days and Seven Nights* (1998). Heche stars in *Six Days and Seven Nights* along with Harrison Ford.

★ **Ransom** (1996) – Ron Howard
Tom Mullen (Mel Gibson) offers the name 'John Smith' as a pseudonym; John Smith was the name of the character for whom Gibson provided the voice in *Pocahontas* (1995).

★ **Saving Private Ryan** (1998) – Steven Spielberg
The soldiers question the meaning of the Edith Piaf song prior to the final battle, as do the men of *The Dirty Dozen* (1967).

★ **Scream** (1996) – Wes Craven
'The first one was scary, but the rest sucked!' So said Casey (Drew Barrymore) talking about the *Nightmare on Elm Street* sequels which, unlike the original *A Nightmare on Elm Street* (1984), weren't directed by Craven.

★ **Speed** (1994) – Jan de Bont
The aeroplane that explodes in the latter half of the movie is named Pacific Courier. This was also the name on the terrorist van in *Die Hard* (1988), for which Jan de Bont was cinematographer.

★ **Speed 2: Cruise Control** (1997) – Jan de Bont
The oil tanker that the ship strikes is the Eindhoven; Eindhoven is Jan de Bont's hometown.

★ **Star Trek: First Contact** (1996) – Jonathan Frakes
The Borg eyepieces flash the names of the production crew in Morse code.

★ **The Sure Thing** (1985) – Rob Reiner
A poster for Reiner's *This Is Spinal Tap* (1984) can be seen in Gib's (John Cusack's) college room.

★ **Swingers** (1996) – Doug Liman
Trent's (Vince Vaughn's) car has the number plate 'THX 1138', which is of course a reference to George Lucas.

★ **Terminator 2: Judgment Day** (1991) –
James Cameron
The cyro-truck carries the name
Benthic Petroleum, as do the petrol pumps
at the garage from where the station wagon
was stolen – the same name as the company
in *The Abyss* (1989), also directed by
James Cameron.

★ **Titanic** (1997) – James Cameron
It is James Cameron's hands we see when
Jack (Leonardo DiCaprio) is drawing Rose
(Kate Winslet). Cameron actually drew all
of the sketches contained within Jack's
sketchbook himself.

★ **Tomorrow Never Dies** (1997) –
Roger Spottiswoode
The registration B MT 2144 used on Bond's
BMW follows on from *Goldfinger* (1964), in
which Bond's Aston Martin has the registration
BMT 216A. The Aston Martin DB5 featured in
GoldenEye (1995) and *Tomorrow Never Dies*
has the plate BMT 214A.

★ **Twister** (1996) – Jan de Bont
Twister, as do *Terminator 2* (1991) and
The Abyss (1989), includes a reference
to Benthic Petroleum, namely the oil truck
carried off by the twister.

★ **When Harry Met Sally** (1989) – Rob Reiner
Harry (Billy Crystal) is seen reading a copy of
Misery by Stephen King. Reiner subsequently
directed *Misery* (1990).

Stephen King's Creepy Showings!

Movies in Which the Writer has Appeared

★ *Knightriders* (1981) – Hoagie Man

★ *Creepshow* (1982) – Jordy Verrill

★ *Maximum Overdrive* (1986) – man at
a cashpoint

★ *Creepshow 2* (1987) – as a truck driver

★ *Pet Sematary* (1989) – as a minister

★ *Sleepwalkers* (1992) – as the cemetery
caretaker

★ *Thinner* (1996) – as Dr Bangor

Will the Real Alan Smithee Please Stand Up!

If you've ever seen a movie or rented a video
purporting to be directed by Alan Smithee,
then the odds are that you probably haven't
seen a movie by Alan Smithee! You see, Alan
Smithee doesn't really exist, well at least not in
Movieland. Alan Smithee is a made-up name.

It's a name used by directors when they
no longer wish to be identified with their
creations. Smithee made his directorial debut
with the 1969 movie *Death of a Gunfighter*,
following creative differences between the
film's star, Richard Widmark, and its true
directors, Don Siegel and Robert Totten.
As a result, both Siegel and Totten withdrew
their names from the movie. However, the
movie had to be directed by somebody, and
so the matter was taken before the Directors
Guild of America, who came up with the
pseudonym, Alan Smithee.

And finally, should you come across the
name, Alan Smithee Jr, then you're actually
seeing the work of Sam Raimi, director of
The Evil Dead.

Below we offer, for your future comfort,
a filmography of one of Hollywood's most
revered directors, the one, the only
Alan Smithee.

Wherever possible we've adopted
a policy of 'name and shame', as indicated
by a name appearing on the right.
Anyway, here it is:

★ *Death of a Gunfighter* (1969) – Don Siegel
and Robert Totten

★ *The Challenge* (1970) (TV)

★ *The Barking Dog* (1978)

★ *Gypsy Angels* (1980)

★ *Fun and Games* (1980) (TV) – Paul Bogart

★ *City in Fear* (1980) (TV) – Judson Taylor

★ *Moonlight* (1982) (TV) – Jackie Cooper and
Rod Holcomb

★ *Dune* (1984) – David Lynch
(the unauthorised longer TV versions only)

★ *Stitches* (1985) – Rod Holcomb

★ *Dalton: Code of Vengeance II* (1986) (TV)

★ *Let's Get Harry* a.k.a. *The Rescue* (1986) –
Stuart Rosenberg

★ *Riviera* (1987) (TV) – John Frankenheimer

★ *Appointment with Fear* (1987) –
Razmi Thomas

★ *Ghost Fever* (1987) – Lee Madden

★ *Morgan Stewart's Coming Home*
a.k.a. *Home Front* (1987) – Paul Aaron and
Terry Windsor

★ *I Love N.Y.* (1988) – Gianni Bozzacchi

★ *Ganheddo* a.k.a. *GUNHED* (1989) –
Masata Harada (US version only)

★ *Backtrack* a.k.a. *Catchfire* a.k.a.
Do It the Hard Way (1989) – Dennis Hopper
(European release only)

★ *The Guardian* (1990) – William Friedkin
(the much-cut TV version only)

★ *The Shrimp on the Barbie*
a.k.a. *The Boyfriend from Hell* (1990)

★ *Solar Crisis* a.k.a. *Crisis 2050*
a.k.a. *Starfire* (1990) – Richard C Sarafian

★ *Bloodsucking Pharaohs in Pittsburgh*
a.k.a. *Picking Up the Pieces* (1991) –
Dean Tschetter

★ *The Owl* (1991) (TV)

★ *Thunderheart* (1992) – Michael Apted
(TV version only)

★ *Fatal Charm* (1992) (TV) – Fritz Kiersch

★ *Bay City Story* a.k.a. *Deadline* (1992) (TV)

★ *Scent of a Woman* (1992) – Martin Brest
(the much-cut airline version only)

★ *Call of the Wild* (1993) (TV) – Michael Uno

★ *Rudy* (1993) – David Anspaugh
(the much-cut TV version only)

★ *While Justice Sleeps* (1994) (TV)

★ *The Birds II: Land's End* (1994) (TV) –
Rick Rosenthal

★ *Heat* (1995) – Michael Mann
(the much-cut TV version only)

★ *Raging Angels* (1995)

★ *The O.J. Simpson Story* (1995) (TV) –
Jerrold Freedman

★ *Hellraiser: Bloodline* a.k.a. *Hellraiser IV*
(1996) – Kevin Yagher

★ *Sub Down* (1997) – Gregg Champion

★ *Le Zombi de Cap-Rouge* (1997)

★ *An Alan Smithee Film: Burn Hollywood
Burn* (1997) – Arthur Hiller

★ *Firehouse* (1997)

★ *Illusion Infinity* (1998)

Registered Trademark – Directors' Specialities Revealed

★ James Cameron

The question that we must ask ourselves is: does Mr Cameron have a foot fetish? It would appear so, judging by the feet of the T800 (Arnold Schwarzenegger) in *The Terminator* (1984) crushing the headphones of Sarah Connor's friend after he has killed her and the romantically charged shots of Rose's and Jack's feet as they dance aboard the Titanic in the 1997 film of the same name. However, we must add to this Cameron's fascination with nuclear war as cheerily delivered in the *Terminator* movies.

★ John Carpenter

Carpenter likes to name characters in one film after the crew of a previous one. For example in *The Fog* (1980) the character Nick Castle, played by Tom Atkins, refers to the actor who played 'the shape' in *Halloween* (1978), and the character Tommy Wallace, played by George 'Buck' Flower, refers to the Mr T Wallace responsible for film editing and production design on *Halloween*.

★ Coen Brothers

The Coen Brothers employ actors as their trademark, namely the two Johns, Goodman and Turturro. Goodman appears in *Raising Arizona* (1987), *Barton Fink* (1991), *The Hudsucker Proxy* (1994) and *The Big Lebowski* (1998). Turturro can be seen in *Miller's Crossing* (1990), *Barton Fink* and *The Big Lebowski*.

★ Brian De Palma

De Palma is a keen admirer of Hitchcock and will often show his respect for the master by means of camera work or place names. In *Carrie* (1976) the name of the high school is Bates High, after Norman Bates of *Psycho* (1960) infamy. In *The Untouchables* (1987), De Palma's scene of Elliot Ness in the airline reproduces Hitchcock's *Foreign Correspondent* (1940).

★ Renny Harlin

The Finnish director can't resist reminding us of his homeland: *Die Hard 2: Die Harder* (1990) incorporates segments of the tone poem Finlandia, by the Finnish composer Jean Sibelius, throughout the movie's soundtrack; in *Cliffhanger* (1993) one of the parachutes is remarkably similar to the Finnish flag; and in *The Long Kiss Goodnight* (1996) characters drink Finlandia vodka, not to mention the graffiti 'Hell Sink', a play on the name of the Finnish capital, on a payphone.

★ Stanley Kubrick

Kubrick, for reasons known only to himself, had an obsession with the number 114. It has featured in most of his films. In *Dr. Strangelove or: How I Learned to Stop Worrying and Love the Bomb* (1964) it is the B-52's message decoder reference – CRM-114. In *2001: A Space Odyssey* (1968) the serial number of the Jupiter Explorer is CRM-114. *In A Clockwork Orange* (1971), Alex (Malcolm McDowell) is given Serum 114 during the Ludovico treatment.

A further reference to the mark of Kubrick is seen in *Back to the Future* (1985), when Marty (Michael J Fox) plugs his guitar into the Doc's super amp, labelled CRM-114.

★ John 'See You Next Wednesday' Landis

Landis likes to incorporate the phrase 'See You Next Wednesday' in his films; it is usually to be found featured on posters in the background of scenes.

In *The Blues Brothers* (1980) we see a policeman hiding behind a billboard for the movie *See You Next Wednesday* – 'Coming Soon to a Theatre Near You.' In *An American Werewolf in London* (1981) it is the name of the porn film showing when David (David Naughton) meets his rotting new friends in Soho.

In *Coming to America* (1988) the words appear on a subway movie poster. The film purports to star Jamie Lee Curtis, who actually starred in the Landis-directed *Trading Places* (1983).

★ George Lucas

The trademark of George Lucas is THX 1138 – the title of his first feature film, made in 1971 and starring Robert Duvall as the character THX 1138 seeking to escape a futuristic world of computerised tyranny. *THX 1138* was originally made by Lucas during his time as a film student, though subsequently adapted for the big screen.

Lucas plays upon the reference frequently: it is the number of Chewbacca's holding cell in *Star Wars* (1977) and the registration of John Milner's roadster in *American Graffiti* (1973).

Other directors will also employ the reference when wishing to pay homage to Lucas in their works.

★ Martin Scorsese

Aside from the use of slow-motion techniques, as in *Taxi Driver* (1976) and *Raging Bull* (1980), Scorsese frequently casts his mother, Catherine Scorsese. In *GoodFellas* (1990) for example, she plays Tommy's (Joe Pesci's) mother, while in *Casino* (1995), she plays the mother of Piscano (Vinny Vella).

★ Steven Spielberg

Spielberg's trademark is somewhat hard-hitting. Throughout his films he seeks to emphasise the impact of bad or absent fathers on the family unit. In *Jaws* (1975) Mrs Kintner (Lee Fierro) is a single mother. In *Schindler's List* (1993) Oskar Schindler (Liam Neeson) tells his wife that he can't commit to a family. And in *The Lost World: Jurassic Park* (1997) Dr Ian Malcolm (Jeff Goldblum) admits that he is a bad father.

★ Quentin Tarantino

Tarantino employs Big Kahuna Burgers and Red Apple Cigarettes as his screen trademark. Both of them make their debut in *True Romance* (1993). We subsequently see Bruce Willis and Uma Thurman smoking Red Apple cigarettes in *Pulp Fiction* (1994). In the same movie, Samuel L Jackson can be seen promoting the nutritional benefits of Big Kahuna burgers.

George Clooney can also be seen carrying a Big Kahuna burger bag in *From Dusk Till Dawn* (1996); a pack of Red Apples can be seen in his car.

In Tarantino's segment of *Four Rooms* (1995), a pack of Red Apples can be seen near the switchboard.

A Big Kahuna bag can also be spotted in *Romy and Michelle's High School Reunion* (1997), directed by David Mirkin. The only connection to Tarantino is, as far as we can see, that Tarantino's ex, Mira Sorvino, stars in the film. Perhaps Mirkin is having a laugh at Tarantino's expense.

DRUGSTORE COWBOY (1989)

★ Gus Van Sant

Gool old Gus is particularly fond of Matt Dillon, having cast him in both *To Die For* (1995) and *Drugstore Cowboy* (1989).

Chapter 18
And Now
for Something
Completely Different

CASTAWAY (1986)

As the title suggests, in this chapter we take a look at a wide and somewhat unconnected array of movie-related topics: from an armchair guide through sport to a list of those celebrities who've graced the pages of *Playboy* magazine, stopping in between to look at the politicians, the Scientologists and those who are not averse to a little bit of onscreen flashing.

Eyes Wide Shut!

10 Members of Hollywood's 'Fairer Sex' at Their Fairest

★ Drew Barrymore
If her performance to date is anything to go by, she'll have more and more *Boys on the Side* (1994).

★ Neve Campbell
Campbell offers her entry for rear of the year in *Northern Passage* (1994).

SALMA HAYEK – DESPERADO (1995)

★ Salma Hayek
Hayek turns many a male *Desperado* (1995).

★ Nicole Kidman
Mrs Cruise bares more than her soul in *Billy Bathgate* (1991).

★ Gwyneth Paltrow
If *Shakespeare in Love* (1998) whetted your appetite you might try *Mrs. Parker and the Vicious Circle* (1994).

★ Michelle Pfeiffer
Mee-aiow – see the Catwoman in *Into the Night* (1985).

★ Julia Roberts
Yes, the very beginning aside, that's really Roberts's body in *Pretty Woman* (1990).

★ Meg Ryan
Camera-shy Meg relaxes momentarily during *The Doors* (1991).

★ Charlize Theron
2 Days in the Valley (1996) with the *Devil's Advocate* (1997). Interested?

★ Uma Thurman
Thurman goes without additional support in *Dangerous Liaisons* (1988), *Where the Heart Is* (1990) and *Mad Dog and Glory* (1993).

And 10 of the Not So Fair

★ Alan Bates
See *Women in Love* (1986) with Mr Bates!

★ Jeff Bridges
Winter Kills (1979); luckily for Bridges it didn't kill his acting career!

★ Michael Douglas
All's bare in love and *The War of the Roses* (1989).

★ John Hurt
The Osterman Weekend (1983) – but was it a long one?

★ William Hurt
Turn up the heat – *Body Heat* (1981)

★ Don Johnson
More vice than Miami in *The Magic Garden of Stanley Sweetheart* (1970).

★ Ryan O'Neal
Partners (1982) to the end!

★ Al Pacino
Pacino drifts along in *Scarecrow* (1973).

★ Oliver Reed
See both Mr Reed and his clothes get *Castaway* (1986).

★ Sylvester Stallone
Stallone flexes his muscles and more, in *A Party at Kitty and Stud's* (1970).

Movie Mates

Baring it all for Playboy Magazine: a Selection

★ Maud Adams – October 1981

★ Pamela Anderson – February 1990, July 1992, August 1993, November 1994, January 1996, September 1997, June 1998, February 1999

★ Ursula Andress – June 1965, July 1966, November 1973, April 1976, January 1982

★ Ann-Margret – October 1966

★ Rosanna Arquette – September 1990

★ Barbara Bach – June 1977, January 1981

★ Brigitte Bardot – March 1958, November 1958, December 1959, July 1964, April 1969, January 1975

★ Drew Barrymore – January 1995

★ Kim Basinger – February 1983, January 1988

★ Jane Birkin – November 1970

★ Sonia Braga – October 1984

★ Claudia Cardinale – February 1962, September 1963

★ Barbara Carrera – July 1977, March 1982

★ Rae Dawn Chong – May 1982

★ Joan Collins – March 1969, December 1983

★ Cindy Crawford – July 1988, October 1998

★ Maryam d'Abo – September 1987

★ Catherine Deneuve – October 1965

★ Bo Derek – March 1980, August 1980, September 1981, July 1984

★ Shannen Doherty – March 1994

★ Diana Dors – April 1956

★ Anita Ekberg – October 1955, August 1956, November 1961

★ Erika Eleniak – July 1989, August 1990, December 1993

★ Linda Evans – July 1971, January 1982, June 1986

★ Farrah Fawcett – December 1978, December 1995, July 1997

★ Sherilyn Fenn – December 1990

★ Jane Fonda – October 1966, March 1968

★ Zsa Zsa Gabor – March 1957

★ Robin Givens – September 1994

★ Melanie Griffith – December 1975, January 1986

★ Margaux Hemingway – June 1978, May 1990

★ Mariel Hemingway – April 1982, January 1984

★ **Barbara Hershey** – August 1972

★ **Grace Jones** – July 1985

★ **Margot Kidder** – March 1975

★ **Nastassja Kinski** – August 1979, May 1983

★ **Sylvia Kristel** – March 1976, February 1982

★ **Sophia Loren** – November 1957,
August 1960

★ **Elle Macpherson** – May 1994

★ **Madonna** – September 1985, July 1992

★ **Jayne Mansfield** – February 1955,
February 1957, November 1957,
February 1958, February 1960, June 1963

★ **Marilyn Monroe** – December 1953,
December 1960, January 1964, January 1984,
January 1987

★ **Julie Newmar** – December 1956,
May 1957, May 1968

★ **Brigitte Nielsen** – September 1985,
August 1986, December 1987

★ **Kim Novak** – October 1959,
December 1963, February 1965

★ **Carré Otis** – June 1990

★ **Victoria Principal** – September 1973

★ **Charlotte Rampling** – March 1974

★ **Vanessa Redgrave** – April 1969

★ **Mimi Rogers** – March 1993

★ **Maria Schneider** – February 1973

★ **Jane Seymour** – July 1973, January 1987

★ **Anna Nicole Smith** – May 1992,
June 1993, February 1994

★ **Elke Sommer** – September 1964,
December 1967, September 1970

★ **Sharon Stone** – July 1990

★ **Sharon Tate** – March 1967

★ **Elizabeth Taylor** – January 1963

★ **Mamie Van Doren** – February 1964,
June 1964

★ **Raquel Welch** – December 1979

★ **Tuesday Weld** – October 1960

★ **Susannah York** – June 1964

★ **Pia Zadora** – March 1982

All the President's Men (and Women)

10 Stars Who've Tried Their Hand at Politics

1. Sonny Bono
Mayor of Palm Springs, California; elected to Congress and US House of Representatives in 1994, where he served until his death in 1998, as the result of a skiing accident.

2. Clint Eastwood
Mayor of Carmel, California (1986–8).

3. Glenda Jackson
Labour Member of Parliament for Hampstead and Highgate (elected 1992); Under-Secretary of State at the Department of the Environment, Transport and the Regions; Minister of Transport in London.

4. Ronald Reagan
Governor of California (1967–75); fortieth President of the United States of America (1981–9).

5. **John Gavin**
US Ambassador to Mexico (1981–6).

6. **Shirley Temple Black**
US ambassador to Ghana (1974–6);
US chief of protocol; appointed US
ambassador to Czechoslovakia in 1989
by President Bush.

7. **Rex Bell**
Elected Lieutenant Governor of Nevada
in 1954; he subsequently failed to win election
as Governor of Nevada in 1958.

8. **Grace Kelly**
Following her marriage to Prince Rainier of
Monaco, she became Her Supreme Highness
Princess Grace.

9. **John Lodge**
Member of the House of Representatives
(1946–8); Governor of Connecticut (1950–4);
US Ambassador to Spain (1955–61);
US Ambassador to Argentina (1969–73);
US Ambassador to Switzerland (1985).

10. **Paul Newman**
Delegate, United Nations Conference on
Disarmament, 1978.

Weird Science

10 Stars Who Are Linked with the Church of Scientology

1. **Anne Archer**

2. **Kirstie Alley**

3. **Tom Cruise**

4. **Jenna Elfman**

5. **Kimberley Kates**

6. **Nicole Kidman**

7. **Juliette Lewis**

8. **Kelly Preston**

9. **Mimi Rogers**

10. **John Travolta**

The Armchair Guide to Sport!

Why bother going to the gym, when you
can participate in an ever increasing range of
sports from the comfort of your own house
or local cinema? To help you on your way
to tip-top condition, here's a list of some of
the better armchair events you may like to
try your hand at. However, remember that
a good warm-up is vital, if you are to avoid
injuring those cold muscles, so always watch
the trailers first! Anyway, without further
ado, let's get fit …

American Football

★ *All The Right Moves* (1983) –
Michael Chapman

★ *Jerry Maguire* (1996) – Cameron Crowe

★ *Heaven Can Wait* (1978) – Warren Beatty

★ *The Last Boy Scout* (1991) – Tony Scott

★ *The Mean Machine* (1974) – Robert Aldrich

★ *Varsity Blues* (1999) – Brian Robbins

★ *The Waterboy* (1998) – Frank Coraci

Baseball

★ *The Bad News Bears* (1976) –
Michael Ritchie

* *Bull Durham* (1988) – Ron Shelton

* *Eight Men Out* (1988) – John Sayles

* *Fear Strikes Out* (1957) – Robert Mulligan

* *Field of Dreams* (1989) – Alden Robinson

* *A League of Their Own* (1992) – Penny Marshall

* *Major League* (1989) – David S. Ward

* *The Natural* (1984) – Barry Levinson

Basketball

* *He Got Game* (1998) – Spike Lee

* *Hoop Dreams* (1994) – Steve James

* *Space Jam* (1996) – Tony Cervone and Joe Pytka

WHITE MEN CAN'T JUMP (1992)

* *White Men Can't Jump* (1992) – Ron Shelton

Boxing

* *The Boxer* (1997) – Jim Sheridan

* *The Champ* (1979) – Franco Zeffirelli

* *Every Which Way But Loose* (1978) – James Fargo

* *Kid Galahad* (1937) – Michael Curtiz

* *Raging Bull* (1980) – Martin Scorsese

* *Rocky* (1976) – John G Avildsen

* *Twenty Four Seven* (1997) – Shane Meadows

Bowling

* *The Big Lebowski* (1998) – Joel Coen

Car Racing

* *The Cannonball Run* (1981) – Hal Needham

* *Days of Thunder* (1990) – Tony Scott

* *Death Race 2000* (1975) – Paul Bartel

* *Grand Prix* (1966) – John Frankenheimer

* *Le Mans* (1971) – Lee H. Katzin

* *The Love Bug* (1969) – Robert Stevenson

* *Genevieve* (1953) – Henry Cornelius

Cycling

* *Breaking Away* (1979) – Peter Yates

Football

★ *Escape to Victory* (1981) – John Huston

★ *Fever Pitch* (1997) – David Evans

★ *Gregory's Girl* (1981) – Bill Forsyth

Golf

★ *Caddyshack* (1980) – Harold Ramis

★ *Tin Cup* (1996) – Ron Shelton

Horse-Racing

★ *A Day at the Races* (1937) – Sam Wood

★ *International Velvet* (1978) – Bryan Forbes

★ *National Velvet* (1944) – Clarence Brown

Hunting

★ *Deliverance* (1972) – John Boorman

★ *The Ghost and the Darkness* (1996) – Stephen Hopkins

★ *Jaws* (1975) – Steven Spielberg

★ *Moby Dick* (1956) – John Huston

★ *Predator* (1987) – John McTiernan

★ *White Hunter Black Heart* (1990) – Clint Eastwood – probably based on the life of John Huston, in particular the filming of *The African Queen* (1951)

Ice-Skating

★ *The Cutting Edge* (1992) – Paul Michael Glaser (Yes, the Starsky of *Starsky and Hutch*)

Mountaineering

★ *Cliffhanger* (1993) – Renny Harlin

★ *The Eiger Sanction* (1975) – Clint Eastwood (who apparently did his own climbing)

★ *Five Days One Summer* (1982) – Fred Zinnermann

★ *K2* (1991) – Franc Roddam

★ *Seven Years in Tibet* (1997) – Jean-Jacques Annaud

Pool

★ *The Baltimore Bullet* (1980) – Robert Ellis Miller

★ *The Color of Money* (1986) – Martin Scorsese

★ *The Hustler* (1961) – Robert Rossen

Rugby

★ *Up 'n' Under* (1998) – John Godber

Running

★ *Chariots of Fire* (1981) – Hugh Hudson

★ *Gallipoli* (1981) – Peter Weir

★ *The Loneliness of the Long Distance Runner* (1962) – Tony Richardson

★ *Marathon Man* (1976) – John Schlesinger

★ *The Running Man* (1987) – Paul Michael Glaser

Skateboarding

★ *Gleaming the Cube* (1989) – Graeme Clifford

★ *Kids* (1995) – Larry Clark

★ *Thrashin'* (1986) – David Winters

Skiing

★ *Aspen Extreme* (1993) – Patrick Hasburgh

★ *Downhill Racer* (1969) – Michael Ritchie

★ *Snowball Express* (1972) – Norman Tokar

Surfing

★ *Big Wednesday* (1978) – John Milius

★ *Point Break* (1991) – Kathryn Bigelow

Tennis

★ *Hard, Fast and Beautiful* (1951) – Ida Lupino

★ *Players* (1979) – Anthony Harvey

Chapter 19
On Her Majesty's Secret Service

HONOR BLACKMAN – GOLDFINGER (1974)

As the ad-line to *GoldenEye* (1995) runs, 'You know the name, you know the number.' The question is, though: just how much more do you know about Britain's most successful secret agent?

Whatever your answer, don't worry. We recently donned the balaclavas and, at exceptional personal risk, made our way into MI6's inner sanctum, where we were able to obtain all manner of highly sensitive information. Sensing no danger to national security, we have decided to print our findings in their entirety. So read on at your own peril! Oh, and one more thing: don't forget to eat the chapter once you've read it!

Bond's Baddies

JOSEPH WISEMAN – DR NO (1962)

★ Dr. No (1962)

Dr No (Joseph Wiseman), member of SPECTRE

Professor Dent (Anthony Dawson), Dr No's henchman

'The Three Blind Mice', hired assassins in the employ of Dr No

Miss Taro (Zena Marshall), by day the secretary to Pleydell-Smith, the British foreign secretary; by night, a spy for Dr No

The Photographer (Margaret LeWars), surveillance operative, also in the employ of Dr No

Mr Jones (Reggie Carter), agent in the employ of Dr No

★ From Russia With Love (1963)

Ernst Stavro Blofeld (Anthony Dawson), the mastermind of SPECTRE

Rosa Klebb (Lotte Lenya), SPECTRE agent number three, reporting directly to Ernst Stavro Blofeld

Donald 'Red' Grant (Robert Shaw), ruthless SPECTRE killing machine selected by Rosa Klebb to eliminate James Bond and Tatiana Romanova

Krilencu (Fred Haggerty), Bulgarian assassin in the employ of the Soviets

Kronsteen (Vladek Sheybal), international chess champion and SPECTRE agent number five, reporting directly to Ernst Stavro Blofeld

Morzeny (Walter Gotell), head of the agent training school on SPECTRE island

HAROLD SAKATA (LEFT) – GOLDFINGER (1964)

★ Goldfinger (1964)

Auric Goldfinger (Gert Frobe), British billionaire and megalomaniac whose driving desire is to control the world's gold market

Oddjob (Harold Sakata), Goldfinger's Korean manservant, best remembered for his steel-rimmed bowler hat

Mr Ling (Burt Kwouk), Red Chinese nuclear-fission expert and adviser to Goldfinger

Mr Solo (Martin Benson), Mafia don and smuggler of nuclear weapons for Goldfinger

Kisch (Michael Mellinger), henchman, in the employ of Goldfinger

★ Thunderball (1965)

Emilio Largo (Adolfo Celi), SPECTRE agent number two, masquerades as a millionaire playboy

Vargas (Philip Locke), SPECTRE assassin and right-hand man to Largo

Fiona Volpe (Luciana Paluzzi), SPECTRE assassin who likes to make love to her victims before dispatching them to the grave

Count Lippe (Guy Doleman), blundering SPECTRE agent

Ladislav Kutze (George Pravda), Polish atomic scientist in the employ of SPECTRE

Angelo Palazzi (Paul Stassino), SPECTRE agent, undergoes extensive plastic surgery in order to double for the NATO pilot Derval

Quist (Bill Cummings), SPECTRE assassin

Jacques Boitier (Bob Simmons and Rose Alba), successful SPECTRE assassin

★ You Only Live Twice (1967)

Ernst Stavro Blofeld (Donald Pleasance), the definitive characterisation of Blofeld (more recently parodied by Mike Myers in *Austin Powers: The Spy Who Shagged Me*)

Mr Osato (Teru Shimada), Japanese industrialist and owner of Osato Chemicals and Engineering, also in the employ of SPECTRE

Helga Brandt (Karin Dor), 'confidential secretary' to Mr Osato; also works for SPECTRE

★ On Her Majesty's Secret Service (1969)

Ernst Stavro Blofeld (Telly Savalas), SPECTRE mastermind

Irma Bunt (Ilse Steppat), henchwoman to Blofeld and mother-figure to his 'Angels of Death'

Grunther (Yuri Borienko), hired-hand of Blofeld and Irma Bunt; responsible for security at Piz Gloria, Blofeld's alpine headquarters

★ Diamonds Are Forever (1971)

Ernst Stavro Blofeld (Charles Gray), a somewhat more charming, and consequently less convincing, incarnation of the SPECTRE mastermind than previously

Kidd and Wint (Bruce Glover and Putter Smith), hired killers of Blofeld known for their penchant for wit of the worst possible taste

Bambi and Thumper (Trina Parks and Donna Garrett), glamorous, gymnastically skilled nymphettes, employed by Blofeld as members of his security team

Professor Dr Metz (Joseph Furst), gifted scientist, committed to the destruction of all nuclear weapons. Unwitting partner-in-crime of Blofeld

Morton Slumber (David Bauer), proprietor of the Slumber Funeral Home in Las Vegas; diamond smuggler

Peter Franks (Joe Robinson), British diamond smuggler

Shady Tree (Leonard Barr), past-it comedian and diamond courier

Bert Saxby (Bruce Cabot), hired hand of Blofeld

★ Live and Let Die (1973)

Dr Kananga/Mr Big (Yaphet Kotto), dictator of the Caribbean island of San Monique, base of his international heroin-trafficking business

Baron Samedi (Geoffrey Holder), Kananga's mystical henchman, supposedly equipped with voodoo powers

Tee Hee (Julius W Harris), Kananga's intimidating henchman, complete with steel arm (he lost his own to a crocodile) and pincer hook

Whisper (Earl Jolly Brown), Kananga's softly spoken henchman

Rosie Carver (Gloria Hendry), clumsy CIA agent, also working for Kananga

CHRISTOPHER LEE – THE MAN WITH THE GOLDEN GUN (1974)

★ The Man with the Golden Gun (1974)

Francisco Scaramanga (Christopher Lee), not only the man with the golden gun but also the man with a third nipple; the world's most effective assassin, he demands a one-million-dollar fee per assignment, never needing more than a single bullet to get the job done.

Nick Nack (Herve Villechaize). Scaramanga's midget henchman is a man of many talents, equally at ease whether playing assassin or rustling up a gourmet meal

Hai Fat (Richard Loo), Hong Kong industrialist and man of few morals; Fat hires Scaramanga to steal the Solex Agitator for him

Chula (Chan Yiu Lam), star pupil at the Kung Fu school run by Hai Fat

★ The Spy Who Loved Me (1977)

Karl Stromberg (Curt Jurgens), billionaire shipping magnate who dreams of a new Atlantis from where he will preside over the affairs of the world

Jaws (Richard Kiel) – his name says it all

Sandor (Milton Reid), another of Stromberg's henchmen

Naomi (Caroline Munro), Stromberg's assistant pilot

Fekkesh and Max Kalba (Nadim Sawalha and Vernon Dobtcheff); Kalba, a nightclub owner, and Fekkesh play a key role in the search for the sub tracking device

MOONRAKER (1979)

★ Moonraker (1979)

Hugo Drax (Michael Lonsdale), billionaire owner of Drax Industries, makers of Space Shuttles for the US government

Jaws (Richard Kiel) – following the demise of his former employer Stromberg, he has since found employment with Drax Industries

Chang (Toshiro Suga), Drax's oriental assassin

★ For Your Eyes Only (1981)

Aris Kristatos (Julian Glover), a former member of the wartime Resistance and now a well-respected shipping magnate; also a patron of athletics, heroin smuggler and all-round opportunist

Emile Leopold Locque (Michael Gothard), member of the Brussels underworld and assassin in the employ of Kristatos

General Gogol (Walter Gotell), KGB general

Eric Kriegler (John Wyman), agent for the KGB; masquerades as an East German skiing champ

Hector Gonzales (Stefan Kalipha), Cuban assassin, works for Kristatos

★ Octopussy (1983)

Kamal Khan (Louis Jordan) corrupt Afghan prince living in India

Gobinda (Kabir Bedi), the right-hand man of Kamal Khan

General Orlov (Steven Berkoff), hard-line communist whose one wish is to see nuclear war in Europe

Mischka and Grischka (David and Tony Meyer), circus knife throwers; not averse to throwing their knives at British agents

★ A View to a Kill (1985)

Max Zorin (Christopher Walken), the product of a Nazi doctor's death-camp experiments to manufacture suitable candidates for a German super-race, he is both genius and psychopath; his goal is to control the world's production of microchips

Max Day (Grace Jones), martial arts expert, assassin and girlfriend of Zorin

Dr Carl Mortner (Willoughby Gray), who, during the war, tested his theory that injecting pregnant women with steroids would result in the birth of superintelligent individuals; as a result the world was given Max Zorin

Scarpine (Patrick Bauchau), Zorin's chief of security

WG Howe (Daniel Benzali), director of oil and mines for the state of California – also in collusion with Zorin

Bob Conley (Manning Redwood), Zorin's all-too-willing mining supervisor

★ The Living Daylights (1987)

General Georgi Koskov (Jeroen Krabbe), a man whose loyalties ultimately lie with neither East nor West: his only aim to further his own ends, which he attempts to do by means of his partnership with Brad Whitaker

Brad Whitaker (Joe Don Baker), arms dealer and budding megalomaniac, who models himself on the great dictators of old, such as Napoleon and Hitler

Necros (Andreas Wisniewski) ruthless and deadly assassin in the employ of Koskov and Whitaker

★ Licence to Kill (1989)

Franz Sanchez (Robert Davi), dictatorial owner of a palatial estate in the fictional South American country of Isthmus, who will let no man come between him and his desire to lead an international drugs cartel

Milton Krest (Anthony Zerbe) provides a respectable front to the drugs- and money-trafficking operations of Sanchez, by means of his Florida-based marine research company

Killifer (Everett McGill), double-crossing colleague of Felix Leiter

Professor Joe Butcher (Wayne Newton), well-regarded TV evangelist and owner of a religious retreat close to Isthmus City; but in reality, his work provides the drugs equivalent of the stock exchange: daily prices are sent out in the form of evangelical broadcasts; buyers consequently signal their offers in the form of charitable donations

Truman-Lodge (Anthony Starke), the financial brains of Sanchez's operation; able to quote the market price of heroin at an instant

Dario (Benicio Del Toro), cold-blooded assassin and ex-Contra, now working for Sanchez – a man who fully appreciates the talents that Dario has to offer

Heller (Don Stroud), Sanchez's head of security

★ **GoldenEye** (1995)

Alec Trevelyan (Sean Bean), as Agent 006, was a colleague and best friend of Bond. Dies at the hands of Soviet General Ourumov, only to resurface years later as the criminal mastermind Janus

General Ourumov (Gottfried John) is, in the eyes of Bond, the man responsible for the death of Trevelyan; if the truth be known, he has been in league with Trevelyan since the end of the Cold War

Boris Grishenko (Alan Cumming), Trevelyan's computer whiz

★ **Tomorrow Never Dies** (1997)

Elliott Carver (Jonathan Pryce), media mogul and megalomaniac (sound familiar?) who seeks to fully exploit the link between world affairs and media manipulation, so as to maximise his own power base

Henry Gupta (Ricky Jay), techno-terrorist in the employ of Carver

Stamper (Gotz Otto), blond-haired, blue-eyed, cold-hearted but enthusiastic henchman of Carver

Dr Kaufman (Vincent Schiavelli), one of the world's greatest assassins; a man for whom torture is no more than a 'hobby'

★ **The World is Not Enough** (1999)

Renard (Robert Carlyle), his world viewpoint no doubt affected by his inability to feel pain, as a result of a bullet lodged in his brain

The Man and His Motors

★ **Dr. No** (1962)

Sunbeam Alpine: in reality the car was hired, in Jamaica, at a cost of fifteen shillings (75 pence) a day

★ **From Russia With Love** (1963)

Bentley Mark IV Convertible: prior to delivery of his now legendary Aston Martin, the Bentley constituted Bond's preferred form of transport

★ **Goldfinger** (1964)

Aston Martin DB5: the first, and without a doubt most famous, of Bond's gadget-laden sports cars

★ **Thunderball** (1965)

Aston Martin DB5

★ **You Only Live Twice** (1967)

Toyota 2000 GT Convertible: incidentally, Toyota never actually manufactured the convertible version as a production model, the film instead utilising two specially adapted vehicles

Little Nellie (Bond's multi-armed mini-helicopter): in fact, a working gyrocopter built and flown by Wing Commander Ken Wallis

★ On Her Majesty's Secret Service (1969)

Aston Martin DBS: in contrast to the DB5, its only modification is a telescopic rifle incorporated into the glove box

★ Diamonds Are Forever (1971)

Moonbuggy: designed by the production designer, Ken Adam

Mustang Mach 1: owned by the diamond smuggler Tiffany Case; Bond uses it to evade the police, as they pursue him through the streets of Las Vegas

★ Live and Let Die (1973)

Glastron Speedboat: fitted with Evinrude jet propulsion motors – in all 48 boats were used to film the spectacular chase sequence, filmed on the waterways of Louisiana

London bus: the top section of the bus was placed on rollers in order to facilitate the scene where Bond drives it under an overpass, shearing the upper deck off in the process.

★ The Man with the Golden Gun (1974)

AMC Hornet Hatchback: memorable for the 360-degree spin, as it leaps over the remains of a bridge, Bond at the wheel.

★ The Spy Who Loved Me (1977)

Lotus Esprit: specially modified for amphibious operation; it gained the nickname of 'Wet Nellie'

★ Moonraker (1979)

The 'Bondola': gondola/speedboat/hovercraft, all in one

Glastron Boat: combination motorboat/hang glider.

★ For Your Eyes Only (1981)

Lotus Esprit: two cars were used during filming: the first is shown self-destructing; the second, fitted with a turbo and capable of speeds up to 150 m.p.h., can be see when Bond drives to Cortina.

Citroën 2CV: Bentley, Aston Martin, Lotus, and now Citroën! – well, at least the film's makers had a sense of humour

★ Octopussy (1983)

Acrostar Mini Jet: the world's smallest jet, capable of speeds just over 300 m.p.h.

★ A View to a Kill (1985)

1962 Vintage Rolls-Royce: Bond's chauffeur-driven 'Roller' is used to add credibility to his masquerade as a wealthy buyer of racehorses, during his initial investigations of Max Zorin

★ The Living Daylights (1987)

Aston Martin V8 Volante: for filming purposes, two models were used: a hardtop Volante and a convertible Vantage; and, as is to be expected, the car is equipped with the usual Bond extras such as tyre-slashing equipment and bulletproof body; less usual extras include concealed missiles and built-in skis (a car for all seasons, one might say)

★ Licence to Kill (1989)

Kenworth Tanker Lorry: driven by Bond, as he pursues Sanchez, during the film's edge-of-the-seat finale

★ GoldenEye (1995)

BMW Z3 Roadster: the car, having appeared in the film months before it was publicly available, became, for those with the funds, a must-have object and consequently a marketing coup for BMW – so much so that order books for the limited-edition '007' model were filled in just one day

Aston Martin DB5: the definitive Bond car makes a welcome return, as it is put through its paces, during the high-speed chase with the Ferrari 355 of Xenia Onatopp

★ **Tomorrow Never Dies** (1997)

BMW 750 iL: the ultimate executive war machine, it can even be driven, when outside of the vehicle, by means of an Ericsson mobile phone

BMW R1200 Motorcycle: used by Bond and Wai Lin, as they seek to escape their pursuers on the streets of Saigon

★ **The World is Not Enough** (1999)

BMW Z8: Bond's latest vehicle (now known as the Z8), which first saw the light of day at the 1997 Tokyo motor show, as the Z08 concept car, a modern-day interpretation of the 1956 BMW 507, is built around a five-litre, eight-cylinder, M5 engine, producing 400 b.h.p. and capable of 0–62 m.p.h. in less than five seconds; a supercar no less!

50 Bond Film Facts

1. Eon, the name of the production company formed by Cubby Broccoli and Harry Saltzman to produce the Bond films, is an acronym of 'Everything or Nothing'.

2. Sean Connery was chosen for the role of James Bond, after Cubby Broccoli and his wife saw him in Disney's *Darby O'Gill and the Little People*.

3. So as to make Sean Connery, who had come from humble beginnings, feel more comfortable with the sophisticated character of James Bond, the director Terence Young

made him sleep in a Savile Row suit, complete with shirt and tie.

4. The voice of Ursula Andress, as Honey Ryder, in *Dr. No*, was dubbed.

5. Bob Simmons, the man who stood in for Connery during the tarantula scene, claimed that the stunt was the most frightening of his career.

6. Jack Lord, who plays Felix Leiter in *Dr. No*, later found fame as the star of TV's *Hawaii Five-O*.

7. SPECTRE is an acronym of the Special Executive for Counterintelligence, Terrorism, Revenge and Extortion.

8. *Dr. No* went on to gross £60 million at the worldwide box office. It had cost $1 million.

9. Lotte Lenya, who played Rosa Klebb in *From Russia With Love*, became popular as a result of working with her husband, the composer Kurt Weil, on stage productions such as *The Threepenny Opera*.

10. The voice of Anthony Dawson, as Ernst Stavro Blofeld in *From Russia With Love*, was dubbed by Eric Pohlman.

11. *From Russia With Love* featured in the former American President John F Kennedy's top-ten list of favourite books as published in *Life* magazine.

12. The then playwright Robert Shaw, as a result of his performance as Red Grant in *From Russia With Love*, embarked upon a successful acting career, and went on to star in such films as *Jaws* (1975) and *The Deep* (1977).

13. Harold Sakata, who plays Oddjob in *Goldfinger*, was discovered when the film's director, Guy Hamilton, saw him appear in a wrestling match under the name of Tosh Togo. Born in Hawaii, Sakata won a silver medal for the USA in the light heavyweight contest of the 1948 Olympics. After the film, Sakata apparently returned to wrestling as Oddjob, and wearing the character's full Bond outfit.

14. One of the most famous scenes from any Bond movie occurs when Bond discovers the 'golden' body of Jill Masterson, played by Shirley Eaton, gilded and motionless on his bed, having died as a result of skin suffocation. To create the scene, the paint was applied over a two-hour period, throughout which Miss Eaton's vital signs were monitored. This brief but memorable appearance on screen brought Miss Eaton much attention, and she subsequently re-created her role for the cover of *Life* magazine.

15. Burt Kwouk, who plays the nuclear expert Mr Ling in *Goldfinger*, is best remembered for the role of Cato, manservant to Inspector Clouseau (Peter Sellers), in the *Pink Panther* films.

16. In *Thunderball*, when Bond leaves the Shrublands Health Spa, he remarks to Patricia Fearing, 'Another time, another place.' This was a reference to one of Connery's earlier films, *Another Time, Another Place*, which co-starred Lana Turner.

17. Claudine Auger, who plays Domino Derval in *Thunderball*, was a former Miss France.

18. So as to put Connery at ease during the fight sequence against a SPECTRE agent in the shark pool, all of the sharks were drugged. However, the shark that attempts to bite Connery as he leaves the pool was in fact dead, and wires were used to give the impression of life.

19. The title of the fifth Bond movie and twelfth Fleming novel, *You Only Live Twice*, is drawn from a poem by the seventeenth-century Japanese poet Bassho, which reads thus:

You only live twice:
Once when you're born,
And once when you look death in the face.

20. The script for *You Only Live Twice* was penned by the novelist Roald Dahl, author of such children's classics as *James and the Giant Peach* (1961) and *Charlie and the Chocolate Factory* (1964). He also wrote the script for *Chitty Chitty Bang Bang* (1968).

21. The production designer for *You Only Live Twice*, Ken Adam, was given $1 million with which to construct the set of SPECTRE's volcano headquarters.

22. The role of Ernst Stavros Blofeld in *You Only Live Twice* was originally meant to be played by the Czech actor Jan Werich. However, when Werich fell ill, Donald Pleasence was brought in as a last-minute replacement.

23. Teru Shimada, who plays the Japanese industrialist Mr Osata in *You Only Live Twice*, had previously appeared in the *Man From U.N.C.L.E.* film, *One Spy Too Many*. In spite of his previous success, Shimada had been working as a janitor when Broccoli offered him the role of Mr Osata.

24. Akiko Wakabayashi, who plays Aki in *You Only Live Twice*, could not actually drive a car, in spite of the fact that she is seen rescuing Bond in her convertible Toyota 2000 GT. Her driving was in fact the result of manual labour on the part of the film's crew, who had to pull the car.

25. *On Her Majesty's Secret Service* features both Diana Rigg (as Tracy Di Vicenzo), who had previously made a name for herself as Emma Peel in *The Avengers*, and Joanna Lumley (as one of Blofeld's 'Angels of Death'), who went on to find fame as Purdey in *The New Avengers*.

26. Piz Gloria, Blofeld's alpine headquarters in *On Her Majesty's Secret Service*, was in reality a part-finished restaurant atop the 10,000-foot Schilthorn mountain in the Swiss Alps. In return for filming permission, the producers offered to finish the interior and build a helipad at a cost of $125,000. The restaurant, in acknowledgement of the success the Bond connection brought it, still bears the name of Piz Gloria.

27. Raquel Welch, Jane Fonda and Faye Dunaway were all considered for the role of Tiffany Case in *Diamonds Are Forever*. The role ultimately went to Jill St John.

28. Sean Connery, who as a result of *Diamonds Are Forever* became the then highest-paid actor in history, donated all $1,250,000 of his salary to a charity for the underprivileged, the Scottish International Trust.

29. Prior to casting Roger Moore for the role of Bond in *Live and Let Die*, the studio considered such stars as Burt Reynolds, Robert Redford and Paul Newman.

30. Jane Seymour, as Solitaire, gained her first taste of the big screen in *Live and Let Die*. She had previously appeared in BBC TV's *The Onedin Line*.

31. Dr Kananga's name is taken from Ross Kananga, owner of the crocodile farm, where the scene of Bond running across the backs of the crocodiles was filmed. In reality Kananga himself doubled for Bond in this potentially very dangerous stunt.

32. Christopher Lee, who plays Scaramanga, villain of *The Man with the Golden Gun*, is the first cousin of the Bond creator Ian Fleming. Fleming had previously offered Lee the role of *Dr No*, but he had declined.

33. Filming of Scaramanga's hideaway, for *The Man with the Golden Gun*, took place on the now popular tourist destination of Phuket island off Thailand.

34. Maud Adams, who plays Andrea Anders in *The Man with the Golden Gun*, went on to play the role of *Octopussy* in the 1983 film of the same name. It had previously been a rule of Broccoli's that no actress make more than one major appearance in a Bond film.

35. *The Man with the Golden Gun* has the honour of being the first Bond movie to be shown at the Kremlin.

36. *The Spy Who Loved Me* bears no relationship to the content of the novel from which it draws its title. Fleming, displeased with his writing, made it a condition of the film rights that only the title could be used – the script would have to be rewritten.

37. In order to accommodate the dramatic sets of *The Spy Who Loved Me*, the world's largest sound stage was built at Pinewood Studios. The '007 Stage', as it came to be known, measures 374 feet long (with an exterior tank of 38 feet), 160 feet wide and 53 feet high.

38. *For Your Eyes Only* features Cassandra Harris, the late wife of the future Bond incarnation Pierce Brosnan. Harris played Countess Lisl, mistress of the smuggler Milos Columbo.

39. Roger Moore later said of the scene in *For Your Eyes Only* where Bond attempts to climb the sheer face of the mountain, atop which sits the fortress occupied by Kristatos, 'I was paralysed … I felt like I was going to fall to my death, or else I was going to throw myself over the edge. It took a lot of Valium to get me up there. I always looked heroic when I really couldn't stand heights.'

40. The Indian tennis professional Vijay Amritraj appears in *Octopussy*. He can be seen driving Bond through the marketplace in a three-wheeled taxi; hence his display of sporting prowess, as he fends off henchmen with an oh-so-convenient tennis racquet. He can subsequently be seen disguised as a snake charmer.

41. Shortly before filming of *A View to a Kill* was due to begin, the '007 Stage' burnt to the ground. Undaunted, Cubby Broccoli had the stage rebuilt in less than four months. In honour of Broccoli's efforts, Pinewood renamed it 'The Albert R Broccoli 007 Stage'.

42. Andreas Wisniewski, who plays the henchman Nekros in *The Living Daylights*, was not only a successful actor but also a famed ballet dancer.

43. Wayne Newton, who plays the TV evangelist Professor Joe Butcher in *Licence to Kill*, was already a legend in his own right as a singer on the Las Vegas club circuit.

44. *GoldenEye's* bungee jump required a stunt man, Wayne Michaels, to plunge a distance of 640 feet, reaching a speed of 100 miles per hour.

45. As a reward for his promotion of the BMW Z3, as featured in *GoldenEye*, Brosnan was given a BMW 850 CSI by the car manufacturer. Shortly afterwards, though, he was caught by police driving at a speed of 120 miles per hour! However, they chose not to issue Brosnan with a speeding ticket as they were more interested in getting the lowdown on the bungee-jump sequence.

46. London's Brent Cross shopping centre provided the location for the gripping BMW chase sequence in *Tomorrow Never Dies*.

47. Among the companies who had product tie-ins with *Tomorrow Never Dies* were BMW, Omega watches, Brioni clothing, Church's shoes, Bollinger champagne, Ericsson mobile phones and Avis rental cars.

48. The sinking of the Devonshire, in *Tomorrow Never Dies*, took place in the same enormous water tank as that used in *Titanic*, at Baja Studios in Mexico.

49. *The World is Not Enough* is the fifteenth Bond film to be shot at Pinewood, the spiritual home of James Bond. For Brosnan it is his first time at Pinewood as Bond. *GoldenEye* was filmed at Leavesden and *Tomorrow Never Dies* was shot at Frogmore; on both occasions the sound stages were already booked.

50. The drum and bass supremo Goldie makes an appearance in *The World is Not Enough*, as Valentin Zukovsky's (Robbie Coltrane's) driver.

The Man and His Ladies

Since the early days of his career, James Bond has always stared death in the face, his life being one fraught with danger, though not without rewards. Bond has always been popular with the women – or should we say Bond Girls? From Honeychile Rider to Elektra King, they have all adored him.

★ **Dr. No** (1962)
Ursula Andress as Honeychile Rider

★ **From Russia With Love** (1963)
Daniella Bianchi as Tatiana Romanova

★ **Goldfinger** (1964)
Honor Blackman as Pussy Galore

★ **Thunderball** (1965)
Claudine Auger as Domino Vitali

★ **You Only Live Twice** (1967)
Mie Hama as Kissy Suzuki

★ **On Her Majesty's Secret Service** (1969)
Diana Rigg as Teresa, Countess di Vicenzo

★ **Diamonds Are Forever** (1971)
Jill St John as Tiffany Case

★ **Live and Let Die** (1973)
Jane Seymour as Solitaire

★ **The Man with the Golden Gun** (1974)
Britt Ekland as Mary Goodnight

★ **The Spy Who Loved Me** (1977)
Barbara Bach as Major Anya Amasova

★ **Moonraker** (1979)
Lois Chiles as Holly Goodhead

★ **For Your Eyes Only** (1981)
Carole Bouquet as Melina Havelock

★ Octopussy (1983)
Maud Adams as Octopussy

★ Never Say Never Again (1983)
Kim Basinger as Domino Petachi

★ A View to a Kill (1985)
Tanya Roberts as Stacey Sutton

★ The Living Daylights (1987)
Maryam D'Abo as Kara Milovy

★ Licence to Kill (1989)
Carey Lowell as Pam Bouvier

★ GoldenEye (1995)
Izabella Scorupco as Natalya Simonova

★ Tomorrow Never Dies (1997)
Michelle Yeoh as Wai Lin

★ The World is Not Enough (1999)
Sophie Marceau as Elektra King

The Language Barrier

The James Bond formula has achieved worldwide success, and as a result many language barriers have been broken. Just take a look at how some of the movie titles have been changed to suit the non-English-speaking countries of the world; sometimes, it would seem that the intended meaning really has been lost in the translation.

★ Dr. No
Agent 007 Vs. The Satanic Dr. No – Spain
James Bond Chases Dr. No – Germany

★ From Russia With Love
Love Greetings from Moscow – Germany
Hearty Kisses from Russia – France

★ Thunderball
Fireball – Germany
Thunderball Fighting – Japan

★ You Only Live Twice
One Doesn't Live More Than Twice – France

★ Diamonds Are Forever
Diamond Fever – Germany

★ Live and Let Die
The Dead Slave – Japan

★ Moonraker
Moonraker: Operation Space – Italy

★ For Your Eyes Only
A Deadly Mission – Germany

★ Octopussy
Operation Octopus – Italy

★ A View to a Kill
In the Face of Death – Germany
A Panorama to Kill – Spain

★ The Living Daylights
The Skin of a Corpse – Germany

★ Licence to Kill
Private Revenge – Italy
The Cancelled Licence – Japan

Bond – James Bond: The Man and His Music

★ Dr. No (1962) – 'The James Bond Theme'

The first of the Bond movies, made with a budget of about $1 million, and starring Sean Connery as James '007' Bond, with an unforgettable appearance by Ursula Andress, offers us probably the most infectious movie theme tune of all time. The two-minute-long composition was written by John Barry and went on to reach Number 13 in the UK charts.

★ From Russia With Love (1963) –
'From Russia With Love'

The vocal version of the theme to Bond's second outing was penned by Lionel Bart and sung by Matt Monro. It went on to reach Number 27 in the UK charts.

★ Goldfinger (1964) – 'Goldfinger'

The Tiger Bay chanteuse Shirley Bassey gives her all and more to this the first title vocal of the Bond movies. The song itself was composed and written by John Barry with Leslie Bricusse and Anthony Newley. The song's strength was reflected by its chart position. It reached Number 8 in the singles charts.

★ Thunderball (1965) – 'Thunderball'

The main title music features the vocal flair of a certain Mr Tom Jones singing a tune written by John Barry and Don Black. The single reached Number 25 in the charts.

However, it wasn't always intended that 'Thunderball' would act as the title theme. Up until the very last minute, the title vocal was set to be 'Mr Kiss Kiss Bang Bang', in honour of Bond's nickname in Japan and other parts of the world. Leslie Bricusse and John Barry once more collaborated on the composition, with Dionne Warwick performing vocal duties. Ultimately, only this instrumental version of the track was used, and then only to highlight the *Thunderball* score.

★ You Only Live Twice (1967) – 'You Only Live Twice'

Nancy Sinatra brings to life the melody of John Barry and the lyrics of Leslie Bricusse, a combination that caused the single to reach Number 11 in the UK charts.

★ On Her Majesty's Secret Service (1969) – 'On Her Majesty's Secret Service'

The sixth Bond movie saw the advent of a new Bond – the Australian George Lazenby – Connery, having decided to call it a day with the completion of *You Only Live Twice*, his fifth movie in the Bond role.

Barry reverted to an instrumental score for the main title, deciding not to use the lyrics provided by Bricusse. The final composition, performed by the John Barry Orchestra, provides a lively and moving accompaniment to the action scenes, in particular the ski-chase scene, that so typify a Bond movie.

★ Diamonds Are Forever (1971) – 'Diamonds Are Forever'

Shirley Bassey returns, both teasing and tantalising, as she performs John Barry and Don Black's title theme.

★ Live and Let Die (1973) – 'Live And Let Die'

The first in the Roger Moore series of Bond movies marks the first title theme to be provided by a rock band. 'Live And Let Die', performed with gusto by Paul McCartney and Wings, went on to reach Number 9 in the UK charts.

★ The Man with the Golden Gun (1974) – 'The Man With The Golden Gun'

The diminutive Scottish pop singer Lulu provides the vocals to the title tune, written by Don Black.

★ The Spy Who Loved Me (1977) – 'Nobody Does It Better'

With 'Nobody Does It Better', the Bond tunesmiths Marvin Hamlisch and Carole Bayer Sager had a hit on their hands. The title tune, performed by Carly Simon, made it to Number 7 in the UK charts. In contrast with the previous Bond films, this was the first time the producers decided on a song that didn't share the title of the film. However, the line 'The Spy Who Loved Me' does crop up in the lyrics.

★ Moonraker (1979) – 'Moonraker'

A John Harry and Hal David composition with vocals provided by Shirley Bassey.

★ For Your Eyes Only (1981) – 'For Your Eyes Only'

The title tune, penned by Bill Conti and Michael Leeson and performed by the then pop sensation Sheena Easton, captured the feel of the moment – disco. As a result it reached Number 8 in the UK charts. It also marked the first onscreen appearance by the song's performer.

★ Octopussy (1983) – 'All Time High'

The film's title song, 'All Time High', written and composed by Tim Rice and John Barry, features the vocals of Rita Coolidge.

★ A View to a Kill (1985) – 'A View To A Kill'

An energetic title song, performed by Duran Duran, only added to the excitement levels of this, the fourteenth Bond movie. It also became the highest-charting Bond tune of its time when it reached Number 2 in the UK charts.

★ The Living Daylights (1987) – 'The Living Daylights'

Performed by the Norwegian rock band A-ha and co-written by John Barry and A-ha's own Pal Waaktaar, the title song reached Number 5 in the UK charts.

Notably *The Living Daylights* was the last Fleming title to be used for a Bond movie.

★ Licence to Kill (1989) – 'Licence To Kill'

With Gladys Knight at the helm, the title track reached Number 6 in the UK charts.

★ GoldenEye (1995) – 'GoldenEye'

GoldenEye sees the introduction of a new Bond, Pierce Brosnan. The title tune, written by Bono and the Edge, of the Irish rock band U2, is performed by the legendary Tina Turner.

★ Tomorrow Never Dies (1997) – 'Tomorrow Never Dies'

For Brosnan's second appearance as Bond, we find Sheryl Crow fulfilling vocal duties on the title track, in a song co-written by herself and Mitchell Froom.

★ The World is Not Enough (1999) – 'The World Is Not Enough'

No longer a 'Wannabe', the Spice Girl Mel C, fresh from her successful collaboration with the Canadian rocker Bryan Adams on 'When You're Gone', was the choice to record the title tune to this next, eagerly awaited Bond movie.

Chapter 20
Elvis - The Way It Is

Elvis Aron Presley was born in Tupelo, Mississippi, USA, on 8 January 1935, and died on 16 August 1977. He was indeed one of the world's most phenomenal performers. During the course of his life, Elvis appeared in 31 feature films and two documentaries and has sold in excess of 200 million records.

In this chapter we look at all of his movies, and the hit songs that came from them, together with some fascinating and intriguing behind-the-scenes facts.

100 Elvis Film Facts

LOVE ME TENDER (1956)

1. On April Fool's Day, 1956, Elvis had his one and only screen test at Paramount Studios in Hollywood. He might have thought it to be a prank when Hal Wallis gave him a seven-year nonexclusive contract and an advance of $450,000 for his first three films.

2. In 1956 Hal Wallis was about to commence filming *The Rainmaker*, starring Katharine Hepburn and Burt Lancaster. Elvis consequently performed a scene from the movie as his screen test for Wallis.

3. To this day, Elvis's first onscreen appearance, in the twenty-minute short *The Pied Piper of Cleveland: A Day in the Life of a Famous Disc Jockey*, remains locked in the archives of Universal Studios, on account of a dispute over ownership of the film.

4. One of Presley's biggest acting influences was James Dean; his favourite film was *Rebel Without a Cause* (1955). It has been said that Elvis could recite every word of Dean's script from memory.

5. Robert Wagner was originally considered for the part of Clint Reno, the part played by Elvis, in *Love Me Tender*.

6. The original working title of *Love Me Tender* was *The Reno Brothers*.

7. The original end scene of *Love Me Tender*, in which Clint dies in Cathy's arms, so much distressed not only Elvis's mother but thousands of his fans, that the film company decided to add a silhouette presence of Clint singing the title song over the end credits. An alternative ending, in which Clint lives, was also filmed but not used.

8. Within three days of its release, all production costs for *Love Me Tender*, of just under $1 million, were recouped.

9. Elvis was named 'Worst Supporting Actor' by the Harvard Lampoon for his supporting role in *Love Me Tender*. This was the only film for which Elvis did not receive star billing: he was third on the cast listing behind Richard Egan and Debra Paget.

10. The original title for *Loving You* was *The Lonesome Cowboy*. However, this was subsequently changed to *Running Wild*. *Something for the Girls* was also briefly considered.

11. Elvis's parents, Gladys and Vernon, were extras in an audience scene during the TV broadcast at the Freegate, in *Loving You*.

12. Elvis received his first screen kiss in *Loving You* from Jana Lund, in a dressing room in Amarillo.

13. Unlucky for some? Elvis's thirteenth film, *Fun in Acapulco*, had thirteen songs featured on the soundtrack album and, coincidentally, there are thirteen letters in the film's title.

14. During the production of *Jailhouse Rock*, Elvis ended up in hospital as a result of swallowing a tooth cap.

15. Elvis's three-minute love scene with Jennifer Holden in *Jailhouse Rock* took over four hours to film.

16. On her last day of filming, the electric heater in Miss Holden's dressing room caught fire. As her room burnt, the dashing hero Elvis carried her to safety.

17. Glenn Strange, who played Mr Simpson in *Jailhouse Rock*, also played the Frankenstein monster on three occasions, *House of Frankenstein* and *House of Dracula* (1945), and *Abbot and Costello Meet Frankenstein* (1948). He also played Sam the Bartender for many seasons in the TV series *Gunsmoke*.

18. Dean Jones, who played Teddy Talbot in *Jailhouse Rock*, is probably best remembered for his role in Disney's charming *The Love Bug* (1969), as Jim Douglas, driver of Herbie the VW Beetle.

19. Elvis himself devised the dance routine in *Jailhouse Rock*.

20. On 9 March 1960 *Jailhouse Rock* was re-released to coincide with Elvis's 5 March discharge from the army, where he had served just over two years in the Tank Batallion.

21. Two previous working titles for *King Creole* were *Danny* and *Sing, You Sinners*.

22. At the time, Carolyn Jones, who played Ronnie in *King Creole*, had the distinction of being nominated for Best Supporting Actress for her role in the 1957 movie, *The Bachelor Party*, in spite of having appeared on screen for only a few minutes. She is probably best remembered for her role

as Morticia Addams in TV's *The Addams Family*.

23. Candy Candido, who played a doorman in *King Creole*, was the voice of Popeye in the 1930s.

24. Michael Curtiz, director of *King Creole*, had more than one hundred films to his name by the end of his career, including the Oscar-nominated *Angels with Dirty Faces* (1938), *Yankee Doodle Dandy* (1942) and *Casablanca* (1942), for which he ultimately won.

25. Elvis's character in *G.I. Blues* was Tulsa McLean. However, before the start of production he was called Tulsa McCauley. Many reviews at the time, as well as reference books, still incorrectly use the original name.

26. Among the titles originally considered for *G.I. Blues* were *Café Europa* and *Dog Face*.

27. Elvis can be seen with a swollen hand in scenes at the Café Europa, on account of his having broken a small bone in his hand while practising karate during the making of *G.I. Blues*.

28. A screening of *G.I. Blues* in Mexico City resulted in a riot: seats were ripped up and windows were smashed. Consequently, the Mexican government banned the screening of all subsequent Elvis films.

29. *Flaming Star* was directed by Don Siegel, who went on to direct, among others, *Invasion of the Body Snatchers* (1956), *Dirty Harry* (1971), *Two Mules for Sister Sarah* (1970) and *Escape from Alcatraz* (1979), which he also produced and appeared in.

30. The director Don Siegel fought with Colonel Tom Parker and Twentieth Century Fox not to have Elvis sing in *Flaming Star*. The end result was the title song, performed over the opening credits, and 'A Cane And A High Starched Collar', which he performed just a few minutes into the film. Two other numbers, 'Britches' and 'Summer Kisses, Winter Tears', were cut from the film prior to release.

31. RCA records presented Elvis with a platinum watch during the filming of *Wild in the Country*, for having sold over 75 million records for the company.

32. Alternative endings were made for *Wild in the Country*. In one ending the Hope Lange character died, and in the other she lived. The decision as to which to use was placed in the hands of a preview audience, and, as a result, she lived.

33. The director of *Wild in the Country*, Philip Dunne, went on to serve as a speech writer for John F Kennedy during his 1960 presidential campaign, wherein he capitalised upon his screenwriting talents, used in such films as *How Green Was My Valley* (1941), *Forever Amber* and *The Ghost of Mrs. Muir* (both 1947).

34. As a result of their performance in *Wild in the Country*, Elvis and his co-star Tuesday Weld were given the Damp Raincoat Award for Most Disappointing Performers of 1961 by the readers of *Teen* magazine.

35. Two songs, 'Lonely Man' and 'Forget Me Never', were cut from the soundtrack of *Wild in the Country*. However, some movie reviews and reference books list the songs in the movie credits.

36. Christina Crawford, the adopted daughter of Joan Crawford, made her movie debut in *Wild in the Country*.

37. The original title of *Blue Hawaii* was *Hawaii Beach Boy*.

38. Juliet Prowse was originally signed to play Maile Duval in *Blue Hawaii*, but because of her excessive contract demands she was replaced by Joan Blackman.

39. Roland Winters, who played Fred Gates in *Blue Hawaii*, was one of six non-Chinese actors to play Charlie Chan in the movies, having starred in six Chan movies in the 1940s.

40. Angela Lansbury, star of TV's *Murder She Wrote*, considers her part as Sarah Lee Gates in *Blue Hawaii* as one of the true low points in her acting career.

41. Within weeks of finishing filming scenes for MGM's *Double Trouble*, Elvis began work on *Easy Come, Easy Go* for Paramount. *Double Trouble* was released two months after *Easy Come, Easy Go*, even though it was completed earlier.

42. There are two notable goofs in *Easy Come, Easy Go*. In one, Ted takes Jo home; however, during the journey her orange top mysteriously changes its colour to white. Another scene depicts Gil surfacing before Ted after an underwater fight. By the time he reaches Dina's boat, he's managed to change and blow-dry his hair, all before Ted's arrival.

43. Charles O'Curran, the choreographer for *Blue Hawaii*, was married to one of Elvis's favourite singers, Patti Page.

44. *Pioneer Go Home* was the original working title of *Follow That Dream*. However, the songwriters found it impossible to find a word that rhymed with 'Pioneer'. As a result the title was then changed to *What a Wonderful Life*; another short-lived title suggestion was *Here Come the Kwimpers*.

45. With gambling illegal in Florida, two anonymous mobsters and a member of the local chamber of commerce were hired to supply the casino equipment necessary for *Follow That Dream*.

46. The director of *Follow That Dream*, Gordon Douglas, was also responsible for the 1954 film *Young at Heart*, making him the only person to have directed both Elvis Presley and Frank Sinatra.

47. Joan Blackman, who played Rose Grogan in *Kid Galahad*, had previously been Elvis's leading lady in *Blue Hawaii*.

48. Ed Asner, probably most famous for his role as TV's Lou Grant, made his film debut as Frank Garson in *Kid Galahad*.

49. For his role in *Kid Galahad*, Elvis was trained by the former junior world welterweight boxing champion Mushy Callahan, who also trained Burt Lancaster and Kirk Douglas for their roles as boxers in the movies.

50. Jack Good, the TV producer responsible for many of the top television shows of the 50s and 60s, including *Boy*, *Shindig* and *Boy Meets Girl*, played Mr Hathaway in *Clambake*. Good later went on to produce *Elvis the Musical* at the Astoria theatre in London, which opened on 28 November 1977.

51. *A Girl in Every Port* and *Welcome Aboard* were two titles considered for *Girls! Girls! Girls!* However, a few months before filming began, the working title was *Gumbo Ya-Ya*, a Creole expression for 'everybody talks at once'.

52. Upon arriving in Hawaii to begin filming of *Girls! Girls! Girls!*, Elvis lost his diamond ring, tie clip and watch when he was mobbed by several thousand fans. The following day a young girl actually returned the ring to Elvis's hotel.

53. One press release for *Girls! Girls! Girls!* claimed, 'first nude in a Hal Wallis movie'. The truth was that a four-year-old child was seen in vision diving naked into the sea.

54. One of the earlier titles for *It Happened at the World's Fair* was *Mister, Will You Marry Me*.

55. A twelve-year-old Kurt Russell makes two brief appearances in *It Happened at the World's Fair*, billed on the credits as the 'boy who kicks Elvis'. Sixteen years later Russell portrayed Elvis in the TV movie *Elvis*.

56. One of the gang of mountain girls in *Kissin' Cousins* was played by Maureen Reagan, eldest daughter of Ronald Reagan and Jane Wyman.

57. *Kissin' Cousins* was produced in just over three weeks with hardly any rehearsal time and a budget of $800,000. On more than one occasion, Presley had to be enticed out of his dressing room because he was so embarrassed about having to wear a blond wig for his part as Jodie, one of the cousins.

58. At the time of release *Viva Las Vegas* was entitled *Love in Las Vegas* for the European market.

59. George Sidney, director of *Viva Las Vegas*, had previously worked on hit movies such as *Show Boat* (1951), *Kiss Me Kate* (1953) and *Pal Joey* (1957). In 1978 he married Jane Robinson, widow of Edward G Robinson.

60. Work on *Roustabout* commenced on 9 March 1964, and for the interior shots three main sound stages at Paramount were opened out and combined for the first time in the history of the studio.

61. *Roustabout* gave the sixties sex goddess Raquel Welch her first screen appearance – playing a college student – with the (un)forgettable line, 'Uh, how come they call this place a tea house, dear?'

62. Richard Kiel had a small role in *Roustabout* as a strongman. He later went on to find fame and fortune as the villainous Jaws in the James Bond movies, *The Spy Who Loved Me* and *Moonraker*.

63. It is alleged that the part of Maggie Morgan in *Roustabout* was originally offered to Mae West, who declined the role; it subsequently went to Barbara Stanwyck.

64. With the release of *Tickle Me*, Elvis's first film with Allied Artists, the company were saved from bankruptcy when the movie became its third greatest box office success in its history, behind *55 Days at Peking* (1963) and *El Cid* (1961). The studio's success story continued with such films as *Papillon* (1973) and *The Man Who Would Be King* (1975).

65. In 1925 Cecil B DeMille built a temple, at a cost of approximately $4,000 for his movie *King of Kings*. The same temple was used in *Harum Scarum* – but not until the set had been extensively remodelled by MGM at a cost of $40,000. With so much money being spent on the set of *Harum Scarum*, it was decided that the one hundred extras would wear costumes

from the 1944 movie *Kismet*. These were later retailored for the 1955 remake of the same film. While not wishing to accuse MGM of being cheapskates, we must note that Elvis's dagger was also a hand-me-down, having made its movie debut in the 1939 film, *Lady of the Tropics*, starring Robert Taylor.

66. *Harum Scarum* went under the title *Harum Holiday* in Britain. Philip Reed, who played King Toranshah, Ruler of Lunarkand, was once married to Joan Crawford; Fran Jeffries, who played Aishah, was married to the singer Dick Haynes.

67. *Jim Dandy, After Midnight* and *Always at Midnight* were originally considered as titles for *Spinout*. In the early stages of production the movie's title was *Never Say No*; it was later changed to *Never Say Yes*. For the European market the film went under the title of *California Holiday*.

68. Before filming commenced on *Paradise Hawaiian Style* Elvis donated $50,000 to the Motion Picture Relief Fund – the largest donation ever made according to the then honorary heads of the charity, Frank Sinatra and Barbara Stanwyck.

69. Annette Day, who co-starred as Jill Conway in *Double Trouble*, was discovered by the producer Judd Bernard in her father's antiques shop on London's Portobello Road. Prior to her appearance in the movie, Day had not had any previous acting experience whatsoever.

70. During the shooting of the sequences aboard a ship that was moored in the particularly treacherous confines of the MGM lot, sixteen of the *Double Trouble* extras allegedly became seasick and had to be replaced.

71. The trained dolphin Susie (yes, that's her real name!), star of TV's *Flipper*, made a guest appearance in *Clambake*.

72. Elvis's $10,000 white suit, as worn in *Clambake*, was later cut up into thousands of small pieces, and given away with his four-record box set *Elvis: The Other Sides – Worldwide Gold Award Hits, Vol. 2*.

73. Among the titles originally buzzing around the studio for *Stay Away Joe* were *Bumblebee, Oh Bumblebee* and *Born Rich*.

74. *Stay Away Joe* was criticised by many columnists on account of its racist regard for Native Americans: it portrayed them as being lazy and incompetent.

75. Nancy Sinatra's co-starring role in *Speedway*, as Susan Jacks, was originally offered to Petula Clark, who turned it down. The singing duo Sonny and Cher also turned down parts in the film.

76. The working title for *Live a Little, Love a Little* was *Kiss My Firm But Pliant Lips* – also the title of the Dan Greenburg novel on which the movie was based.

77. During the filming of *Live a Little, Love a Little*, Elvis was knocked to the ground by autograph hunters – in the menacing shape of two little old women rushing to meet Rudy Vallee, who played Louis Penlow in the movie.

78. Eddie Hodges, who played the delivery boy in *Live a Little, Love a Little*, was once a contestant on the American TV quiz show *Name That Tune*, where he won $25,000. His fellow contestant was none other than the future astronaut and US senator, John Glenn.

79. On account of Elvis's declining status as a movie star, *Live a Little, Love a Little* was not made available on general release in the UK.

80. The working title for *Charro!* was *Come Hell, Come Sundown. Charro!* was the first Presley movie not to include him performing a song, although he was heard singing the title song over the opening credits.

81. The music for *Charro!*, title song aside, was composed by Hugo Montenegro. The previous year, 1968, Montenegro had a number-one hit in England, with the theme music to Clint Eastwood's *The Good, the Bad, and the Ugly*.

82. Bobbie Gentry was originally considered for the role of Charlene in *The Trouble with Girls*.

83. During the opening scene of *A Change of Habit*, a bus passes by advertising a Los Angeles radio station. Someone should have told the continuity team that the film was set in New York!

84. Mary Tyler Moore picked up a Golden Turkey Award for Worst Performance by an Actor or Actress as a Clergyman or Nun, for her performance in *Change of Habit*.

85. A dozen large rats used in a downtown apartment scene in *Change of Habit* escaped and ran riot on the set, which had to be evacuated until animal handlers were able to round up the vermin.

86. James J Jamison III in *Clambake* and Kenny Donford in *Speedway* were both played by Bill Bixby, famous for his role as Dr David Banner in the TV series *The Incredible Hulk*.

87. Elvis Presley found it impossible to watch *Jailhouse Rock* owing to the tragic death of Judy Tyler, killed in a car accident in July 1957, just prior to the film's release.

88. Upon its release in America, *The Trouble with Girls* was paired in the cinemas with the Japanese science-fiction movie, *The Green Slime*.

89. *The Trouble with Girls* featured Frank Welker, who later earned a living providing cartoon voiceovers, in particular, that of Freddy in *Scooby-Doo, Where Are You?*

90. Ann-Margret, the female lead in *Viva Las Vegas*, starred in *Kitten with a Whip*, also made in 1963, in which she played a young temptress who captivates a middle-aged politician.

91. *Kissin' Cousins* was shot in just over two weeks. Sam Katzman, the film's producer, was known in the industry as 'King of the Quickies'.

92. Of *Spinout*, *Time* magazine said, 'Elvis is pitching his act at some sort of adult audience – possibly adult chimpanzees.'

93. Offscreen feuding between Elvis and his *Clambake* co-star Shelley Fabares can be felt on screen, especially during such 'tender' moments as when the pair are seen embracing.

94. The album *G.I. Blues* remained on the charts of *Billboard* for 111 weeks, thereby eclipsing any other Elvis record.

95. By the time *Clambake* went into production, Elvis's weight was already beginning to cause problems. On the first day of filming, he slipped, suffered a concussion, and was put out of action for several weeks, delaying filming in the process.

96. In reviewing *Love Me Tender*, *Time* magazine asked of Presley, 'Is it a sausage? It certainly is smooth and damp looking, but whoever heard of a 172-lb. sausage, six feet tall? Is it a Walt Disney Goldfish? It has the same sort of big, soft beautiful eyes and long curly lashes, but whoever heard of a goldfish with sideburns? Is it a corpse? The face just hangs there limp and white with its little drop-seat mouth, rather like Lord Byron in the wax museum.' With like enthusiasm *Films in Review* wrote of *Love Me Tender*, 'Presley is a pied piper who could lead his followers to an end more socially deleterious than their permanent disappearance in a cave.'

97. Millie Perkins must have slapped Elvis a little too hard during a scene from *Wild in the Country* – she broke her wrist!

98. The last major film role offered to Presley was opposite Barbra Streisand in *A Star is Born* (1976). Unfortunately, as a result of Elvis's manager, Colonel Tom Parker, arguing over who got top bill, in addition to his exorbitant demands regarding Elvis's salary, the part ultimately went to Kris Kristofferson.

99. Stanley Kramer wanted Elvis to co-star as a convict with Sidney Poitier in the Academy-Award-winning 1958 movie, *The Defiant Ones*. However, Tom Parker turned down the part on account of its racial prejudice and because Kramer wouldn't allow Presley to sing. The part went to one of Elvis's favourite actors, Tony Curtis.

100. Two other major movie roles were turned downed by Colonel Parker, owing to his not accepting second billing for Elvis. One was the Oscar-winning 1961 movie, *West Side Story*, playing opposite Natalie Wood. Elvis's role went to George Chakiris, who went on to win an Oscar for Best Supporting Actor, for his performance in the movie. Previously, Elvis was approached to star alongside Elizabeth Taylor in the 1958 Tennessee Williams film, *Cat on a Hot Tin Roof*; the part eventually went to Paul Newman.

Whole Lot of Actin' Goin' on!

The complete list of movies featuring Elvis Aron Presley

★ **Love Me Tender** (1956);
with Elvis as Clint Reno

★ **Loving You** (1957);
with Elvis as Jimmy Tompkins

★ **Jailhouse Rock** (1957);
with Elvis as Vince Everett

★ **King Creole** (1958);
with Elvis as Danny Fisher

★ **G.I. Blues** (1960);
with Elvis as Tulsa McLean

★ **Flaming Star** (1960);
with Elvis as Pacer Burton

★ **Wild in the Country** (1961);
with Elvis as Glenn Tyler

★ **Blue Hawaii** (1961);
with Elvis as Chad Gates

★ **Follow That Dream** (1962);
with Elvis as Toby Kwimper

★ **Kid Galahad** (1962);
with Elvis as Walter Gulick

★ **Girls! Girls! Girls!** (1962);
with Elvis as Ross Carpenter

★ **It Happened at the World's Fair** (1963);
with Elvis as Mike Edwards

★ **Fun in Acapulco** (1963);
with Elvis as Mike Windgren

★ **Kissin' Cousins** (1964);
with Elvis as Josh Morgan and Jodie Tatum

★ **Viva Las Vegas** (1964);
with Elvis as Lucky Jackson

★ **Roustabout** (1964);
with Elvis as Charlie Rogers

★ **Girl Happy** (1965);
with Elvis as Rusty Wells

★ **Tickle Me** (1965);
with Elvis as Lonnie Beale

★ **Harum Scarum** (1965);
with Elvis as Johnny Tyronne

★ **Frankie and Johnny** (1966);
with Elvis as Johnny

★ **Paradise, Hawaiian Style** (1966);
with Elvis as Greg (Rick) Richards

★ **Spinout** (1966);
with Elvis as Mike McCoy

★ **Easy Come, Easy Go** (1967);
with Elvis as Ted Jackson

★ **Double Trouble** (1967);
with Elvis as Guy Lambert

★ **Clambake** (1967);
with Elvis as Scott Hayward

★ **Stay Away, Joe** (1968);
with Elvis as Joe Lightcloud

★ **Speedway** (1968);
with Elvis as Steve Grayson

★ **Live a Little, Love a Little** (1968);
with Elvis as Greg Nolan

★ **Charro!** (1969);
with Elvis as Jess Wade

★ **The Trouble with Girls** (1969);
with Elvis as Walter Hale

★ **Change of Habit** (1969);
with Elvis as Dr John Carpenter

★ **Elvis – That's the Way It Is** (1970)
(Documentary)

★ **Elvis on Tour** (1972)
(Documentary)

Biographical Films

★ **Elvis** (1979);
with Kurt Russell as Elvis

★ **Elvis and the Beauty Queen** (1981);
with Don Johnson as Elvis

★ **This is Elvis** (1981);
with Paul Boensh III, David Scott,
Dana Mackay and Johnny Harra, as Elvis

★ **Elvis and Me** (1988);
with Dale Midkiff as Elvis

Presley's Pick of the Pops: the Man, the Movies, the Hits

(Highest chart position indicated in brackets)

★ **Love Me Tender** (1956)
'Love Me Tender' (11)

★ **Loving You** (1957)
'(Let's Have A) Party' (2); '(Let Me Be Your)
Teddy Bear' (3); 'Got A Lot O' Livin' To
Do' (17); 'Loving You' (24)

★ **Jailhouse Rock** (1957)
'Jailhouse Rock' (1)

★ **King Creole** (1958)
'King Creole' (2); 'Hard Headed Woman' (2)

★ **G.I. Blues** (1960)
'Wooden Heart' (1); the film also features
Presley's version of 'Blue Suede Shoes',
which is played on a jukebox in the
Rathskeller Club by a disgruntled customer

★ **Flaming Star** (1960)
No hit singles

★ **Wild in the Country** (1961)
'Wild In The Country' (4)

★ **Blue Hawaii** (1961)
'Rock-A-Hula Baby'/'Can't Help Falling
In Love' (1) (as a double-A-sided single)

★ **Follow That Dream** (1962)
EP containing songs, including the title track,
from the movie reached number 34

★ **Kid Galahad** (1962)
No hit singles

★ **Girls! Girls! Girls!** (1962)
'Return To Sender' (1)

★ **It Happened at the World's Fair** (1963)
'One Broken Heart For Sale' (12)

★ **Fun in Acapulco** (1963)
'Bossa Nova Baby' (13)

★ **Kissin' Cousins** (1964)
'Kissin' Cousins' (10)

★ **Viva Las Vegas** (1964)
'Viva Las Vegas' (17)

★ **Roustabout** (1964)
No hit singles

★ **Girl Happy** (1965)
'Do The Clam' (19)

★ **Tickle Me** (1965)
No hit singles

★ **Harum Scarum** (1965)
No hit singles

★ **Frankie and Johnny** (1966)
'Frankie And Johnny' (21)

★ **Paradise Hawaiian Style** (1966)
No hit singles

★ **Spinout** (1966)
'All That I Am' (18)

★ **Easy Come Easy Go** (1967)
'You Gotta Stop'/'Love Machine' (38)

★ **Double Trouble** (1967)
'Long Legged Girl (With The Short
Dress On)' (49)

★ **Clambake** (1967)
No hit singles

★ **Stay Away Joe** (1968)
No hit singles

★ **Speedway** (1968)
'Your Time Hasn't Come Yet Baby' (22)

★ **Live a Little, Love a Little** (1968)
No hit singles

★ **Charro!** (1969)
No hit singles

★ **The Trouble with Girls** (1969)
'Clean Up Your Own Backyard' (22)

★ **Change of Habit** (1969)
no hit singles

The subsequent features, *Elvis –
That's the Way It Is* (1970) and *Elvis on
Tour* (1972), were documentaries, and as such,
while featuring many of Elvis's earlier hits,
did not feature any new releases.

Chapter 21
The Empire Strikes
Back

STAR WARS (1977)

Ask yourself this: what kind of movie book would this be if we didn't include some reference to the phenomenon of *Star Wars*? An incomplete one! we hear you cry. At a time when the prayers of moviegoers the world over have been answered by the release of *Episode 1: The Phantom Menace* (1999), we felt that it was only fair to devote a few pages solely to *Star Wars*. So, beginning in a galaxy far, far away and ending somewhere near Wantage, we've collated a selection of the most tantalising trivia for your satisfaction.

50 Star Wars Facts

1. As *Star Wars* premiered in Hollywood, in May of 1977, George Lucas and his wife sat eating in a restaurant near the cinema; they observed a lane of traffic being closed, limousines being parked outside the theatre, dozens of police in attendance, and long queues of people going both ways around the block. To their amazement, they realised that it was all because of his film, the now legendary *Star Wars*.

2. *Star Wars* achieved an opening-day figure of $254,309 in only thirty-two cinemas.

3. The original script title for *Star Wars* was *The Adventures of Luke Skywalker as Taken from the Journal of the Whills: Saga One: The Star Wars*.

4. *Star Wars* entered into production with a budget of only $3.5 million. Its final cost was more than $10 million, a considerable sum at the time.

5. *Star Wars* was turned down as a marketable concept by both Universal Studios (who had first option, having already distributed Lucas's previous film, the successful *American Graffiti*) and United Artists, before being given the go-ahead at Twentieth Century Fox, by the studio's development executive, Alan Ladd Jr.

6. In the original script for *Star Wars*, Ben Kenobi isn't killed by Vader. Instead, the light-sabre duel finishes with Kenobi hitting a door, which slams shut, thereby allowing Kenobi and the others to run to safety. However, during filming Lucas felt that the script was weak and, at the suggestion of his wife Marcia, he rewrote the script, incorporating the death of Kenobi at the hands of Vader.

7. Mark Hamill made his acting debut on TV's *The Bill Cosby Show* in 1970.

8. It is claimed that the plot of *Star Wars* closely mirrors that of *The Hidden Fortress* (*Kakushi Toride No San Akunin*), by the legendary Japanese director Akira Kurosawa. The plot of *The Hidden Fortress* concerns the journey of a deposed princess, accompanied by a general, away from the hidden fortress of her father, into a friendly province wherein lies the family treasure. The princess is also aided in her escape by two soldiers, named Tahei and Matashichi.

9. The characters of R2D2 and C3PO are inspired by the work of JRR Tolkien and Akira Kurosawa – in particular the characters of Samwise Gamgee and Pippin Took, as featured in Tolkien's *The Lord of the Rings* – and the characters of Tahei and Matashichi by those from Kurosawa's *The Hidden Fortress* (*Kakushi Toride No San Akunin*).

10. Han Solo was originally intended to be a large green-skinned smuggler.

11. Right up to the moment filming made it a necessity, Luke's full name was in doubt – Luke Starkiller or Luke Skywalker. Lucas finally decided upon Skywalker the day before filming.

12. The following literary works all had an influence upon the evolution of the *Star Wars* storyline: *The Narnia Chronicles* by CS Lewis; *The Hobbit* and *The Lord of the Rings*, both by JRR Tolkien; *The Golden Bough* by Frazer; and *The Hero with a Thousand Faces* by Joseph Campbell.

13. The name 'Wookie' is the inspired creation of the Californian DJ Terry McGovern. McGovern apparently improvised the word while doing voiceovers for Lucas's *THX-1138*. Lucas picked up on the term, and the rest, as they say, is history.

14. Jodie Foster was considered for the role of Princess Leia; however, she was rejected because of her age: she was only thirteen at the time.

15. Robert Englund, prior to becoming *A Nightmare on Elm Street's* Freddy Krueger, tested for the role of Luke Skywalker; although he failed to win the part, he subsequently persuaded a young friend and successful television actor, named Mark Hamill, to try for it.

16. Koo Stark holds the unfortunate honour of never having made it past the cutting room floor. Her contribution to *Star Wars*, a night out on the town with Luke Skywalker, was cut following a disastrous reception by the film company's executive Alan Ladd Jr.

17. Peter Mayhew, the man behind Chewbacca, is seven foot two tall; David Prowse, the man behind Darth Vader, is six foot seven; both in stark contrast to Kenny Baker, the man inside R2D2, who is only three foot eight.

18. The principal actors of *Star Wars*, Sir Alec Guinness aside, all agreed to work for the very modest fee of $1,000 per week.

19. Carrie Fisher, as Princess Leia, had to have her breasts taped down during filming so as to avoid unwanted uplift; apparently she was prohibited from wearing a bra since there are none in space.

20. The voice of Greedo was supplied by an expert in linguistics from Berkeley University named Larry Ward, who utilised the no-longer-practised Inca tongue of Quechua.

21. During the final stages of filming *Star Wars* Mark Hamill was involved in a serious car accident. He suffered injuries to his face and had to have his nose rebuilt using cartilage from his ear.

22. The vocals of Chewbacca were the result of a sound mix of the voices of various animals, including a walrus, a seal, a badger and four different types of bear.

23. In order to create the sound effects of R2D2, the following items were called into use:

dry ice, bits of metal and, finally, a length of piping.

24. A swordsmith, Bob Anderson, substituted for David Prowse, as Darth Vader, during the light-sabre duels.

25. A specially trained, and suitably attired, elephant was used to create the Banthas.

26. David Prowse was nicknamed 'Darth Farmer' by Carrie Fisher, as a result of his broad West Country accent. Consequently, James Earl Jones was enlisted to provide a suitably more sinister voice.

27. The introduction to the *Star Wars* story, which begins with the words, 'It is a period of civil war ...', was rewritten, from George Lucas's version, by Brian De Palma and Jay Cocks.

28. The scene in *The Empire Strikes Back*, where a monster shoots out of a swamp, attempting to grab R2D2, was actually filmed in George Lucas's half-finished swimming pool, in his new San Rafael home. The pool was filled with muddy water and George shot the footage personally.

THE EMPIRE STRIKES BACK (1980)

29. The veteran writer Leigh Brackett, responsible for such movie classics as *El Dorado* (1967) and *The Long Goodbye* (1973), was hired to write the first draft of *The Empire Strikes Back*, based on Lucas's original story, but died of cancer halfway through the project. Lawrence Kasden, who had worked with Lucas and Steven Spielberg

on *Raiders of the Lost Ark*, was brought in to finish the project.

30. The Ice Planet Hoth scenes, of *The Empire Strikes Back*, were filmed on a Norwegian glacier over a period of ten days.

31. During the Hoth battle scenes of *The Empire Strikes Back*, members of the Norwegian Red Cross Mountain Rescue team played the parts of both Rebel and Imperial forces. Their knowledge of local climatic conditions proved invaluable on account of Norway's subzero temperatures.

32. Sixty-four different sets, on seven stages, were used for *The Empire Strikes Back*.

33. Frank Oz, creator and voice of Miss Piggy, as featured in TV's *The Muppets*, operated Yoda in *The Empire Strikes Back*.

34. To give the puppet of Yoda lifelike facial movements, concealed wires were attached to its lips, tongue, cheeks, ears, eyeballs and eyelids, which were then operated by Oz and his team of puppeteers. It took about four hours to film two lines of dialogue.

35. Richard Marquand, the British director of *Return of the Jedi*, previously worked on the successful 1971 BBC 2 drama series, *The Search for the Nile*, which starred Norman Rossington (who died in May 1999) and Kenneth Haigh. He later went on to direct the 1985 hit movie, *Jagged Edge*, which starred Jeff Bridges and Glenn Close. In 1987, at the age of 49, he died of a heart attack following a stroke.

36. During the making of *The Empire Strikes Back*, Mark Hamill sprained his thumb, filming the scene of him falling from the antenna beneath Cloud City. Consequently one week of filming was lost.

37. Harrison Ford wanted to kill off his character, Han Solo, in *Return of the Jedi*, as he believed that he was no longer involved in the story; George Lucas refused on the grounds that it would be too depressing for his upbeat movie.

38. Kenny Baker, who played R2D2 in the trilogy, can also be seen (though, as before, in costume) playing the Ewok that becomes infatuated with Princess Leia.

39. When filming of *Return of the Jedi* moved to America, Lucas, eager to prevent the plot being leaked in advance of the film's release, attempted to conceal the cast and crew's activities by assigning them to a supposedly forthcoming horror film, *Blue Harvest*.

40. *Return of the Jedi* was released in America on 28 May 1983, exactly six years to the day after *Star Wars*.

41. *Episode 1: The Phantom Menace* was shot over a 65-day period on sound stages in Leavesden, England, and on location in Caserta, Italy, and near Tozeur, Tunisia.

42. In playing the part of Jar Jar Binks in *Episode 1: The Phantom Menace*, Ahmed Best had to endure temperatures of 154 degrees while wearing the character's outfit, made from foam-latex and plastic.

43. Ewan McGregor, who plays the young Obi-Wan Kenobi in *Episode 1*, is not the first of his family to appear in film from the *Star Wars* series. His uncle, Denis Lawson, appeared in the original *Star Wars*, as the Rebel pilot Wedge Antilles.

44. The veteran actor and persistent mountaineer Brian Blessed provides the voice of Boss Nass, leader of the Gunguns.

45. The name of the character Newt Gunray is apparently derived from the names of the former US President Ronald Reagan and former Speaker of the House Newt Gingrich.

46. On 29 July 1997, during the filming of Tatooine sets for *Episode 1: The Phantom Menace*, history repeated itself when a sandstorm struck the camp, scattering equipment and props. Nature had similarly affected the filming of *Star Wars* back in 1976. George Lucas remained undaunted, though, and even considered the storm a good omen!

47. George Lucas cut his fee for directing *Star Wars* by $500,000 in return for rights to the sequels and all merchandising.

48. Merchandise associated with *Star Wars* has generated approximately $4.5 billion in sales since the film's release in 1977.

49. George Lucas owns a 4,700-acre estate, known as 'Skywalker Ranch', situated in Nacisio, California. The *Star Wars* creator's home has a full-time staff of 35, including its own fire brigade.

50. Beneath the foundations of Skywalker Ranch lies a time capsule, placed there in 1981, containing various items of *Star Wars* memorabilia as well as the letter from his then attorney confirming the go-ahead on *Star Wars*.

The Special Editions: an Itemised Account

Star Wars

At 125 minutes long, the Special Edition of *Star Wars* is four minutes longer than the original 1977 release. So just what did George Lucas do with roughly $10 million?

Well, below, we detail where the money went, with our listing of the major changes.

1. The Dewbacks (lizard-like creatures) that roam the desert of Tatooine have been enhanced by the use of new Industrial Light and Magic effects. Previously, puppets stood motionless on the horizon; now the creatures move about on all fours.

2. The background scenes used in the Tatooine sequences have been improved by the use of new matte paintings, to provide greater depth and realism.

3. The shots of Luke's landspeeder have been digitally enhanced so as to strengthen the illusion that the speeder is in fact gliding several feet above the ground. Previously Lucas had smeared the lens of the camera with Vaseline in order to blur the distinction between the speeder and the ground.

4. Much has been added to the scenes in and around Mos Eisley Spaceport. Making full use of digital effects, additional footage of actors, robots and other creatures has now been intercut with detailed overhead shots. Consequenty Mos Eisley now has the feel of a bustling spaceport and Lucas finally has his 'wretched hive of scum and villainry'.

5. Han Solo's meeting with Greedo at Mos Eisley has been changed. We now see Greedo fire at Han first, rather than the other way round. Han, of course, returns fire, but now only in self-defence and not murder.

6. Jabba returns! Technological limitations behind him, Lucas has been able to insert the Jabba of *Return of the Jedi* into *Star Wars*, thereby enabling the meeting between Han Solo and Jabba the Hut. So as to enhance the illusion further, Lucas even has Solo step on the tail of Jabba, as he is walking around him.

7. The destruction of Alderaan, Princess Leia's home planet, has been digitally enhanced.

8. Seeing double! During the scene where Han Solo chases several stormtroopers in the Death Star, following them, as they turn into a corridor, we now see Solo literally run straight into a waiting battalion of stormtroopers, many times the number featured in the original release. The comic effect is, of course, increased similarly.

9. The meeting between Luke and Biggs on Yavin, home of the Rebel base, has been expanded so as to allow the two greater time to reminisce about the good old days on Tatooine.

10. Footage of the Rebel ship take-off from Yavin has been enhanced by the inclusion of more highly detailed effects.

11. The Rebel attack on the Death Star, and resultant dog-fight with the TIE fighters, has been improved considerably. Craft are now seen moving past the camera in all dimensions and consequently the battle is far more convincing.

12. The Death Star's explosion has been enhanced.

13. The presentation ceremony that ends *Star Wars* now includes additional actors, inserted digitally. Previously, matte paintings made up the bulk of those standing to the left- and right-hand sides of the screen.

14. James Earl Jones, the voice behind the man behind the mask of Darth Vader, finally gets credit where credit's due. Previously only *Return of the Jedi* mentioned his contribution to the trilogy.

The Empire Strikes Back

At 127 minutes long, the Special Edition of *The Empire Strikes Back* has an additional three minutes added.

1. The Special Edition features more footage of the Wampa, both feeding in its cave and as it attacks Luke. Previously only a brief shot of a glove puppet was used.

2. The battle scenes on Hoth have been digitally improved, in particular the blending in of the matte paintings, for example the view from within the snowspeeders. The shots of the Rebels leaving Hoth, and of the *Falcon* escaping from the Star Destroyer, have also been enhanced, by the insertion of computer-generated effects.

3. Additional shots of the *Millennium Falcon* arriving at the Cloud City of Bespin, complete with accompanying music by John Williams, have been added.

4. Digitally created backdrops and new matte scenes have been added throughout the footage of Bespin, so as to create a more breathtaking and dramatic sense of location, as would befit a city in the clouds.

5. The general populace of Bespin are shown listening to Lando, as he warns them that the city has been taken over by the Empire.

6. The shot of Luke falling down a ventilation shaft, following Vader's admittance that he is indeed Luke's father, is now accompanied by a scream. Previously Luke had fallen in silence.

7. The scene of Luke hanging from an antenna attached to Cloud City has been intercut with footage of Vader walking to his shuttle and subsequently landing in an Imperial Star Destroyer.

8. Credit, as with *Star Wars*, is once more rightfully given to James Earl Jones.

Return of the Jedi

At 135 minutes long, the Special Edition includes an additional four minutes of film.

1. *Return of the Jedi* now features a particularly jazzed-up musical number, 'Jedi Rocks', in place of 'Lapti Nek'. The band, too, has benefited from technological advances: not only have its members increased but gone are the puppeteer's wires, which once constrained the movements of the singer, Sy Snootles. Revelling in his new-found freedom, Snootles even performs a duet with a Yazim.

2. The shot of a girl inside the rancour pit has been inserted just as the band's performance draws to a close.

3. A scene-setting shot of the Tatooine desert, complete with a herd of Bantha, has been inserted.

4. Extra tentacles and a beak have been digitally added to the Sarlacc pit creature.

5. The ending of *Jedi* now features the following additions: a new composition, entitled 'Victory Celebration' by John Williams; footage of people the galaxy over celebrating the end of the Empire: and finally the shots of Obi-Wan, Yoda and the now saved Anakin Skywalker.

Chapter 22
Postcards from
the Edge

SAVING PRIVATE RYAN (1998)

Location Landmarks

So That's Where They Shot It!

Whether it be a matter of money, weather or whatever, movies often aren't filmed where you might think. Want to know more? Well, read on!

★ An American Werewolf in London (1981)

One of the most memorable scenes occurs when the two American backpackers, played by David Naughton and Griffin Dunne, decide to seek food and shelter in the Slaughtered Lamb public house. Their reception is far from hospitable and soon the boys find themselves back out on the moors.

If you have ever tried to find the Slaughtered Lamb in Yorkshire then you will have been disappointed. It's in Surrey! Equally confusing perhaps is that the pub is actually called the Black Swan and it is in Effingham, near Leatherhead. Don't worry: you won't find any werewolves there, just stockbrokers!

As for the moors, well, two locations were used: Windsor Great Park for the close shots, and the Brecon Beacons in Wales for the wider shots.

★ Batman (1989)

The director Tim Burton's interpretation of the *Batman* story was shot almost entirely at London's Pinewood Studios, using the giant sound stages to create Burton's apocalyptic vision of Gotham. However, for Wayne Manor, home of Bruce Wayne and his alter ego Batman, a combination of two English stately homes was used: Knebworth House for the exterior shots, and Hatfield House for the interior shots.

★ Braveheart (1995)

The screen depiction of William Wallace's attempts to liberate Scotland from the English was for the most part shot in Ireland, as a result of tax incentives, an abundance of suitable castles and the provision of regular soldiers as extras.

Dunsoghly Castle near Dublin was used to represent Edinburgh Castle; apparently, the film makers believed that most people wouldn't spot the difference. However, for scenes of York and London, only one castle was used, Trim Castle, approximately 25 miles northwest of Dublin. One side of the castle was used for scenes of York, the other for scenes of London. The battle of Stirling Bridge was filmed at the Curragh Plains, in County Kildare, while the Battle of Falkirk was filmed at nearby Ballymore Eustace.

★ The Bridges of Madison County (1995)

The actual bridges, as featured in the film, are to be found at Winterset, Iowa – as is the house of Francesca, which, prior to restoration, was an abandoned 1800s homestead.

★ Chaplin (1992)

Richard Attenborough's biopic of the Hollywood legend charts the life of Chaplin from his impoverished childhood in London's East End through his exile in Switzerland to his eventual return to Hollywood, to collect a special Academy Award, in 1972.

However, Attenborough, owing to the irreversible passage of time and resultant change in architecture, decided not to film in the East End; instead, he chose to create the East End of Chaplin's time in Cheney Road, situated just behind London's King's Cross Station. To complete the transformation, the set designers added 'additional' houses to the scene.

London's St Pancras chambers, situated only minutes from King's Cross Station, also feature in the film. Attenborough uses the red-bricked building and former railway hotel to stand in for London's Cane Hill Asylum, to which Chaplin has his mother committed.

★ Dirty Dancing (1987)

If you've ever fancied a bit of 'dirty dancing' then you'd better get yourself up to the resort of Mountain Lake in Virginia. There, approximately an hour west of Roanoke, you'll find the Mountain Lake Hotel, which was transformed into the Catskills resort for the duration of filming. Just for the record, Patrick Swayze stayed in Room 232; Jennifer Grey and her family stayed in the Virginia cottage.

★ Field of Dreams (1989)

'If you build it, he will come' – or so a heavenly voice tells the farmer Ray Kinsella (Kevin Costner) as he stands in the middle of his Iowa cornfield. Sure enough, Kevin the farmer takes the advice of his spiritual mentor, and builds a baseball diamond in the middle of his cornfield. And come *they* did: apparently, 10,000 people visited the empty field, just outside of Dyersville, Iowa, the summer after the release of the film! Since then some 40,000 people have visited the site each year; some get married there; one man even had his ashes scattered there.

★ First Knight (1995)

In order to create their Camelot, the film makers went to North Wales, more specifically, Trawsfynydd Lake near Ffestiniog. The location proved perfect for their needs, in particular the road previously built as a link to the nearby power station, which meant that the script's requirement that Camelot be approached from across water could be adhered to.

★ Full Metal Jacket (1987)

Stanley Kubrick's study of the Vietnam war, and the personal transformations that it generates, brings to mind bleak and harrowing images: images of death, killing and gasworks. Yes, gasworks!

The film was actually shot on the north bank of the Thames, at the derelict Beckton Gas Works, hundreds of miles from Vietnam.

In order to add the finishing touches to his battle-scarred landscape, Kubrick undertook extensive remodelling of the 300-acre site, blowing up the already crumbling buildings and planting palm trees.

★ The Last of the Mohicans (1992)

Chimney Rock National Park in North Carolina, with its stunning views of the Blue Ridge Mountains, provided a most suitable location for the filming of James Fenimore Cooper's classic tale of adventure. Memorable scenes were filmed at Hickory Nut Falls, Inspiration Point (5,000 feet) and Groundhog Slide.

Notting Hill (1999)

Surprisingly enough, a film that for once was filmed in and around the area referred to in its title, that of *Notting Hill*, West London, in particular Portobello Road. Sights that feature in the film include the Warwick Castle public house, the interior of the Coronet cinema, Base Cuts (a hairdresser's), Saints Tattoo Parlour and several shots of market stalls on Portobello Road.

The film used hundreds of local residents as extras, and the author of Notting Hill, Richard Curtis, is himself a local resident; his blue front door features heavily in the film. However, Curtis, not one to miss a trick, put the house on the market shortly before the film's release, with a local estate agent, making the movie possibly the last word in product placement. Oh, and the asking price, a cool £1.3 million!

★ 1984 (1984)

Michael Radford's adaptation of George Orwell's political commentary upon the implications of totalitarianism was filmed in Wiltshire aside from one crucial location: that used to represent 'Victory Square'. The film makers needed to find a location that they could not only dress convincingly but also close to traffic and accommodate several thousand extras. They found their answer in the burnt-out remains of North London's Alexandra Palace. Gutted by fire in 1980, the former exhibition hall was little more than four walls at the time of filming. Consequently, it was a more than suitable site for 'Victory Square'.

★ Octopussy (1983)

Of all the Bond films, *Octopussy*, Bond's thirteenth outing, features some of the most memorable locations, in particular the white marble palace belonging to Octopussy herself. In reality the film makers used the palace on Lake Pichola, built in the eighteenth century, by the Maharana of Udaipur. The palace has since become the luxury Lake Palace Hotel.

The scenes of the US Air Force base at Feldstadt in West Germany were actually filmed at RAF Upper Heyford in Oxfordshire, while the sequence showing Octopussy's train involved turning the Nene Valley Railway in Cambridgeshire into the east–west border of Germany.

★ Oklahoma! (1955)

Any guesses where *Oklahoma!* was filmed? Well it wasn't Oklahoma! The film makers shot the musical in Arizona. Apparently, location scouts recommended Arizona because of its perfect weather – plenty of sunshine and no rain. Oklahoma, on the other hand, got the thumbs down, on account of the countless oil derricks and buzzing aeroplanes overhead, which would have inevitably interfered with filming. At least they had good old dependable Arizona, where it rained relentlessly!

★ Patriot Games (1992)

If you've seen this film, you may be wondering just how they got to shoot the scene where the IRA terrorists attack the car of the Queen's cousin at Buckingham Palace. Well, they didn't. The film makers used the Royal Naval College at Dartmouth as a stand-in. The college is also used to represent the naval college, where the

ex-CIA analyst Jack Ryan, played by Harrison Ford, gives his lecture.

★ Reds (1981)

Produced, directed, co-written by and starring Warren Beatty, this three-hour epic chronicles the romance of a journalist, John Reed, with a feminist, Louise Bryant, in the years before and after the Russian Revolution, both in the Soviet Union and the United States.

Filming took place in the United States, Spain, Finland and England. However, in order to keep costs at a minimum, and with the production based at Twickenham Studios, it made sense to film as many scenes as possible in England.

As a result many of the interior shots were filmed there, in particular the capital. Consequently, Lancaster House stood in for the interior of St Petersburg's Winter Palace (the exterior shots of the palace were filmed in Finland); while the Zion Institute in Hulme, Manchester, stood in for Chicago's Town Hall.

★ Revolution (1985)

The director Hugh Hudson's historical drama, set during the American Revolution and starring Al Pacino, was actually filmed in England.

For scenes of New York the Norfolk port of King's Lynn was used. The area around the port's seventeenth-century Custom House doubling for New York harbour. The battle scene was shot southeast of Plymouth, with scenes of the British camp being filmed at Barrator Reservoir near Dartmoor, and the American camp at Thetford, in Norfolk.

★ Saving Private Ryan (1998)

The Normandy landings were filmed on a remote beach in Ireland's County Wexford. It had been intended to film entirely in England, but the MOD in their wisdom were unwilling to aid the director Steven Spielberg, who had asked for the provision of 1,000 soldiers as extras.

★ The Shining (1980)

This exploration of madness by the writer Jack Torrance (Jack Nicholson) at the isolated Overlook Hotel in Colorado was actually filmed at the Timberline Lodge, Mount Hood National Forest, in Oregon. Family holiday anyone? Well, book early to avoid disappointment!

★ Star Wars (1977)

George Lucas took cast and crew to Chott el-Djerid, a dry salt-lake bed in the Saharan desert land of Tunisia. Here he built his Tatooine and the setting of Luke Skywalker's uncle's farm. The interior of the homestead was shot deep within the hotel Sidi Driss, in the town of Matmata.

The scenes of Luke skimming above the ground in his landspeeder were filmed back in the States, at Death Valley. The scenes had previously been shot in Tunisia but had to be reshot because the supports, wheels and tracks of the landspeeder had been caught on film.

★ Superman IV (1987)

If you had to pick one place in England to represent the fictional city of Metropolis, where would it be? Milton Keynes in Buckinghamshire, perhaps? Well, that's where it was filmed – the close-up shots anyway. The long shots were filmed in North America.

★ Wuthering Heights (1939)

In order to film Emily Brontë's haunting tale of love and tragedy, one thing stood in the film makers' way: the Yorkshire Moors, or rather the lack of the Yorkshire Moors in Hollywood, where the film was being made. Never ones to let the small matter of geography stand in their way, they built their own moors, about fifty miles from Hollywood.

With the use of a 540-acre tract in the Canejo Hills, the moors of Yorkshire were replicated. First, the land was cleared of the native wild lilac and greasewood, and in their place were planted 14,000 tumbleweeds, collected by schoolchildren at a rate of pay of one cent each. The weeds were individually anchored to the ground and sawdust, which had been dyed purple, was sprinkled everywhere so as to resemble heather when filmed from a distance.

For the close-up shots, 1,000 heather plants were bought; however, as a result of a trade embargo, the plants could not be transported across the state line until they were fumigated and debugged, and the seed pods were sterilised. Final bill: $100,000.

Chapter 23
Hook

Witty and Not So Witty Ways to Make You Want to See Their Movies

The tagline – or tag as it is known – is that oh so witty line that appears on movie posters. It is the movie's catchphrase, the bait with which to hook us, tempt us, make us want to go and see the movie!

Though often dull and unimaginative, they can also be funny, scary or just plain stupid. Below we offer one hundred and fifty of our favourite tags.

1. On the air. Unaware. – *The Truman Show* (1998)

2. Man is the warmest place to hide. – *The Thing* (1982)

3. Think fast. Look alive. Die hard. – *Die Hard with a Vengeance* (1995)

4. Make Your Last Breath Count. – *Scream* (1996)

5. For God's sake, get out of that house! – *The Amityville Horror* (1979)

6 Stealing, Cheating, Killing. Who said romance is dead? – *True Romance* (1993)

7. A long time ago in a galaxy far, far away ... – *Star Wars* (1977)

8. Kiss me and I'll claw you to death. – *The Cat People* (1942)

9. You'll Believe a Man Can Fly! – *Superman* (1978)

10. It knows what scares you. – *Poltergeist* (1982)

11. Nothing on Earth could come between them. – *Titanic* (1997)

12. Something has survived. – *The Lost World: Jurassic Park* (1997)

13. Love means never having to say you're sorry. – *Love Story* (1970)

14. What if someone you never met, someone you never saw, someone you never knew was the only someone for you? – *Sleepless in Seattle* (1993)

15. From the brother of the director of *Ghost*. – *Naked Gun 33⅓: The Final Insult*

16. Good morning. You are one day closer to the end of the world. You have been warned. *The Omen* (1976)

17. Just ring for doom service! – *Horror Hotel* a.k.a. *City of the Dead* (1960)

18. It will tear your soul apart. – *Hellraiser* (1987)

19. You'll laugh. You'll cry. You'll hurl. – *Wayne's World* (1992)

20. You'll be sick, sick, sick – from laughing! – *A Bucket of Blood* (1959)

21. Let's go to work. – *Reservoir Dogs* (1992)

22. Hang on! – *Cliffhanger* (1993)

23. Power can be murder to resist. – *The Firm* (1993)

24. In space no one can hear you scream. – *Alien* (1979)

25. They're young ... they're in love ... and they kill people. – *Bonnie and Clyde* (1967)

26. What's slower than a speeding bullet, and able to hit tall buildings at a single bound? – *Airplane* (1980)

27. Get ready for rush hour. – *Speed* (1994)

28. On every street in every city, there's a nobody who dreams of being a somebody. – *Taxi Driver* – (1976)

43. Check in. Relax. Take a shower. – *Psycho* (1998)

29. Introducing the plans for a new business venture. – *The Italian Job* (1969)

30. They lost half a million at cards but they've still got a few tricks up their sleeve. – *Lock, Stock & Two Smoking Barrels* (1998)

31. Herbert West has a very good head on his shoulders – and another one in his desk. – *Re-Animator* (1985)

32. Love Never Dies. – *Dracula* (1992)

33. Size Does Matter. – *Godzilla* (1998)

34. Lock your doors. Bolt your windows. There's something in THE FOG! – *The Fog* (1980)

35. Flesh seduces. Passion kills. – *Basic Instinct* (1992)

36. What happened is true.
Now the motion picture that's just as real. – *The Texas Chainsaw Massacre* (1974)

37. The story of a homosexual who married a nymphomaniac. – *The Music Lovers* (1971)

38. Sex is power. – *Disclosure* (1994)

39. Be afraid. Be very afraid. – *The Fly* (1986)

40. What went down on the way to the top. – *Primary Colors* (1998)

41. A comedy about sex, murder and seafood. – *A Fish Called Wanda* (1988)

42. Someone knows their secret, someone knows they're scared, and someone knows what they did last summer. – *I Know What You Did Last Summer* (1997)

44. You'll never close your eyes again. – *Invasion of the Body Snatchers* (1978)

45. Living with a roommate can be murder. – *Single White Female* (1992)

46. A murdered wife. A one-armed man. An obsessed detective. The chase begins. – *The Fugitive* (1993)

47. Protecting the earth from the scum of the universe. – *Men in Black* (1997)

48. Choose life. Choose a job. Choose a starter home. Choose dental insurance, leisure wear and matching luggage. Choose your future. But why would anyone want to do a thing like that? – *Trainspotting* (1996)

49. Whatever you do, don't stop for The Hitcher. – *The Hitcher* (1986)

50. The scream you hear may be your own! – *Play Misty for Me* (1971)

51. No More Mr. Nice Guy. – *Payback* (1999)

52. Believe Everything Except Your Eyes. – *Snake Eyes* (1998)

53. Somewhere … somehow … someone's going to pay! – *Commando* (1985)

54. You have nothing to lose but your mind. – *Asylum* (1972)

55. Seven deadly sins. Seven ways to die. Seven ways to kill. – *Seven* (1995)

56. Justice Is Coming. – *Tombstone* (1993)

57. It could happen to you. – *Breakdown* (1997)

58. The first casualty of war is innocence. – *Platoon* (1986)

59. An epic of miniature proportions. – *A Bug's Life* (1998)

60. Life gets complicated when you love one woman and worship eleven men. – *Fever Pitch* (1997)

61. … an army of one. – *The Outlaw Josey Wales* (1976)

62. No one thought she had the courage. The nerve. Or the lingerie. – *Shirley Valentine* (1989)

63. Sleep all day, party all night. It's fun to be a vampire. – *The Lost Boys* (1987)

64. Every man dies, not every man really lives. – *Braveheart* (1995)

65. Drink from me and live forever. – *Interview with the Vampire* (1994)

66. Somebody said get a life … so they did. – *Thelma and Louise* (1991)

67. When he pours, he reigns. – *Cocktail* (1988)

68. Women want him for his wit. The CIA wants him for his body. All Nick wants is his molecules back. – *Memoirs of an Invisible Man* (1992)

69. Nice planet. We'll take it! – *Mars Attacks!* (1996)

70. What do you get for the man who has everything? – *The Game* (1997)

71. It's the land of hospitality … unless you don't belong. – *Southern Comfort* (1981)

72. How do I loathe thee? Let me count the ways. – *10 Things I Hate About You* (1999)

73. Part man. Part machine. All cop. The future of law enforcement. – *RoboCop* (1987)

74. Weird is relative. – *The Addams Family* (1991)

75. He is afraid. He is alone. He is three million light years from home. – *E.T. – The Extra-Terrestrial* (1982)

76. It's Not Paranoia if They're Really After You. – *Enemy of the State* (1998)

77. Leave your inhibitions at the door. – *Showgirls* (1995)

78. All it takes is a little confidence! – *The Sting* (1973)

79. Things are about to get a little hairy. – *An American Werewolf in Paris* (1997)

80. Meet Joe Black: Sooner or later everyone does. – *Meet Joe Black* (1998)

81. Cocktails first. Questions later. – *Swingers* (1996)

82. When he said I do, he didn't say what he did. – *True Lies* (1994)

83. Never let her out of your sight. Never let your guard down. Never fall in love. – *The Bodyguard* (1992)

84. This is the weekend they didn't play golf. – *Deliverance* (1972)

85. If you love being scared, it'll be the night of your life. – *Fright Night* (1985)

86. To avoid fainting, keep repeating: It's only a movie ... it's only a movie ... – *The Last House on the Left* (1972)

87. Expect the impossible. – *Mission: Impossible* (1996)

88. Play Or Be Played. – *Existenz* (1999)

89. They'll never get caught. They're on a mission from God. – *The Blues Brothers* (1980)

90. Off the record, on the QT, and very hush-hush ... – *L.A. Confidential* (1997)

91. Every ant has his day. – *Antz* (1998)

92. Five criminals. One line-up. No coincidence. – *The Usual Suspects* (1995)

93. Just when you thought it was safe to go back into the water. – *Jaws 2* (1978)

94. Dare you say his name 5 times. – *Candyman* (1992)

95. Eight legs, two fangs and an attitude. – *Arachnophobia* (1990)

96. Fridays will never be the same again. – *Friday the 13th* (1980)

97. 10 Seconds: The pain begins. 15 Seconds: You can't breathe. 20 Seconds: You explode. – *Scanners* (1981)

98. And now! At last! Another film completely different from some of the other films which aren't quite the same as this one is. – *Monty Python and the Holy Grail* (1974)

99. One man's struggle to take it easy. – *Ferris Bueller's Day Off* (1986)

100. Fear can hold you prisoner. Hope can set you free. – *The Shawshank Redemption* (1994)

101. They had a date with fate in Casablanca! – *Casablanca* (1942)

102. Mothered by an ape – he knew only the law of the jungle – to seize what he wanted! – *Tarzan, the Ape Man* (1932)

103. He loved the American Dream. With a Vengeance. – *Scarface* (1983)

104. Is the price of stardom a broken heart? – *A Star is Born* (1934)

105. A story about a gal who lost her reputation – and never missed it! – *I'm No Angel* (1933)

106. If there was an Eleventh Commandment, they would have broken that too. – *The Postman Always Rings Twice* (1981)

107. The city under the city – *The Asphalt Jungle* (1950)

108. The bride gets the THRILLS! Father gets the BILLS! – *Father of the Bride* (1950)

109. The greatest adventure a man ever lived ... with a woman! – *The African Queen* (1951)

110. The story of a man who was too proud to run. – *High Noon* (1952)

111. What we've got here is failure to communicate. – *Cool Hand Luke* (1967)

112. You don't assign him to murder cases, you just turn him loose. – *Dirty Harry* (1971)

113. See Barbarella do her thing! – *Barbarella* (1967)

114. How fast must a man go to get from where he's at? – *Downhill Racer* (1969)

115. You just can't keep a good man down! – *Dracula Has Risen from the Grave* (1968)

116. The Ultimate Trip. – *2001: A Space Odyssey* (1968)

117. God created woman, but the Devil created Brigitte Bardot. – *And God Created Woman* (1957)

118. MASH gives a damn. – *M*A*S*H* (1970)

119. How would you like to tussle with Russel? – *The Outlaw* (1943)

120. Nobody's as good as Bette when she's bad. – *Beyond the Forest* (1949)

121. Vigilante, city style – Judge, Jury, and Executioner. – *Death Wish* (1974)

122. The motion picture with something to offend everyone! – *The Loved One* (1965)

123. Somewhere in the Universe, there must be something better than man! – *Planet of the Apes* (1968)

124. Unchanged men in a changing land. Out of step, out of place and desperately out of time. – *The Wild Bunch* (1969)

125. Garbo talks! – *Anna Christie* (1930)

126. Consider the possibilities. – *Bob & Carol & Ted & Alice* (1969)

127. If this doesn't make your skin crawl ... it's on too tight! – *Black Christmas* (1975)

128. Do you know what the most FRIGHTENING thing in the world is ...? – *Peeping Tom* (1959)

129. Nothing says goodbye like a bullet. – *The Long Goodbye* (1973)

130. The birds Is coming! – *The Birds* (1963)

131. One tiny spark becomes a night of blazing suspense. – *The Towering Inferno* (1974)

132. Some days business is good – and some days it's murder! – *The Big Sleep* (1978)

133. She's brown sugar and spice but if you don't treat her nice she'll put you on ice! – *Foxy Brown* (1974)

134. She was the woman of his dreams. She had large dark eyes, a beautiful smile and a great pair of fins. – *Splash!* (1984)

135. The Night HE Came Home. – *Halloween* (1978)

136. The only thing more terrifying than the last twelve minutes of this film is the first eighty! – *Suspiria* (1976)

137. Don't pronounce it – see it! – *Phffft* (1954)

138. His whole life was a million-to-one shot! – *Rocky* (1976)

139. Pray for Rosemary's baby! – *Rosemary's Baby* (1968)

140. Guaranteed not to make you think. – *Fighting American* (1924)

141. This movie will haunt your future ... because it's almost here! – *Rollerball* (1975)

142. Where there's smoke, there must be someone smoking! – *Easy Living* (1937)

143. If you've got a taste for terror ... take Carrie to the prom. – *Carrie* (1976)

144. You know the name. You know the number. – *GoldenEye* (1995)

145. You can't prepare for where the truth will take you. – *8MM* (1999)

146. ... A comedy about the greatest love story almost never told ... – *Shakespeare in Love* (1998)

147. Sister, sister, oh so fair, why is there blood all over your hair? – *What Ever Happened to Baby Jane?* (1962)

148. He went from the eye of the storm, into the arms of a hurricane. – *Forces of Nature* (1999)

149. Fear thy neighbour. – *Arlington Road* (1999)

150. We are not alone ... – *Close Encounters of the Third Kind* (1977)

Chapter 24
The Last Picture
Show

DAZED & CONFUSED (1993)

The Cult of...

Just what is a cult film? Ultimately, it is one that generates a fanatical following; it is a movie that is viewed over and over again, each time as enjoyable as the last, if not more so. Cult movies aren't generally big productions and don't usually perform so well at the box office. Cult-movie fans scrutinise their chosen movie, they can cite quotes at the drop of a hat, they avidly discuss all relevant trivia – but most of all they eat, sleep and dream their cult classic.

The following list is by no means definitive – it constitutes little more than a taster of the weird and wonderful world that is cult movies. Seven decades of cult classics and soon-to-be cult classics.

1930s

★ *Freaks* (1932) – Tod Browning

1940s

★ *Lady in the Lake* (1946) – Robert Montgomery

★ *Rope* (1948) – Alfred Hitchcock

★ *Gun Crazy* (1950) – Joseph H Lewis

1950s

★ *Johnny Guitar* (1954) – Nicholas Ray

★ *Plan 9 From Outer Space* (1959) – Edward D Wood Jr

1960s

★ *Peeping Tom* (1960) – Michael Powell

★ *Psycho* (1960) – Alfred Hitchcock

★ *Carnival of Souls* (1962) – Herk Harvey

★ *What Ever Happened to Baby Jane?* (1962) – Robert Aldrich

★ *Shock Corridor* (1963) – Samuel Fuller

★ *Dr. Strangelove or: How I Stopped Worrying and Learned to Love the Bomb* (1964) – Stanley Kubrick

★ *Django* (1965) – Sergio Corbucci

★ *Blowup* (1966) – Michelangelo Antonioni

★ *Valley of the Dolls* (1967) – Mark Robson

★ *Yellow Submarine* (1968) – George Dunning

★ *Barbarella* (1968) – Roger Vadim

★ *Night of the Living Dead* (1968) – George A Romero

★ *Easy Rider* (1969) – Dennis Hopper

1970s

★ *Performance* (1970) – Nic Roeg

★ *Trash* (1970) – Andy Warhol

★ *A Clockwork Orange* (1971) – Stanley Kubrick

★ *Harold and Maude* (1971) – Hal Ashby

★ *Fritz the Cat* (1971) – Ralph Bakshi

★ *And Now for Something Completely Different* (1971) – Terry Gilliam and Ian MacNaughton

★ *Pink Flamingos* (1972) – John Waters

★ *American Graffiti* (1973) – George Lucas

★ *Badlands* (1973) – Terrence Malick

★ *The Wicker Man* (1973) – Robin Hardy

★ *Don't Look Now* (1973) – Nicolas Roeg

★ *The Exorcist* (1973) – William Friedkin

★ *The Texas Chainsaw Massacre* (1974) –
Tobe Hooper

★ *Dark Star* (1974) – John Carpenter

★ *Monty Python and the Holy Grail* (1974) –
Terry Gilliam

★ *The Rocky Horror Picture Show* (1975) –
Jim Sharman

★ *Tommy* (1975) – Ken Russell

★ *Death Race 2000* (1975) – Paul Bartel

★ *Shivers* (1975) – David Cronenberg

★ *The Man Who Fell to Earth* (1976) –
Nicolas Roeg

★ *Suspiria* (1976) – Dario Argento

★ *Saturday Night Fever* (1977) – John Badham

★ *Star Wars* (1977) – George Lucas

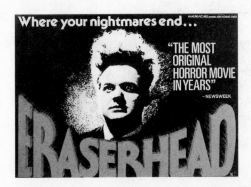

★ *Eraserhead* (1977) – David Lynch

★ *Animal House* (1978) – John Landis

★ *Grease* (1978) – Randal Kleiser

★ *Up In Smoke* (1978) – Lou Adler

★ *Caligula* (1979) – Tinto Brass

★ *Apocalypse Now* (1979) –
Francis Ford Coppola

★ *Quadrophenia* (1979) – Franc Roddam

★ *The Warriors* (1979) – Walter Hill

★ *Star Trek – The Motion Picture* (1979) –
Robert Wise

★ *Attack of the Killer Tomatoes* (1979) –
John De Bello

★ *Zombie Flesh Eaters* (1979) – Lucio Fulci

★ *Life of Brian* (1979) – Terry Jones

★ *Rock 'N' Roll High School* (1979) –
Allan Arkush

★ *Ultravixens* (1979) – Russ Meyer

★ *Alien* (1979) – Ridley Scott

1980s

★ *Motel Hell* (1980) – Kevin Connor

★ *Scanners* (1980) – Steve Barnett

★ *Mad Max* (1980) – George Miller

★ *Friday the 13th* (1980) – Sean S Cunningham

★ *The Blues Brothers* (1980) – John Landis

★ *Polyester* (1981) – John Waters

★ *An American Werewolf in London* (1981) –
John Landis

★ *Xtro* (1982) – Harry Bromley Davenport

★ *Mad Max 2* a.k.a. *The Road Warrior* (1982) – George Miller

★ *Pink Floyd The Wall* (1982) – Alan Parker

★ *Diva* (1982) – Jean-Jacques Beineix

BLADE RUNNER (1982)

★ *Blade Runner* (1982) – Ridley Scott

★ *Fast Times at Ridgemont High* (1982) – Amy Heckerling

★ *Monty Python's The Meaning of Life* (1983) – Terry Jones

★ *Evil Dead* (1983) – Sam Raimi

★ *Videodrome* (1983) – David Cronenberg

★ *The Outsiders* (1983) – Francis Ford Coppola

★ *This is Spinal Tap* (1984) – Rob Reiner

★ *Repo Man* (1984) – Alex Cox

★ *A Nightmare on Elm Street* (1984) – Wes Craven

★ *Dune* (1984) – David Lynch

★ *Re-Animator* (1985) – Stuart Gordon

★ *Legend* (1985) – Ridley Scott

★ *Real Genius* (1985) – Martha Coolidge

★ *The Toxic Avenger* (1985) – Michael Herz

★ *Pee-Wee's Big Adventure* (1985) – Tim Burton

★ *Brazil* (1985) – Terry Gilliam

★ *Blood Simple* (1985) – Joel Coen

★ *The Hitcher* (1986) – Robert Harmon

★ *Withnail & I* (1986) – Bruce Robinson

★ *Manhunter* (1986) – Michael Mann

★ *Highlander* (1986) – Russell Mulcahy

★ *Blue Velvet* (1986) – David Lynch

★ *Raising Arizona* (1987) – Joel Coen

★ *Bad Taste* (1987) – Peter Jackson

★ *The Lost Boys* (1987) – Joel Schumacher

★ *Hairspray* (1988) – John Waters

★ *Dead Heat* (1988) – Mark Goldblatt

HEATHERS (1989)

★ *Heathers* (1989) – Michael Lehmann

★ *Leningrad Cowboys Go America* (1989) – Aki Kaurismaki

★ *Meet the Feebles* (1989) – Pete Jackson

★ *The Killer* (1989) – John Woo

1990s

★ *Wild at Heart* (1990) – David Lynch

★ *Jacob's Ladder* (1990) – Adrian Lyne

★ *Henry: Portrait of a Serial Killer* (1990) – John McNaughton

★ *Miller's Crossing* (1990) – Joel Coen

★ *Barton Fink* (1991) – Joel Coen

★ *Slacker* (1991) – Richard Linklater

★ *Johnny Suede* (1991) – Tom DiCillo

★ *Delicatessen* (1992) – Jean-Pierre Jeunet

★ *Man Bites Dog* (1992) – Rémy Belvaux and André Bonzel

★ *Reservoir Dogs* (1992) – Quentin Tarantino

★ *Dazed and Confused* (1993) – Richard Linklater

★ *Clerks* (1994) – Kevin Smith

★ *The Hudsucker Proxy* (1994) – Joel Coen

★ *Reality Bites* (1994) – Ben Stiller

★ *Killing Zoe* (1994) – Roger Avary

★ *Pulp Fiction* (1994) – Quentin Tarantino

★ *The Crow* (1994) – Alex Proy

★ *Fargo* (1996) – Joel Coen

★ *Trainspotting* (1996) – Danny Boyle

★ *Funny Games* (1997) – Michael Haneke

★ *Pecker* (1998) – John Waters

★ *Lock, Stock & Two Smoking Barrels* (1998) – Guy Ritchie

★ *The Big Lebowski* (1998) – Joel Coen

★ *Fear and Loathing in Las Vegas* (1998) – Terry Gilliam

Back to Black

Just what does blaxploitation refer to? Essentially, it's a term used to describe a type of film that came to life in the early 1970s, a genre best typified by the likes of *Shaft* (1970) and *Sweet Sweetback's Baadasssss Song* (1971), both of which were low-budget movies featuring black performers. They portrayed black heroes and villains overcoming seemingly insurmountable obstacles, with more than liberal amounts of sex and violence thrown in for good measure.

In its day the genre was accused of portraying black people as stereotypical private eyes, pimps, drug dealers and prostitutes – which indeed it did. Ironically, this only made it more difficult for black actors to land the better roles in mainstream productions. The advent of the blockbuster mentality, typified by movies such as *Star Wars* (1977), marked the beginning of the end for blaxploitation films. Blaxploitation movies have, however, not been forgotten. Quentin Tarantino, for example, openly acknowledges his admiration for the genre, and recently cast the blaxploitation queen Pam Grier as the lead in *Jackie Brown* (1997).

A Blaxploitation Filmography

★ *Cotton Comes to Harlem* (1970)

★ *Shaft* (1971)

★ *Sweet Sweetback's Baadasssss Song* (1971)

★ *Come Black, Charleston Blue* (1972)

★ *Cool Breeze* (1972)

★ *Top of the Heap* (1972)

★ *Melinda* (1972)

★ *Hammer* (1972)

★ *Hit Man* (1972)

★ *Slaughter* (1972)

★ *Across 110th Street* (1972)

★ *Blacula* (1972)

★ *Shaft's Big Score* (1972)

★ *Superfly* (1972)

★ *Black Caesar* (1973)

★ *Black Vampire* (1973)

★ *Blackenstein* (1973)

★ *Cleopatra Jones* (1973)

★ *Coffy* (1973)

★ *Detroit 9000* (1973)

★ *Ganja and Hess* (1973)

★ *Hell Up in Harlem* (1973)

★ *The Mack* (1973)

★ *Savage!* (1973)

★ *Scream, Blacula, Scream* (1973)

★ *Shaft in Africa* (1973)

★ *Slaughter's Big Rip-Off* (1973)

★ *Superfly TNT* (1973)

★ *Abby* (1974)

★ *Black Eye* (1974)

★ *Black Gunn* (1974)

★ *Black Belt Jones* (1974)

★ *Black Godfather* (1974)

★ *Foxy Brown* (1974)

★ *No Way Back* (1974)

★ *Hangup* a.k.a. *Superdude* (1974)

★ *Three the Hard Way* (1974)

★ *Truck Turner* (1974)

★ *The Black Six* (1974)

★ *Uptown Saturday Night* (1974)

★ *The Black Gestapo* (1975)

★ *Bucktown* (1975)

★ *Cleopatra Jones and the Casino of Gold* (1975)

★ *Dolemite* (1975)

★ *Friday Foster* (1975)

★ *Let's Do It Again* (1975)

★ *Mean Johnny Barrows* (1975)

★ *Sheba Baby* (1975)

★ *Soul Vengeance* (1975)

★ *Black Fist* a.k.a. *The Black Streetfighter* (1976)

★ *Avenging Disco Godfather* (1976)

★ *Dr. Black and Mr. Hyde* a.k.a. *The Watts Monster*; *Dr. Black and Mr. White* (1976)

★ *Dolemite 2 The Human Tornado* (1976)

★ *Hot Potato* (1976)

★ *J.D.'s Revenge* (1976)

★ *The Guy From Harlem* (1977)

★ *Monkey Hustle* (1977)

The Invasion of the Killer Bs!

The Bs, as in B movies, were a direct attempt by Hollywood to recoup falling box-office returns during the early years of the Depression. Whereas previously audiences had been shown just one feature-length film, they were now treated to two presentations, the main feature and a low-budget – i.e. B – movie in support.

From the mid 1930s to the late 1940s, B movies enjoyed great popularity and were shown in three-quarters of all American cinemas. Furthermore, they constituted a launching pad for the careers of many of Hollywood's future stars.

Fred Zinnemann, director of *High Noon* (1952) and *From Here to Eternity* (1953), worked on B movies prior to his big break, as did William Wyler, who went on to direct the Academy-Award-winning *Ben-Hur* (1959). Actors, too, utilised the Bs as a means of gaining that all-too-important 'experience': Glenn Ford, Jane Wyman and Susan Hayward for example.

Remember, though, that B doesn't always stand for 'bad', with that we offer you ...

20 Killer Bs

★ *The Galloping Ghost* (1931)

★ *The Whispering Shadow* (1933)

★ *Mystery Mountain* (1934)

★ *Bulldog Drummond's Revenge* (1937)

★ *Federal Bullets* (1937)

★ *King of Alcatraz* (1938)

★ *Thank You, Mr. Moto* (1938)

★ *Charlie Chan at Treasure Island* (1939)

★ *Heaven With a Barbed Wire Fence* (1939)

★ *Buck Rogers* (1940)

★ *Ellery Queen and the Murder Ring* (1941)

★ *The Falcon's Brother* (1942)

★ *The Man Who Wouldn't Die* (1942)

★ *Phantom Killer* (1942)

★ *Smart Alecks* (1942)

★ *Whistling in Dixie* (1942)

★ *Crime by Night* (1944)

★ *Marshall of Reno* (1944)

★ *Dick Tracy Meets Gruesome* (1947)

★ *Philo Vance's Secret Mission* (1947)

And Finally...

During the 60s, chances are that if you
went to your local cinema you would have
seen an Edgar Wallace second feature,
prior to the feature presentation. Overall,
47 films were made from 1960 to 1963 by
Jack Greenwood at Merton Park in London.
Notable titles included: *The Clue of the
Twisted Candle*; *Game for Three Losers*;
Never Back Losers; *The Clue of the Silver Key*;
A Marriage of Inconvenience; *The Clue of the
New Pin*; *Partners in Crime*; *The £20,000 Kiss*;
Who Was Maddox and *The Man who was
Nobody*. The films always began with a
revolving statue of Wallace, in spite of the
fact that the crime writer had little to do
with most of the stories. Incidentally, the
theme music to the films, 'Man of Mystery',
gave the British pop band the Shadows
a top-ten hit in 1960.

Chapter 25
Celebrating the
Movies

50 Years of Awards 1949-98

Since the inception of the Academy Awards back in 1927, there are now roughly four hundred different movie-award bodies worldwide – all established with one unifying theme in mind: a celebration of film. Of course they don't all carry the kudos of the Oscars. Many of them we'll probably never hear of, and for this perhaps we should be grateful!

So as to avoid producing a book of awards and nothing else, we've whittled the selection down to three: the Academy Awards, the National Lampoon Worst Movie Awards and the Golden Raspberry Awards. Furthermore, we've chosen to list only the principal awards from each awarding body, namely those corresponding to best actor, best supporting actor, best picture, best director, best score, best song, and, to finish, best foreign film. However, should the information presented appear to be at odds with this, don't worry: you'll see from below that some of the awarding bodies seem to have great trouble sticking with an award title once they've chosen it.

Oh, and just in case any of you are asking why we haven't listed the awards given out in 1999 yet, well, we have: you see, the awards given out in 1999 were for films released in 1998. Confused? So were we, but that's the way the industry likes it! Consequently the year listed alongside the awards refers not to the year of the ceremony, but the previous year, i.e. the year for which nominations were invited. Thus, *Shakespeare in Love* won Best Picture in the 1998 Oscars, although the award itself wasn't made until 1999.

And finally, just to be different, we've listed the awards in reverse, starting with the most recent and working back. Anyway, without further ado, here are the listings …

The Academy Awards

On 4 May 1927 the Academy of Motion Picture Arts and Sciences became a legal corporation – the brainchild of the Metro-Goldwyn-Mayer head, Louis B Mayer. Its intended purpose was to be the mediation of labour disputes. However, the Academy's role was soon expanded to include, among other things, the bestowal of 'awards of merit for distinctive achievement'.

Best Actor

★ 1998 (71st) **Roberto Benigni**
Life is Beautiful

★ 1997 (70th) **Jack Nicholson**
As Good As It Gets

★ 1996 (69th) **Geoffrey Rush**
Shine

★ 1995 (68th) **Nicolas Cage**
Leaving Las Vegas

★ 1994 (67th) **Tom Hanks**
Forrest Gump

★ 1993 (66th) **Tom Hanks**
Philadelphia

★ 1992 (65th) **Al Pacino**
Scent of a Woman

★ 1991 (64th) **Anthony Hopkins**
The Silence of the Lambs

★ 1990 (63rd) **Jeremy Irons**
Reversal of Fortune

★ 1989 (62nd) **Daniel Day-Lewis**
My Left Foot

★ 1988 (61st) **Dustin Hoffman**
Rain Man

★ 1987 (60th) **Michael Douglas**
Wall Street

★ 1986 (59th) **Paul Newman**
The Color of Money

★ 1985 (58th) **William Hurt**
Kiss of the Spider Woman

★ 1984 (57th) **F Murray Abraham**
Amadeus

★ 1983 (56th) **Robert Duvall**
Tender Mercies

★ 1982 (55th) **Ben Kingsley**
Gandhi

★ 1981 (54th) **Henry Fonda**
On Golden Pond

★ 1980 (53rd) **Robert De Niro**
Raging Bull

★ 1979 (52nd) **Dustin Hoffman**
Kramer Vs. Kramer

★ 1978 (51st) **Jon Voight**
Coming Home

★ 1977 (50th) **Richard Dreyfuss –**
The Goodbye Girl

★ 1976 (49th) **Peter Finch**
Network

★ 1975 (48th) **Jack Nicholson**
One Flew Over the Cuckoo's Nest

★ 1974 (47th) **Art Carney**
Harry and Tonto

★ 1973 (46th) **Jack Lemmon**
Save the Tiger

★ 1972 (45th) **Marlon Brando**
The Godfather

★ 1971 (44th) **Gene Hackman**
The French Connection

★ 1970 (43rd) **George C Scott**
Patton

★ 1969 (42nd) **John Wayne**
True Grit

★ 1968 (41st) **Cliff Robertson**
Charly

★ 1967 (40th) **Rod Steiger**
In the Heat of the Night

★ 1966 (39th) **Paul Scofield**
A Man For All Seasons

★ 1965 (38th) **Lee Marvin**
Cat Ballou

★ 1964 (37th) **Rex Harrison**
My Fair Lady

★ 1963 (36th) **Sidney Poitier**
Lilies of the Field

★ 1962 (35th) **Gregory Peck**
To Kill a Mockingbird

★ 1961 (34th) **Maximillian Schell**
Judgment at Nuremberg

★ 1960 (33rd) **Burt Lancaster**
Elmer Gantry

★ 1959 (32nd) **Charlton Heston**
Ben-Hur

★ 1958 (31st) **David Niven**
Separate Tables

★ 1957 (30th) **Alec Guinness**
The Bridge on the River Kwai

★ 1956 (29th) **Yul Brynner**
The King and I

★ 1955 (28th) **Ernest Borgnine**
Marty

★ 1954 (27th) **Marlon Brando**
On the Waterfront

★ 1953 (26th) **William Holden**
Stalag 17

★ 1952 (25th) **Gary Cooper**
High Noon

★ 1951 (24th) **Humphrey Bogart**
The African Queen

★ 1950 (23rd) **José Ferrer**
Cyrano de Bergerac

★ 1949 (22nd) **Broderick Crawford**
All the King's Men

Best Supporting Actor

★ 1998 (71st) **James Coburn**
Affliction

★ 1997 (70th) **Robin Williams**
Good Will Hunting

★ 1996 (69th) **Cuba Gooding Jr**
Jerry Maguire

★ 1995 (68th) **Kevin Spacey**
The Usual Suspects

★ 1994 (67th) **Martin Landau**
Ed Wood

★ 1993 (66th) **Tommy Lee Jones**
The Fugitive

★ 1992 (65th) **Gene Hackman**
Unforgiven

★ 1991 (64th) **Jack Palance**
City Slickers

★ 1990 (63rd) **Joe Pesci**
GoodFellas

★ 1989 (62nd) **Denzel Washington**
Glory

★ 1988 (61st) **Kevin Kline**
A Fish Called Wanda

★ 1987 (60th) **Sean Connery**
The Untouchables

★ 1986 (59th) **Michael Caine**
Hannah and Her Sisters

★ 1985 (58th) **Don Ameche**
Cocoon

★ 1984 (57th) **Haing S Ngor**
The Killing Fields

★ 1983 (56th) **Jack Nicholson**
Terms of Endearment

★ 1982 (55th) **Louis Gossett Jr**
An Officer and a Gentleman

★ 1981 (54th) **John Gielgud**
Arthur

★ 1980 (53rd) **Timothy Hutton**
Ordinary People

★ 1979 (52nd) **Melvyn Douglas**
Being There

★ 1978 (51st) **Christopher Walken**
The Deer Hunter

★ 1977 (50th) **Jason Robards Jr**
Julia

★ 1976 (49th) **Jason Robards Jr**
All the President's Men

★ 1975 (48th) **George Burns**
The Sunshine Boys

★ 1974 (47th) **Robert De Niro**
The Godfather, Part 2

★ 1973 (46th) **John Houseman**
The Paper Chase

★ 1972 (45th) **Joel Grey**
Cabaret

★ 1971 (44th) **Ben Johnson**
The Last Picture Show

★ 1970 (43rd) **John Mills**
Ryan's Daughter

★ 1969 (42nd) **Gig Young**
They Shoot Horses, Don't They?

★ 1968 (41st) **Jack Albertson**
The Subject Was Roses

★ 1967 (40th) **George Kennedy**
Cool Hand Luke

★ 1966 (39th) **Walter Matthau**
The Fortune Cookie

★ 1965 (38th) **Martin Balsam**
A Thousand Clowns

★ 1964 (37th) **Peter Ustinov**
Topkapi

★ 1963 (36th) **Melvyn Douglas**
Hud

★ 1962 (35th) **Ed Begley Sr**
Sweet Bird of Youth

★ 1961 (34th) **George Chakiris**
West Side Story

★ 1960 (33rd) **Peter Ustinov**
Spartacus

★ 1959 (32nd) **Hugh Griffith**
Ben-Hur

★ 1958 (31st) **Burl Ives**
The Big Country

★ 1957 (30th) **Red Buttons**
Sayonara

★ 1956 (29th) **Anthony Quinn**
Lust for Life

★ 1955 (28th) **Jack Lemmon**
Mister Roberts

★ 1954 (27th) **Edmond O'Brien**
The Barefoot Contessa

★ 1953 (26th) **Frank Sinatra**
From Here to Eternity

★ 1952 (25th) **Anthony Quinn**
Viva Zapata!

★ 1951 (24th) **Karl Malden**
A Streetcar Named Desire

★ 1950 (23rd) **George Sanders**
All About Eve

★ 1949 (22nd) **Dean Jagger**
Twelve O'Clock High

Best Actress

★ 1998 (71st) **Gwyneth Paltrow**
Shakespeare in Love

★ 1997 (70th) **Helen Hunt**
As Good As It Gets

★ 1996 (69th) **Frances McDormand**
Fargo

★ 1995 (68th) **Susan Sarandon**
Dead Man Walking

★ 1994 (67th) **Jessica Lange**
Blue Sky

★ 1993 (66th) **Holly Hunter**
The Piano

★ 1992 (65th) **Emma Thompson**
Howard's End

★ 1991 (64th) **Jodie Foster**
The Silence of the Lambs

★ 1990 (63rd) **Kathy Bates**
Misery

★ 1989 (62nd) **Jessica Tandy**
Driving Miss Daisy

★ 1988 (61st) **Jodie Foster**
The Accused

★ 1987 (60th) **Cher**
Moonstruck

★ 1986 (59th) **Marlee Matlin**
Children of a Lesser God

★ 1985 (58th) **Geraldine Page**
The Trip to Bountiful

★ 1984 (57th) **Sally Field**
Place in the Heart

★ 1983 (56th) **Shirley McClaine**
Terms of Endearment

★ 1982 (55th) **Meryl Streep**
Sophie's Choice

★ 1981 (54th) **Katharine Hepburn**
On Golden Pond

★ 1980 (53rd) **Sissy Spacek**
Coal Miner's Daughter

★ 1979 (52nd) **Sally Field**
Norma Rae

★ 1978 (51st) **Jane Fonda**
Coming Home

★ 1977 (50th) **Diane Keaton**
Annie Hall

★ 1976 (49th) **Faye Dunaway**
Network

★ 1975 (48th) **Louise Fletcher**
One Flew Over the Cuckoo's Nest

★ 1974 (47th) **Ellen Burstyn**
Alice Doesn't Live Here Anymore

★ 1973 (46th) **Glenda Jackson**
A Touch of Class

★ 1972 (45th) **Liza Minnelli**
Cabaret

★ 1971 (44th) **Jane Fonda**
Klute

★ 1970 (43rd) **Glenda Jackson**
Women in Love

★ 1969 (42nd) **Maggie Smith**
The Prime of Miss Jean Brodie

★ 1968 (41st) **Katharine Hepburn/
Barbra Streisand**
The Lion in Winter/Funny Girl

★ 1967 (40th) **Katharine Hepburn**
Guess Who's Coming to Dinner

★ 1966 (39th) **Elizabeth Taylor**
Who's Afraid of Virginia Woolf?

★ 1965 (38th) **Julie Christie**
Darling

★ 1964 (37th) **Julie Andrews**
Mary Poppins

★ 1963 (36th) **Patricia Neal**
Hud

★ 1962 (35th) **Anne Bancroft**
The Miracle Worker

★ 1961 (34th) **Sophia Loren**
Two Women

★ 1960 (33rd) **Elizabeth Taylor**
Butterfield 8

★ 1959 (32nd) **Simone Signoret**
Room at the Top

★ 1958 (31st) **Susan Hayward**
I Want to Live

★ 1957 (30th) **Joanne Woodward**
The Three Faces of Eve

★ 1956 (29th) **Ingrid Bergman**
Anastasia

★ 1955 (28th) **Anna Magnani**
The Rose Tattoo

★ 1954 (27th) **Grace Kelly**
Country Girl

★ 1953 (26th) **Audrey Hepburn**
Roman Holiday

★ 1952 (25th) **Shirley Booth**
Come Back, Little Sheba

★ 1951 (24th) **Vivien Leigh**
A Streetcar Named Desire

★ 1950 (23rd) **Judy Holiday**
Born Yesterday

★ 1949 (22nd) **Olivia de Havilland**
The Heiress

Best Supporting Actress

★ 1998 (71st) **Dame Judi Dench**
Shakespeare in Love

★ 1997 (70th) **Kim Basinger**
L.A. Confidential

★ 1996 (69th) **Juliette Binoche**
The English Patient

★ 1995 (68th) **Mira Sorvino**
Mighty Aphrodite

★ 1994 (67th) **Dianne Wiest**
Bullets Over Broadway

★ 1993 (66th) **Anna Paquin**
The Piano

★ 1992 (65th) **Marisa Tomei**
My Cousin Vinny

★ 1991 (64th) **Mercedes Ruehl**
The Fisher King

★ 1990 (63rd) **Whoopi Goldberg**
Ghost

★ 1989 (62nd) **Brenda Fricker**
My Left Foot

★ 1988 (61st) **Geena Davis**
The Accidental Tourist

★ 1987 (60th) **Olympia Dukakis**
Moonstruck

★ 1986 (59th) **Dianne Wiest –**
Hannah and Her Sisters

★ 1985 (58th) **Anjelica Huston**
Prizzi's Honor

★ 1984 (57th) **Peggy Ashcroft**
A Passage to India

★ 1983 (56th) **Linda Hunt**
The Year of Living Dangerously

★ 1982 (55th) **Jessica Lange**
Tootsie

★ 1981 (54th) **Maureen Stapleton**
Reds

★ 1980 (53rd) **Mary Steenburgen**
Melvin and Howard

★ 1979 (52nd) **Meryl Streep**
Kramer Vs. Kramer

★ 1978 (51st) **Maggie Smith**
California Suite

★ 1977 (50th) **Vanessa Redgrave**
Julia

★ 1976 (49th) **Beatrice Straight**
Network

★ 1975 (48th) **Lee Grant**
Shampoo

★ 1974 (47th) **Ingrid Bergman**
Murder on the Orient Express

★ 1973 (46th) **Tatum O'Neal**
Paper Moon

★ 1972 (45th) **Eileen Heckart**
Butterflies are Free

★ 1971 (44th) **Cloris Leachman**
The Last Picture Show

★ 1970 (43rd) **Helen Hayes**
Airport

★ 1969 (42nd) **Goldie Hawn**
Cactus Flower

★ 1968 (41st) **Ruth Gordon**
Rosemary's Baby

★ 1967 (40th) **Estelle Parsons**
Bonnie and Clyde

★ 1966 (39th) **Sandy Dennis**
Who's Afraid of Virginia Woolf?

★ 1965 (38th) **Shelley Winters**
A Patch of Blue

★ 1964 (37th) **Lilia Kedrova**
Zorba the Greek

★ 1963 (36th) **Margaret Rutherford**
The V.I.P.'s

★ 1962 (35th) **Patty Duke**
The Miracle Worker

★ 1961 (34th) **Rita Moreno**
West Side Story

★ 1960 (33rd) **Shirley Jones**
Elmer Gantry

★ 1959 (32nd) **Shelley Winters**
The Diary of Anne Frank

★ 1958 (31st) **Wendy Hiller**
Separate Tables

★ 1957 (30th) **Miyoshi Umeki**
Sayonara

★ 1956 (29th) **Dorothy Malone**
Written on the Wind

★ 1955 (28th) **Jo Van Fleet**
East of Eden

★ 1954 (27th) **Eva Marie Saint**
On the Waterfront

★ 1953 (26th) **Donna Reed**
From Here to Eternity

★ 1952 (25th) **Gloria Grahame**
The Bad and the Beautiful

★ 1951 (24th) **Kim Hunter**
A Streetcar Named Desire

★ 1950 (23rd) **Josephine Hull**
Harvey

★ 1949 (22nd) **Mercedes McCambridge**
All the King's Men

Best Picture

★ 1998 (71st) *Shakespeare in Love*

★ 1997 (70th) *Titanic*

★ 1996 (69th) *The English Patient*

★ 1995 (68th) *Braveheart*

★ 1994 (67th) *Forrest Gump*

★ 1993 (66th) *Schindler's List*

★ 1992 (65th) *Unforgiven*

★ 1991 (64th) *The Silence of the Lambs*

★ 1990 (63rd) *Dances With Wolves*

★ 1989 (62nd) *Driving Miss Daisy*

★ 1988 (61st) *Rain Man*

★ 1987 (60th) *The Last Emperor*

★ 1986 (59th) *Platoon*

★ 1985 (58th) *Out of Africa*

★ 1984 (57th) *Amadeus*

★ 1983 (56th) *Terms of Endearment*

★ 1982 (55th) *Gandhi*

★ 1981 (54th) *Chariots of Fire*

★ 1980 (53rd) *Ordinary People*

★ 1979 (52nd) *Kramer Vs. Kramer*

★ 1978 (51st) *The Deer Hunter*

★ 1977 (50th) *Annie Hall*

★ 1976 (49th) *Rocky*

★ 1975 (48th) *One Flew Over the Cuckoo's Nest*

★ 1974 (47th) *The Godfather, Part 2*

★ 1973 (46th) *The Sting*

★ 1972 (45th) *The Godfather*

★ 1971 (44th) *The French Connection*

★ 1970 (43rd) *Patton*

★ 1969 (42nd) *Midnight Cowboy*

★ 1968 (41st) *Oliver!*

★ 1967 (40th) *In the Heat of the Night*

★ 1966 (39th) *A Man for All Seasons*

★ 1965 (38th) *The Sound of Music*

★ 1964 (37th) *My Fair Lady*

★ 1963 (36th) *Tom Jones*

★ 1962 (35th) *Lawrence of Arabia*

★ 1961 (34th) *West Side Story*

★ 1960 (33rd) *The Apartment*

★ 1959 (32nd) *Ben-Hur*

★ 1958 (31st) *Gigi*

★ 1957 (30th) *The Bridge on the River Kwai*

★ 1956 (29th) *Around the World in 80 Days*

★ 1955 (28th) *Marty*

★ 1954 (27th) *On the Waterfront*

★ 1953 (26th) *From Here to Eternity*

★ 1952 (25th) *The Greatest Show on Earth*

★ 1951 (24th) *An American in Paris*

★ 1950 (23rd) *All About Eve*

★ 1949 (22nd) *All the King's Men*

Best Director

★ 1998 (71st) **Steven Spielberg**
Saving Private Ryan

★ 1997 (70th) **James Cameron**
Titanic

★ 1996 (69th) **Anthony Minghella**
The English Patient

★ 1995 (68th) **Mel Gibson**
Braveheart

★ 1994 (67th) **Robert Zemeckis**
Forrest Gump

★ 1993 (66th) **Steven Spielberg**
Schindler's List

★ 1992 (65th) **Clint Eastwood**
Unforgiven

★ 1991 (64th) **Jonathan Demme**
The Silence of the Lambs

★ 1990 (63rd) **Kevin Costner**
Dances With Wolves

★ 1989 (62nd) **Oliver Stone**
Born on the Fourth of July

★ 1988 (61st) **Barry Levinson**
Rain Man

★ 1987 (60th) **Bernardo Bertolucci**
The Last Emperor

★ 1986 (59th) **Oliver Stone**
Platoon

★ 1985 (58th) **Sydney Pollack**
Out of Africa

★ 1984 (57th) **Milos Forman**
Amadeus

★ 1983 (56th) **James L Brooks**
Terms of Endearment

★ 1982 (55th) **Richard Attenborough**
Gandhi

★ 1981 (54th) **Warren Beatty**
Reds

★ 1980 (53rd) **Robert Redford**
Ordinary People

★ 1979 (52nd) **Robert Benton**
Kramer Vs. Kramer

★ 1978 (51st) **Michael Cimino**
The Deer Hunter

★ 1977 (50th) **Woody Allen**
Annie Hall

★ 1976 (49th) **John G Avildsen**
Rocky

★ 1975 (48th) **Milos Forman**
One Flew Over the Cuckoo's Nest

★ 1974 (47th) **Francis Ford Coppola**
The Godfather, Part 2

★ 1973 (46th) **George Roy Hill**
The Sting

★ 1972 (45th) **Bob Fosse**
Cabaret

★ 1971 (44th) **William Friedkin**
The French Connection

★ 1970 (43rd) **Franklin J Schaffner**
Patton

★ 1969 (42nd) **John Schlesinger**
Midnight Cowboy

★ 1968 (41st) **Carol Reed**
Oliver!

★ 1967 (40th) **Mike Nichols**
The Graduate

★ 1966 (39th) **Fred Zinnemann**
A Man For All Seasons

★ 1965 (38th) **Robert Wise**
The Sound of Music

★ 1964 (37th) **George Cukor**
My Fair Lady

★ 1963 (36th) **Tony Richardson**
Tom Jones

★ 1962 (35th) **David Lean**
Lawrence of Arabia

★ 1961 (34th) **Robert Wise**
West Side Story

★ 1960 (33rd) **Billy Wilder**
The Apartment

★ 1959 (32nd) **William Wyler**
Ben-Hur

★ 1958 (31st) **Vincente Minnelli**
Gigi

★ 1957 (30th) **David Lean**
The Bridge on the River Kwai

★ 1956 (29th) **George Stevens**
Giant

★ 1955 (28th) **Delbert Mann**
Marty

★ 1954 (27th) **Elia Kazan**
On the Waterfront

★ 1953 (26th) **Fred Zinnemann**
From Here to Eternity

★ 1952 (25th) **John Ford**
The Quiet Man

★ 1951 (24th) **George Stevens**
A Place in the Sun

★ 1950 (23rd) **Joseph Mankiewicz**
All About Eve

★ 1949 (22nd) **Joseph Mankiewicz**
A Letter to Three Wives

Best Score

★ 1998 (71st) *Life is Beautiful*
Nicolo Piovani

★ 1997 (70th) *Titanic*
James Horner

★ 1996 (69th) *The English Patient*
Gabriel Yared

★ 1995 (68th) *The Postman (Il Postino)*
Luis Enríquez Bacalov

★ 1994 (67th) *The Lion King*
Hans Zimmer

★ 1993 (66th) *Schindler's List*
John Williams

★ 1992 (65th) *Aladdin*
Alan Menken

★ 1991 (64th) *Beauty and the Beast*
Alan Menken

★ 1990 (63rd) *Dances With Wolves*
John Barry

★ 1989 (62nd) *The Little Mermaid*
Alan Menken

★ 1988 (61st) *The Milagro Beanfield War*
Dave Grusin

★ 1987 (60th) *The Last Emperor*
David Byrne, Cong Su, Ryuichi Sakamoto

★ 1986 (59th) *Round Midnight*
Herbie Hancock

★ 1985 (58th) *Out of Africa*
John Barry

★ 1984 (57th) *A Passage to India*
Maurice Jarre

★ 1983 (56th) *The Right Stuff*
Bill Conti

★ 1982 (55th) *E.T. – The Extra-Terrestrial*
John Williams

★ 1981 (54th) *Chariots of Fire*
Vangelis

★ 1980 (53rd) *Fame*
Michael Gore

★ 1979 (52nd) *A Little Romance*
Georges Delerue

★ 1978 (51st) *Midnight Express*
Giorgio Moroder

★ 1977 (50th) *Star Wars*
John Williams

★ 1976 (49th) *The Omen*
Jerry Goldsmith

★ 1975 (48th) *Jaws*
John Williams

★ 1974 (47th) *The Godfather, Part 2*
Carmine Coppola, Nino Rota

★ 1973 (46th) *The Way We Were*
Marvin Hamlisch

★ 1972 (45th) *Limelight*
**Charles Chaplin, Raymond Rasch,
Larry Russell**

★ 1971 (44th) *Summer of '42*
Michel Legrand

★ 1970 (43rd) *Love Story*
Francis Lai

★ 1969 (42nd) *Butch Cassidy and the
Sundance Kid*
Burt Bacharach

★ 1968 (41st) *The Lion in Winter*
John Barry

★ 1967 (40th) *Thoroughly Modern Millie*
Elmer Bernstein

★ 1966 (39th) *Born Free*
John Barry

★ 1965 (38th) *Doctor Zhivago*
Maurice Jarre

★ 1964 (37th) *Mary Poppins*
Richard M Sherman, Robert B Sherman

★ 1963 (36th) *Tom Jones*
John Addison

★ 1962 (35th) *Lawrence of Arabia*
Maurice Jarre

★ 1961 (34th) *Breakfast at Tiffany's*
Henry Mancini (dramatic or comedy score);
West Side Story
**Saul Chaplin, Johnny Green, Sid Ramin,
Irwin Kostal** (musical score)

★ 1960 (33rd) *Exodus*
Ernest Gold (dramatic or comedy);
Song Without End
Morris Stoloff, Harry Sukman (musical)

★ 1959 (32nd) *Ben-Hur*
Miklos Rozsa (dramatic or comedy);
Porgy and Bess
André Previn, Ken Darby (musical)

★ 1958 (31st) *The Old Man and the Sea*
Dimitri Tiomkin (dramatic or comedy);
Gigi
André Previn (musical)

★ 1957 (30th) *The Bridge on the River Kwai*
Malcolm Arnold

★ 1956 (29th) *Around the World in 80 Days*
Victor Young (dramatic or comedy);
The King and I
Alfred Newman, Ken Darby (musical)

★ 1955 (28th) *Love Is a Many
Splendored Thing*
Alfred Newman (dramatic or comedy);
Oklahoma!
**Robert Russell Bennett, Jay Blackton,
Adolph Deutsch** (musical)

★ 1954 (27th) *The High and the Mighty*
Dimitri Tiomkin (dramatic or comedy);
Seven Brides for Seven Brothers
Adolph Deutsch, Saul Chaplin (musical)

★ 1953 (26th) *Lili*
Bronislau Kaper (dramatic or comedy);
Call Me Madam
Alfred Newman (musical)

★ 1952 (25th) *High Noon*
Dimitri Tiomkin (dramatic or comedy);
With a Song in My Heart
Alfred Newman (musical)

★ 1951 (24th) *A Place in the Sun*
Franz Waxman (dramatic or comedy);
An American in Paris
Johnny Green, Saul Chaplin (musical)

★ 1950 (23rd) *Sunset Boulevard*
Franz Waxman (dramatic or comedy);
Annie Get Your Gun
Adolph Deutsch, Roger Edens (musical)

★ 1949 (22nd) *The Heiress*
Aaron Copland (dramatic or comedy);
On the Town
Roger Edens, Lennie Hayton (musical)

Best Song

★ 1998 (71st) 'When You Believe' from
The Prince of Egypt – **Stephen Schwartz**

★ 1997 (70th) 'My Heart Will Go On' from
Titanic – **James Horner, Will Jennings**

★ 1996 (69th) 'You Must Love Me' from
Evita – **Andrew Lloyd Webber, Tim Rice**

★ 1995 (68th) 'Colors Of the Wind' from
Pocahontas – **Alan Menken, Stephen Schwartz**

★ 1994 (67th) 'Can You Feel The Love
Tonight?' from *The Lion King* – **Elton John,
Tim Rice**

★ 1993 (66th) 'Streets Of Philadelphia' from
Philadelphia – **Bruce Springsteen**

★ 1992 (65th) 'A Whole New World' from
Aladdin – **Alan Menken, Tim Rice**

★ 1991 (64th) 'Beauty And The Beast' from
Beauty and the Beast – **Howard Ashman,
Alan Menken**

★ 1990 (63rd) 'Sooner Or Later
(I Always Get My Man)' from *Dick Tracy* –
Stephen Sondheim

★ 1989 (62nd) 'Under The Sea' from
The Little Mermaid – **Howard Ashman,
Alan Menken**

★ 1988 (61st) 'Let The River Run' from
Working Girl – **Carly Simon**

★ 1987 (60th) '(I've Had) The Time Of My
Life' from *Dirty Dancing* – **John DeNicola,
Donald Markowitz, Franke Previte**

★ 1986 (59th) 'Take My Breath Away' from
Top Gun – **Giorgio Moroder, Tom Whitlock**

★ 1985 (58th) 'Say You, Say Me' from
White Nights – **Lionel Richie**

★ 1984 (57th) 'I Just Called To Say I Love
You' from *The Woman in Red* –
Stevie Wonder

★ 1983 (56th) 'Flashdance ... What A Feeling'
from *Flashdance* – **Irene Cara, Keith Forsey,
Giorgio Moroder**

★ 1982 (55th) 'Up Where We Belong' from
An Officer and a Gentleman – **Will Jennings,
Jack Nitzsche, Buffy Sainte-Marie**

★ 1981 (54th) 'Arthur's Theme (Best That You Can Do)' from *Arthur* – **Peter Allen, Burt Bacharach, Christopher Cross, Carole Bayer Sager**

★ 1980 (53rd) 'Fame' from *Fame* – **Michael Gore, Dean Pitchford**

★ 1979 (52nd) 'It Goes Like It Goes' from *Norma Rae* – **Norman Gimbel, David Shire**

★ 1978 (51st) 'Last Dance' from *Thank God It's Friday* – **Paul Jabara**

★ 1977 (50th) 'You Light Up My Life' from *You Light Up My Life* – **Joseph Brooks**

★ 1976 (49th) 'Evergreen (Love Theme From A Star Is Born)' from *A Star Is Born* – **Barbra Streisand, Paul Williams**

★ 1975 (48th) 'I'm Easy' from *Nashville* – **Keith Carradine**

★ 1974 (47th) 'We May Never Love Like This Again' from *The Towering Inferno* – **Joel Hirschhorn, Al Kasha**

★ 1973 (46th) 'The Way We Were' from *The Way We Were* – **Alan Bergman, Marilyn Bergman, Marvin Hamlisch**

★ 1972 (45th) 'The Morning After' from *The Poseidon Adventure* – **Joel Hirschhorn, Al Kasha**

★ 1971 (44th) 'Theme From Shaft' from *Shaft* – **Isaac Hayes**

★ 1970 (43rd) 'For All We Know' from *Lovers and Other Strangers* – **James Griffin, Fred Karlin, Robb Royer**

★ 1969 (42nd) 'Raindrops Keep Fallin' On My Head' from *Butch Cassidy and the Sundance Kid* – **Burt Bacharach, Hal David**

★ 1968 (41st) 'The Windmills Of Your Mind' from *The Thomas Crown Affair* – **Alan Bergman, Marilyn Bergman, Michel Legrand**

★ 1967 (40th) 'Talk To The Animals' from *Doctor Dolittle* – **Leslie Bricusse**

★ 1966 (39th) 'Born Free' from *Born Free* – **John Barry, Don Black**

★ 1965 (38th) 'The Shadow Of Your Smile' from *The Sandpiper* – **Johnny Mandel, Paul Francis Webster**

★ 1964 (37th) 'Chim Chim Cher-ee' from *Mary Poppins* – **Richard M Sherman, Robert B Sherman**

★ 1963 (36th) 'Call Me Irresponsible' from *Papa's Delicate Condition* – **Sammy Cahn, James Van Heusen**

★ 1962 (35th) 'Days Of Wine And Roses' from *Days of Wine and Roses* – **Henry Mancini, Johnny Mercer**

★ 1961 (34th) 'Moon River' from *Breakfast at Tiffany's* – **Henry Mancini, Johnny Mercer**

★ 1960 (33rd) 'Never On Sunday' from *Never On Sunday* – **Manos Hadjidakis**

★ 1959 (32nd) 'High Hopes' from *A Hole in the Head* – **Sammy Cahn, James Van Heusen**

★ 1958 (31st) 'Gigi' from *Gigi* – **Alan Jay Lerner, Frederick Loewe**

★ 1957 (30th) 'All The Way' from *The Joker Is Wild* – **Sammy Cahn, James Van Heusen**

★ 1956 (29th) 'Whatever Will Be, Will Be (Que Sera, Sera)' from *The Man Who Knew Too Much* – **Ray Evans, Jay Livingston**

★ 1955 (28th) 'Love Is A Many Splendored Thing' from *Love Is a Many Splendored Thing* – **Sammy Fain, Paul Francis Webster**

★ 1954 (27th) 'Three Coins In The Fountain' from *Three Coins in the Fountain* – **Sammy Cahn, Jule Styne**

★ 1953 (26th) 'Secret Love' from *Calamity Jane* – **Sammy Fain, Paul Francis Webster**

★ 1952 (25th) 'High Noon (Do Not Forsake Me, Oh My Darlin')' from *High Noon* – **Dimitri Tiomkin, Ned Washington**

★ 1951 (24th) 'In The Cool, Cool, Cool Of The Evening' from *Here Comes The Groom* – **Hoagy Carmichael, Johnny Mercer**

★ 1950 (23rd) 'Mona Lisa' from *Captain Carey, U.S.A.* – **Ray Evans, Jay Livingston**

★ 1949 (22nd) 'Baby, It's Cold Outside' from *Neptune's Daughter* – **Frank Loesser**

Best Foreign Language Film

★ 1998 (71st) *Life is Beautiful* – Italy

★ 1997 (70th) *Character* – the Netherlands

★ 1996 (69th) *Kolya* – Czech Republic

★ 1995 (68th) *Antonia's Line* – the Netherlands

★ 1994 (67th) *Burnt by the Sun* – Russia

★ 1993 (66th) *Belle Epoque* – Spain

★ 1992 (65th) *Indochine* – France

★ 1991 (64th) *Mediterraneo* – Italy

★ 1990 (63rd) *Journey of Hope* – Switzerland

★ 1989 (62nd) *Nuovo Cinema Paradiso* – Italy

★ 1988 (61st) *Pelle the Conqueror* – Denmark

★ 1987 (60th) *Babette's Feast* – Denmark

★ 1986 (59th) *The Assault* – the Netherlands

★ 1985 (58th) *The Official Story* – Argentina

★ 1984 (57th) *Dangerous Moves* – Switzerland

★ 1983 (56th) *Fanny & Alexander* – Sweden

★ 1982 (55th) *Volver A Empezar (To Begin Again)* – Spain

★ 1981 (54th) *Mephisto* – Hungary

★ 1980 (53rd) *Moscow Does Not Believe in Tears* – Union of Soviet Socialist Republics

★ 1979 (52nd) *The Tin Drum* – Federal Republic of Germany

★ 1978 (51st) *Get Out Your Handkerchiefs* – France

★ 1977 (50th) *Madame Rosa* – France

★ 1976 (49th) *Black and White in Color* – Ivory Coast

★ 1975 (48th) *Dersu Uzala* – Union of Soviet Socialist Republics

★ 1974 (47th) *Amarcord* – Italy

★ 1973 (46th) *Day for Night* – France

★ 1972 (45th) *The Discreet Charm of the Bourgeoisie* – France

★ 1971 (44th) *The Garden of the Finzi Continis* – Italy

★ 1970 (43rd) *Investigation of a Citizen Above Suspicion* – Italy

★ 1969 (42nd) *Z* – Algeria

★ 1968 (41st) *War and Peace* – Union of Soviet Socialist Republics

★ 1967 (40th) *Closely Watched Trains* – Czechoslovakia

★ 1966 (39th) *A Man and a Woman* – France

★ 1965 (38th) *The Shop on Main Street* – Czechoslovakia

★ 1964 (37th) *Yesterday, Today and Tomorrow* – Italy

★ 1963 (36th) *Federico Fellini's 8½* – Italy

★ 1962 (35th) *Sundays and Cybele* – France

★ 1961 (34th) *Through a Glass Darkly* – Sweden

★ 1960 (33rd) *The Virgin Spring* – Sweden

★ 1959 (32nd) *Black Orpheus* – France

★ 1958 (31st) *My Uncle* – France

★ 1957 (30th) *The Nights of Cabiria* – Italy

★ 1956 (29th) *La Strada* – Italy

★ 1955 (28th) *Samurai, The Legend of Musashi* – Japan

★ 1954 (27th) *Gate of Hell* – Japan

★ 1953 (26th) No award given for this year

★ 1952 (25th) *Forbidden Games* – France

★ 1951 (24th) *Rashomon* – Japan

★ 1950 (23rd) *The Walls of Malapaga* – France/Italy

★ 1949 (22nd) *The Bicycle Thief* – Italy

Harvard Lampoon Movie Worsts

First awarded in 1939, the ''Poonies', an offshoot of America's oldest humour magazine, the *Harvard Lampoon*, are also America's longest-established worst-movie awards. Each year, since 1939, awards have been given to the worst pictures, the worst actors, and the worst of anything else that has taken the fancy of the writers. Since the advent of the 80s, though, and with it the beginning of the 'Razzies' (or Golden Raspberry awards), the ''Poonies' seem to have slipped into obscurity, appearing only intermittently after 1983. A great shame, since they provided by far the most entertaining award categories.

If the award categories listed below appear inconsistent, well, that's because they are. However, we felt it best to adhere to the categories as listed by *Harvard Lampoon* themselves, hence the inconsistencies.

Ten Worst Films

★ **1994** *Forrest Gump, Reality Bites, Philadelphia, The Lion King, Speed, True Lies, Four Weddings and a Funeral, Schindler's List, It Could Happen to You, The Crow*

Ten Worst Pictures

★ **1992** *The Last of the Mohicans, A League of Their Own* … (Apparently the judges hadn't seen any other films that year; as a result they completed the ten with made-up film titles such as *Ballin': The Movie*.)

Worst Movie

★ **1990** *Darkman*

Ten Worst Pictures

★ **1983** *Silkwood, Terms of Endearment, Mr. Mom, Sudden Impact, National Lampoon's Vacation, Broadway Danny Rose, Return of the Jedi, Twilight Zone: The Movie, Yentl, Flashdance*

★ **1982** *Star Trek II: The Wrath of Khan, The Verdict, E.T. – The Extra-Terrestrial, Gandhi, An Officer and a Gentleman, Missing, Tootsie, Rocky III, Annie, Conan the Barbarian*

★ **1981** *On Golden Pond, Tarzan, the Ape Man, Superman II, Stripes, History of the World, Part 1, The Fox and the Hound, Arthur, Reds, The Great Muppet Caper, Raiders of the Lost Ark*

★ **1980** *Xanadu, Altered States, Blue Lagoon, Dressed to Kill, The Jazz Singer, Nine to Five, Yanks, Fame, Flash Gordon, The First Family*

★ **1979** *Manhattan, The Muppet Movie, The Amityville Horror, Apocalypse Now, 10, All That Jazz, Rocky II, 1941, The Rose, Star Trek – The Motion Picture*

★ **1978** *Sgt. Pepper's Lonely Hearts Club Band, Rabbit Test, Interiors, Superman, Foul Play, Up in Smoke, F.I.S.T., Magic, Ice Castles, Same Time, Next Year*

★ **1977** *Looking for Mr. Goodbar, It's Alive, The Turning Point, A Nightful of Rain, New York, New York, Coming Home, Oh, God, Semi-Tough, The Goodbye Girl, The Gauntlet*

★ **1976** *A Star is Born, The Enforcer, Murder by Death, Slapshot, The Omen, Lipstick, Mikey and Nicky, The Missouri Breaks, Car Wash, King Kong*

★ **1975** *Barry Lyndon, Tommy, At Long Last Love, The Other Side of the Mountain, The Hindenberg, The Day of the Locust, The Story of O, Mahogany, Shampoo, Once Is Not Enough*

★ **1974** *Lenny, S*P*Y*S, Harry and Tonto, Airport 1975, Blazing Saddles, The Night Porter, The Trial of Billy Jack, Murder on the Orient Express, Daisy Miller, The Front Page*

★ **1973** *The Great Gatsby, Day of the Dolphin, Jonathan Livingston Seagull, The Seven-Ups, A Touch of Class, Blume in Love, The Way We Were, The Exorcist, Save the Tiger, American Graffiti*

★ **1972** *Last Tango in Paris, The Candidate, The Getaway, Sounder, Deliverance, Play It As It Lays, The Emigrants, What's Up, Doc?, Man of La Mancha, The Man*

★ **1971** *A Clockwork Orange, Carnal Knowledge, Summer of '42, Fiddler on the Roof, The Last Movie, T.R. Baskin, Kotch, Willard, The Music Lovers, Dealing*

★ **1970** *Love Story, Airport, Patton, Joe, Soldier Blue, Getting Straight, The Strawberry Statement, Little Fauss and Big Halsey, Julius Caesar, The Statue*

★ **1969** *Easy Rider, Medium Cool, Putney Swope, Bob & Carol & Ted & Alice, Topaz, The Maltese Bippy, True Grit, John and Mary, Hello, Dolly!, Last Summer*

★ **1968** *The Lion in Winter, Ice Station Zebra, Rosemary's Baby, Star!, The Boston Strangler, Candy, Barbarella, You Are What You Eat, The Seagull, Boom!*

★ **1967** *Guess Who's Coming to Dinner, Valley of the Dolls, Up the Down Staircase, One Million Years B.C., The Comedians, Reflections in a Golden Eye, Thoroughly Modern Millie, Doctor Dolittle, The Fox, Carmen Baby*

★ **1966** *Is Paris Burning?, Hurry Sundown, The Oscar, The Fortune Cookie, The Bible, A Countess from Hong Kong, The Blue Max, Fantastic Voyage, Torn Curtain, Penelope*

★ **1965** *The Sandpiper, The Hallelujah Trail, Lord Jim, What's New, Pussycat?, The Agony and the Ecstasy, Shenandoah, Genghis Khan, Thunderball, The Great Race, The Yellow Rolls-Royce*

★ **1964** *The Greatest Story Ever Told, The Carpetbaggers, Sylvia, Cheyenne Autumn, Station Six-Sahara, Kiss Me, Stupid* (all tied); *The Outrage, The Fall of the Roman Empire, One Potato, Two Potato, Youngblood Hawke, Kisses for My President, Goodbye Charlie, The Unsinkable Molly Brown, Muscle Beach Party*

★ **1963** *Cleopatra, The V.I.P.'s, The Prize, It's a Mad, Mad, Mad, Mad World, How the West Was Won, Heavens Above!, 55 Days at Peking, Act One; The Birds* and *Bye Bye Birdie* (tied); *Gidget Goes to Rome* and *Tammy and the Doctor* (tied)

★ **1962** *The Chapman Report, If a Man Answers, Hemingway's Adventures of a Young Man, Diamond Head, The Wonderful World of the Brothers Grimm, White Slave Ship, Mutiny on the Bounty, Taras Bulba, Barabbas, The Mongols or The Tartars or The Huns*

★ **1961** *King of Kings* and *Parrish* (tie),
*By Love Possessed, The Devil at 4 O' Clock,
The Last Sunset, The Young Doctors, Ada,
Flower Drum Song, Babes in Toyland,
Sergeants Three*

★ **1960** *Butterfield 8, Strangers When
We Meet, The Gazebo, Ice Palace, Exodus,
It Started in Naples, Pepe, Pollyanna,
Because They're Young, High Time*

★ **1959** *The Best of Everything, The Miracle,
Career, Never So Few, Solomon and Sheba,
The Tempest, A Summer Place, They Came
to Cordura, Say One for Me, Hercules*

★ **1958** *South Pacific, The Vikings,
The Roots of Heaven, The Last Hurrah,
Marjorie Morningstar, The Buccaneers,
The Big Country, The Old Man and the Sea,
A Certain Smile, Windjammer*

★ **1957** *Raintree County, The Pride and
the Passion, Peyton Place, Island in the Sun,
Jeanne Eagels, Funny Face, The Hunchback of
Notre Dame, The Sun Also Rises, Pal Joey,
April Love*

★ **1956** *The Ten Commandments, Alexander
the Great, Trapeze, The Benny Goodman
Story, Gaby, Serenade, Bhowani Junction,
Miracle in the Rain, The Vagabond King,
The Proud and the Profane*

★ **1955** *Not as a Stranger, Ulysses,
The Prodigal, Hit the Deck, The Tall Man,
The Rains of Ranchipur, Battle Cry,
The Last Time I Saw Paris, The Long Grey
Line, Underwater*

★ **1954** *Haaji Baba, There's No Business
Like Show Business, The Egyptian, The High
and the Mighty, Magnificent Obsession,
Beau Brummel, The Student Prince,
Knights of the Round Table, Demetrius and
the Gladiators, White Christmas*

★ **1953** *The Robe, Salome, Beneath the
12-Mile Reef, Hondo, Torch Song, Call Me
Madam, How to Marry a Millionaire, Easy to
Love, I, the Jury, Gentlemen Prefer Blondes*

★ **1952** *Jumping Jacks, The Snows of
Kilimanjaro, Quo Vadis?, Son of Paleface,
Million Dollar Mermaid, Bloodhounds of
Broadway, Niagara, Because You're Mine,
An Affair in Trinidad, The Merry Widow*

★ **1951** *Tales of Hoffman, Valentino,
Alice in Wonderland, That's My Boy, Texas
Carnival, Take Care of My Little Girl,
The Flames of Araby, Here Comes the Groom,
David and Bathsheba, I Want You*

★ **1950** *Our Very Own, Samson and
Delilah, Three Came Home, The Next Voice
You Hear, An American Guerilla in the
Philippines, Cheaper by the Dozen, Stromboli,
The Flame and the Arrow, The Conspirators,
The Duchess of Idaho*

★ **1949** *Joan of Arc, The Great
Gatsby, The Night Has a Thousand Eyes,
Flamingo Road, Look for the Silver Lining,
Top o' the Morning, The Fountainhead,
The Fan, That Midnight Kiss, A Connecticut
Yankee in King Arthur's Court*

Kirk Douglas Award for Worst Actor

★ 1994 **Eric Stolz** as a Harvard student,
Naked in New York

The Kirk Douglas' Son Award

★ 1992 **Michael Douglas** – *Basic Instinct*

Worst Actor

★ 1990 **Patrick Swayze** – *Ghost, Road House*

Kirk Douglas Award for Worst Actor

★ 1983 **Al Pacino** – *Scarface*

★ 1982 **Clint Eastwood** – *Firefox, Honkytonk Man*

★ 1981 **Warren Beatty** – *Reds*

★ 1980 **Jack Nicholson** – *The Shining*

★ 1979 **Marlon Brando** – *Apocalypse Now*

★ 1978 **Warren Beatty** – *Heaven Can Wait's* triple threat (writer/director/idiot Ken-doll impersonator)

★ 1977 **Kris Kristofferson** – *Semi-Tough*

★ 1976 **Clint Eastwood** – *The Enforcer*

★ 1975 **Ryan O'Neal** – *Barry Lyndon*

★ 1974 **Burt Reynolds** – *The Longest Yard*

★ 1973 **Jack Lemmon** – *Save the Tiger*

★ 1972 **Robert Redford** – *The Candidate*

★ 1971 **Jack Nicholson** – *Carnal Knowledge*

★ 1970 **Elliot Gould** – for *Getting Straight* and for dumping Barbra Streisand

★ 1969 **Peter Fonda** – *Easy Rider*

★ 1968 **Sidney Poitier** – *For Love of Ivy*

★ 1967 **Richard Burton** – *Doctor Faustus, The Comedians*

★ 1966 **George Peppard** – *The Blue Max*

★ 1965 No award

★ 1964 **James Franciscus** – *Youngblood Hawke*

★ 1963 **Burt Lancaster** – *The Leopard, Seven Days in May*

★ 1962 **Charlton Heston** – *Diamond Head, The Pigeon That Took Rome*

★ 1961 **Richard Beymer** – *West Side Story*

★ 1960 **Frank Sinatra** – *Can-Can*

★ 1959 **Sal Mineo** – *Tonka*

★ 1958 **Kirk Douglas** – *The Vikings* (the trophy will be retired, Mr Douglas having won it for the third time)

★ 1957 **Rock Hudson** – *A Farewell to Arms*

★ 1956 **Gregory Peck** – *Moby Dick*

★ 1955 **Kirk Douglas** – *Ulysses, Indian Fighter*

★ 1954 No award

★ 1953 **Victor Mature** – *The Robe*

Worst Male Performance

★ 1952 **Jerry Lewis** – *Sailor Beware, Jumping Jacks*, etc.

Worst Actor

★ 1951 **Robert Taylor** – *Quo Vadis?*

★ 1950 **Clifton Webb** – *Cheaper by the Dozen*

Worst Single Performance – Male

★ 1949 **Gregory Peck** – *The Great Sinner*

Worst Supporting Actor

★ 1973 **Dustin Hoffman** – *Papillon*

★ 1970 **Jon Voight** – *Catch-22*

★ 1968 **Rod Steiger** – *No Way to Treat a Lady*

★ 1966 **John Huston** – *The Bible*

★ 1964 **Laurence Harvey** – *The Outrage*

★ 1963 **Roy Cohn** – *Point of Order*

★ 1960 **Eddie Fisher** – *Butterfield 8*

★ 1959 **Dick Nixon** – *The Best of Benson*

★ 1958 **Errol Flynn** – *The Roots of Heaven*

★ 1957 **McGeorge Bundy** – *To the Age That Is Waiting*

★ 1956 **Elvis Presley** – *Love Me Tender*

★ 1953 **Brandon de Wilde** – *Shane*

Worst Supporting Male Performance

★ 1952 **Dean Martin** – *Sailor Beware*, *Jumping Jacks* etc.

Natalie Wood Award for Worst Actress

★ 1994 **Moira Kelly** as a Harvard student – *With Honours*

★ 1992 **Lorraine Bracco** – *Medicine Man*

Worst Actress

★ 1990 **Bette Midler** – *Beaches*

Natalie Wood Award for Worst Actress

★ 1983 **Natalie Wood** – *Brainstorm*

★ 1982 **Meryl Streep** – *Sophie's Choice*. Jonathan Winters could have done a better job with that accent.

Jane Fonda Award for Worst Actress

★ 1981 **Katharine Hepburn** as the Creature from the *Golden Pond*

★ 1980 **Shelley Duvall** – *Popeye*

★ 1979 **Jane Fonda** – *The Electric Horseman*

Natalie Wood Award for Worst Actress

★ 1978 We couldn't decide whether to give it to **Jane Fonda** for *Coming Home*, **Jane Fonda** for *Comes a Horseman*, or **Jane Fonda** for *Come the China Syndrome*. So we decided to give it to you, Jane, just for being you.

★ 1977 **Marthe Keller** – *Black Sunday*

★ 1976 **Barbra Streisand** – *A Star is Born* Her performance should delight those who can't tell the difference between Eydie Gormé and Patti Smith

★ 1975 **Diana Ross** – *Mahogany*

★ 1974 **Julie Andrews** – *The Tamarind Seed*

★ 1973 **Barbra Streisand** – *The Way We Were*

★ 1972 **Ali MacGraw** – *The Getaway*

★ 1971 **Candice Bergen** – *T.R. Baskin*

★ 1970 **Ali MacGraw** – *Love Story*

★ 1969 **Jane Fonda** – *Spirits of the Dead*, and for marrying Roger Vadim

★ 1968 **Barbra Streisand** – *Funny Girl*

★ 1967 **Raquel Welch** – *One Million Years B.C.*, *The Biggest Bundle of Them All*, *Bedazzled*

Worst Actress

★ 1966 **Ursula Andress** – *Casino Royale*

★ 1965 No award

★ 1964 **Carrol Baker** – *The Greatest Story Ever Told*, *The Carpetbaggers*, *Sylvia*, *Cheyenne Autumn*, *Station Six-Sahara*

★ 1963 **Debbie Reynolds** – *How the West Was Won*, *Mary, Mary*

★ 1962 **Jane Fonda** – *The Chapman Report*

★ 1961 **Susan Hayward** – *Ada*, *Back Street*

★ 1960 **Eva Marie Saint** – *Exodus*

★ 1959 **Lana Turner** – *Imitation of Life*

★ 1958 **Rita Hayworth** – *Separate Tables*

★ 1957 **Kim Novak** – *Jeanne Eagels*, *Pal Joey*

★ 1956 **Jennifer Jones** – *The Man in the Grey Flannel Suit*

★ 1955 **Debbie Reynolds** – *Hit the Deck*, *Susan Slept Here*

★ 1954 No award

★ 1953 **Terry Moore** – *Beneath the 12-Mile Reef*

Worst Female Performance

★ 1952 **Marilyn Monroe** – *Niagara*

Worst Actress

★ 1951 **Corinne Calvet** – *On the Riviera*

★ 1950 **Elizabeth Taylor** – *The Conspirators*

Worst Single Performance – Female

★ 1949 **Shirley Temple** – *Mr. Belvedere Goes to College*

Worst Supporting Actress

★ 1973 **Dyan Cannon** – *Shamus*, *The Last of Sheila*

★ 1970 **Ruth Gordon** – *Where's Poppa?*

★ 1968 **Ewa Aulin** – *Candy*

★ 1966 **Leslie Caron** – *Is Paris Burning?*

★ 1964 **Honor Blackman** – *Pussy Galore*

★ 1963 **Carol Burnett** – *Who's Been Sleeping in My Bed?*

★ 1960 **Annette Funicello** – *The Horse Masters*

★ 1959 **Sandra Dee** – *A Summer Place*

★ 1958 **Christine Carrere** – *A Certain Smile*

★ 1957 **Joan Collins** – *Island in the Sun*

★ 1956 **Anne Baxter** – *The Ten Commandments*

★ 1953 **Zsa Zsa Gabor** – *Moulin Rouge*

And to finish this subsection, a selection of *Harvard Lampoon*'s silliest awards over the years

★ **1994** The From Milton Berle's Private Joke File Award (to the comedy that should have stayed private): *The Mask*. Too bad the computers couldn't write the jokes just like they randomly selected Jim Carrey from a demographic data set to be a movie star

★ **1992** Worst Irishploitation Movie: *Far and Away*, with Tom Cruise. Thank you, midget

★ **1983** The Title Most Overtly Evocative of Genitalia While Retaining a PG Rating Award: *Octopussy*

★ **1982** The Worst Movie with the Most Number 3's in the Title Citation: *Friday the 13th Part 3 in 3-D*

★ **1981** The Brian De Palma 'It Takes a Thief' Award: To Francis Ford Coppola, Alfred Hitchcock, Brian de Palma, Michelangelo Antonioni, Franklin Schaffner, William Friedkin, the Kennedy family, and John Avildsen, all of whom were robbed by Brian De Palma during the making of *Blow Out*

★ **1980** The Watergate Worst (for the most outrageous cover-up job of the year): John Hurt and his make-up man, *The Elephant Man*

★ **1979** Worst Movie Worst Award (for the *Harvard Lampoon* Movie Worst Award of the past forty years which exemplifies their smarmy, undignified and scattershot approach): To the 1955 award to *Rebel Without a Cause*: 'Movie without a plot … to prevent the perpetration of further cinematic abominations, let's pray lead actors (we use the word perhaps too loosely)

Sal Mineo and James Dean meet untimely deaths [Dean died as the result of a car crash in 1955; Mineo was murdered in 1976].'

★ **1978** The Trinitron Memorial (for the most ungraceful transition from small screen to big): Farrah Fawcett-Majors, *Somebody Killed Her Husband*

★ **1976** The Volvo Trophy: Liv Ullmann in *Face to Face* as the Swedish import that always breaks down

★ **1975** The Wrong-Way Corrigan Memorial Flight Jacket (for worst direction): Steven Spielberg, *Jaws*, for turning *Moby Dick* into *King Kong* and attempting to pass this fish story off as great cinematic art

★ **1974** The Curse-of-the-Living-Corpse Award: Gloria Swanson, an actress only slightly older than the mountains she is imperilled above in *Airport '75*

★ **1973** The Charles Manson Memorial Scalpel (for the clumsiest job of cutting): *O Lucky Man!*, whose shooting script was first published as a deck of flash cards by Educational Playthings

★ **1972** The Uncrossed Heart (to the least promising young performer): Cybill Shepherd, who has now gone through two major films without once opening her eyes

★ **1971** HJ Heinz Laurel Clot (to the film that makes most extensive use of the company's various vegetable derivatives): *Dirty Harry*

★ **1970** The OK-Doc-Break-the-Arm-Again Award (for the most flagrant example of miscasting): Dean Martin, who soberly piloted a 707 to a belly-landing in *Airport*

★ **1969** The OhGodohGod, the Lights, the Shapes, the Colors Award (to that movie which makes us glad we have lungs to inhale with): To the revival of Walt Disney's *Fantasia*

★ **1967** The Piltdwon Mandible (to the most obviously and unabashedly spurious scientific phenomena): *One Million Years B.C.*, for the contemporaneous existence of Raquel Welch and a passel of dinosaurs, an unscientific juxtaposition redounding entirely to the credit of the dinosaurs

★ **1966** Der Otto: Awarded annually to Otto Preminger for his yearly excursions into the tawdry, the sordid, and the silly. This year for his direction of *Hurry Sundown*

★ **1964** The Please-Don't-Put-Us-Through-DeMille-Again Award: *The Greatest Story Ever Told*

★ **1963** The Timothy Cratchit Memorial Award (to that Hollywood personality who offers the lamest excuse for unsavoury behaviour): Elizabeth Taylor, for divorcing Eddie Fisher, on the grounds of abandonment

★ **1961** The Roscoe Award: to Natalie Wood, for so gallantly persisting in her career despite a total inability to act

★ **1960** The Bratwurst Award (to the most obnoxious child star of the year): David Ladd, *A Dog of Flanders*

★ **1959** The Wish-It-Were-True Award: Bing Crosby as a celibate priest in *Say One for Me*

★ **1958** The Fauntleroy Bequest (a stipend set up in the will of the late Lord Fauntleroy to send a young lad to acting school): Awarded to James (*A Light in the Forest*) MacArthur, with all dispatch

★ **1955** First Annual Award for Crude Symbolism: The fireworks in mounting crescendo as a backdrop for Grace Kelly and Cary Grant in their big scene in *To Catch a Thief*

★ **1954** Saddest Evidence of Rapid Aging: Jimmy Stewart impassively receiving a massage from Grace Kelly in *Rear Window*

★ **1951** Finest Example of Idyllic Young Love: Ava Gardner and Frank Sinatra

★ **1950** Worst Insult to the American Fighting Man: John Wayne

The Golden Raspberry Awards

The Golden Raspberry, or 'Razzie', as it's lovingly referred to, is probably the one award an actor tries hardest not to win! It is a celebration of the worst Hollywood has to offer. Its aim is to rightfully acknowledge the big-budget turkey's contribution to the legend that is Hollywood.

The award itself is an all-expense-spared, gold-painted, imitation raspberry, on top of a 35mm film core, with a Lipton can lid for its base. A truly priceless award! Founded by the Los Angeles copywriter John Wilson, the Association, whose numbers are made up mostly by the industry's lesser beings, holds its no-name ceremony yearly, on the night before the Oscars. The first ceremony took place in 1980; since then popular winners of a Raspberry have included Sly Stallone, Madonna and Kevin Costner, all of whom have several turkeys to their name. However, and perhaps not surprisingly, the awards tend to be given in the absence of those nominated.

Worst Actor

★ 1998 **Bruce Willis**
Armageddon; also for *Mercury Rising* and *The Siege*

★ 1997 **Kevin Costner**
The Postman

★ 1996 **Pauly Shore**
Bio-Dome

★ 1995 **Pauly Shore**
Jury Duty;
Tom Arnold
Big Bully; also for *Carpool* and *The Stupids*

★ 1994 **Kevin Costner**
Wyatt Earp

★ 1993 **Burt Reynolds**
Cop-and-a-Half

★ 1992 **Sylvester Stallone**
Stop! Or My Mom Will Shoot

★ 1991 **Kevin Costner**
Robin Hood: Prince of Thieves

★ 1990 **Andrew 'Dice' Clay**
The Adventures of Ford Fairlane

★ 1989 **William Shatner**
Star Trek 5: The Final Frontier

★ 1988 **Sylvester Stallone**
Rambo 3

★ 1987 **Bill Cosby**
Leonard Part 6

★ 1986 **Prince**
Under the Cherry Moon

★ 1985 **Sylvester Stallone**
Rambo: First Blood, Part 2 and *Rocky 4*

★ 1984 **Sylvester Stallone**
Rhinestone

★ 1983 **Christopher Atkins**
A Night In Heaven

★ 1982 **Laurence Olivier**
Inchon!

★ 1981 **Klinton Spilsbury**
Legend of the Lone Ranger

★ 1980 **Neil Diamond**
The Jazz Singer

Worst Supporting Actor

★ 1998 **Joe Eszterhas**
An Alan Smithee Film: *Burn Hollywood Burn*

★ 1997 **Dennis Rodman**
Double Team

★ 1996 **Marlon Brando**
The Island of Dr. Moreau

★ 1995 **Dennis Hopper**
Waterworld

★ 1994 **OJ Simpson**
Naked Gun 33¹/₃: The Final Insult

★ 1993 **Woody Harrelson**
Indecent Proposal

★ 1992 **Tom Selleck**
Christopher Columbus: The Discovery

★ 1991 **Dan Aykroyd**
Nothing But Trouble

★ 1990 **Donald Trump** (playing himself!)
Ghosts Can't Do It

★ 1989 **Christopher Atkins**
Listen To Me

★ 1988 **Dan Aykroyd**
Caddyshack 2

★ 1987 **David Mendenhall**
Over the Top

★ 1986 **Jerome Benton**
Under the Cherry Moon

★ 1985 **Rob Lowe**
St. Elmo's Fire

★ 1984 **Brooke Shields** (with wig and moustache)
Sahara

★ 1983 **Jim Nabors**
Stroker Ace

★ 1982 **Ed McMahon**
Butterfly

★ 1981 **Steve Forrest**
Mommie Dearest

★ 1980 **John Adams**
Gloria;
Laurence Olivier
The Jazz Singer

Worst Actress

★ 1998 **Melanie Brown, Emma Bunton, Melanie Chisholm, Geri Halliwell, Victoria Adams**
Spice World

★ 1997 **Demi Moore**
G.I. Jane

★ 1996 **Demi Moore**
Striptease

★ 1995 **Elizabeth Berkley**
Showgirls

★ 1994 **Sharon Stone**
Intersection and *The Specialist*

★ 1993 **Madonna**
Body of Evidence

★ 1992 **Melanie Griffith**
A Stranger Among Us and *Shining Through*

★ 1991 **Sean Young**
(playing the surviving twin)
A Kiss Before Dying

★ 1990 **Bo Derek**
Ghosts Can't Do It

★ 1989 **Heather Locklear**
Return of the Swamp Thing

★ 1988 **Liza Minnelli**
Rent-A-Cop and *Arthur 2: On the Rocks*

★ 1987 **Madonna**
Who's That Girl?

★ 1986 **Madonna**
Shanghai Surprise

★ 1985 **Linda Blair**
Night Patrol, Savage Island and *Savage Streets*

★ 1984 **Bo Derek**
Bolero

★ 1983 **Pia Zadora**
The Lonely Lady

★ 1982 **Pia Zadora**
Butterfly

★ 1981 **Faye Dunaway**
Mommie Dearest;
Bo Derek
Tarzan, the Ape Man

★ 1980 **Brooke Shields**
The Blue Lagoon

Worst Supporting Actress

★ 1998 **Maria Pitillo**
Godzilla

★ 1997 **Alicia Silverstone**
Batman and Robin

★ 1996 **Melanie Griffith**
Mulholland Falls

★ 1995 **Madonna**
Four Rooms

★ 1994 **Rosie O'Donnell**
Car 54, Where Are You?, Exit to Eden and *The Flintstones*

★ 1993 **Faye Dunaway**
The Temp

★ 1992 **Estelle Getty**
Stop! Or My Mom Will Shoot

★ 1991 **Sean Young** (playing the twin who is murdered)
A Kiss Before Dying

★ 1990 **Sofia Coppola**
The Godfather, Part 3

★ 1989 **Brooke Shields** (playing herself)
Speed Zone

★ 1988 **Kristy McNichol**
Two Moon Junction

★ 1987 **Darryl Hannah**
Wall Street

★ 1986 **Dom DeLuise** (in drag)
Haunted Honeymoon

★ 1985 **Brigitte Nielsen**
Rocky 4

★ 1984 **Lynn-Holly Johnson**
Where the Boys Are '84

★ 1983 **Sybil Danning**
Chained Heart and *Hercules*

★ 1982 **Aileen Quinn**
Annie

★ 1981 **Diana Scarwid**
Mommie Dearest

★ 1980 **Amy Irving**
Honeysuckle Rose

Worst Director

★ 1998 **Gus Van Sant**, *Psycho*

★ 1997 **Kevin Costner**, *The Postman*

★ 1996 **Andrew Bergman**, *Striptease*

★ 1995 **Paul Verhoeven**, *Showgirls*

★ 1994 **Steven Seagal**, *On Deadly Ground*

★ 1993 **Jennifer Lynch**, *Boxing Helena*

★ 1992 **David Seltzer**, *Shining Through*

★ 1991 **Michael Lehmann**, *Hudson Hawk*

★ 1990 **John Derek**, *Ghosts Can't Do It*

★ 1989 **William Shatner**, *Star Trek 5:
The Final Frontier*

★ 1988 **Blake Edwards**, *Sunset* and
Stewart Raffill, *Mac and Me*

★ 1987 **Norman Mailer**, *Tough Guys Don't
Dance* and **Elaine May**, *Ishtar*

★ 1986 **Prince**, *Under the Cherry Moon*

★ 1985 **Sylvester Stallone**, *Rocky 4*

★ 1984 **John Derek**, *Bolero*

★ 1983 **Peter Sasdy**, *The Lonely Lady*

★ 1982 **Ken Annakan**, *Pirate Movie*
and **Terence Young**, *Inchton!*

★ 1981 **Michael Cimino**, *Heaven's Gate*

★ 1980 **Robert Greenwald**, *Xanadu*

Worst Picture

★ 1998 An Alan Smithee Film:
Burn Hollywood Burn

★ 1997 *The Postman*

★ 1996 *Striptease*

★ 1995 *Showgirls*

★ 1994 *Color of Night*

★ 1993 *Indecent Proposal*

★ 1992 *Shining Through*

★ 1991 *Hudson Hawk*

★ 1990 *Ghosts Can't Do It* and
The Adventures of Ford Fairlane

★ 1989 *Star Trek 5: The Final Frontier*

★ 1988 *Cocktail*

★ 1987 *Leonard Part 6*

★ 1986 *Howard the Duck* and
Under the Cherry Moon

★ 1985 *Rambo: First Blood, Part 2*

★ 1984 *Bolero*

★ 1983 *The Lonely Lady*

★ 1982 *Inchon!*

★ 1981 *Mommie Dearest*

★ 1980 *Can't Stop the Music!*

★ 1982 'Pumpin' And Blowin'' from
The Pirate Movie

★ 1981 'Baby Talk' from *Paternity*

★ 1980 Theme from
The Man with Bogart's Face

Worst Song

★ 1998 'I Wanna Be Mike Ovitz!' from
An Alan Smithee Film: *Burn Hollywood Burn*

★ 1997 The Entire Song Score from
The Postman

★ 1996 'Pussy, Pussy, Pussy
(Whose Kitty Cat Are You?)' from *Striptease*

★ 1995 'Walk Into The Wind' from *Showgirls*

★ 1994 'Marry The Mole' from *Thumbelina*

★ 1993 'Whoomp! There It Is' from
Addams Family Values

★ 1992 'High Times, Hard Times'
from *Newsies*

★ 1991 'Addams Groove' from
The Addams Family

★ 1990 'He's Comin' Back (The Devil!)'
from *Repossessed*

★ 1989 'Bring Your Daughter To The
Slaughter' from *Nightmare on Elm Street 5*

★ 1988 'Jack Fresh' from *Caddyshack 2*

★ 1987 'I Want Your Sex' from
Beverly Hills Cop 2

★ 1986 'Love Or Money' from
Under the Cherry Moon

★ 1985 'Peace In Our Life' from *Rambo 2*

★ 1984 'Drinkenstein' from *Rhinestone*

★ 1983 'The Way You Do It' from
The Lonely Lady

Bibliography

Books

★ **The Bare Facts Video Guide** (1999),
Craig Hosoda – Titan Books

★ **The Book of Movie Lists: An Offbeat,
Provocative Collection of the Best and Worst of
Everything in Movies** (1999),
Joseph McBride – Contemporary Books

★ **The Complete Idiot's Guide to Elvis** (1997),
Frank Coffey – Alpha Books

★ **The Elvis Film Encyclopedia** (1997),
Eric Braun – Batsford

★ **Elvis His Life from A to Z** (1989),
Fred L Worth and Steve D Tamerius – Corgi Books

★ **Empire Building The Remarkable,
Real-life Story of Star Wars** (1997),
Garry Jenkins – Simon & Schuster

★ **The Encyclopedia of Movie Awards** (1996),
Michael Gebert – St Martin's Paperbacks
(NB: The *Harvard Lampoon* Movie Awards have been
taken entirely from this book. Gebert acknowledges
that these excerpts are owned and copyrighted
by *Harvard Lampoon* Inc and have been used with
their permission (*Harvard Lampoon*, 44 Bow Street,
Cambridge, MA 02138).)

★ **The Essential Bond: The Authorized Guide
to the World of 007** (1998),
Lee Pfeiffer and Dave Worrall – Boxtree

★ **Film Flubs The Sequel:
Even More Memorable Movie Mistakes** (1992),
Bill Givens – Carol Publishing Group

★ **Film Flubs: Memorable Movie Mistakes** (1990),
Bill Givens – Carol Publishing Group

★ **First Films: Illustrious, Obscure,
and Embarrassing Movie Debuts** (1993),
Jami Bernard – Carol Publishing Group

★ **Frankly, My Dear**: More than 650 of the funniest,
smartest, gutsiest, nastiest, sexiest, and simply the greatest
quotes in celebration of women in the movies (1993),
Jeff Block – Carol Publishing Group

★ **George Lucas: The Creative Impulse** (1992),
Charles Champlin – Harry N Abrams Inc

★ **The Guinness Book of Box Office Hits** (1995),
Phil Swern – Guinness

★ **The Guinness Book of Movie Facts & Feats** (1993),
Patrick Robertson – Guinness

★ **Halliwell's Filmgoers Companion** (1997),
Leslie Halliwell – HarperCollins

★ **High Concept: Don Simpson and
the Hollywood Culture of Excess** (1999),
Charles Fleming – Bloomsbury

★ **The History of Cinema for Beginners** (1998),
Jarek Kupsc – Writers and Readers Publishing Inc

★ **The Hollywood Celebrity Death Book** (1993),
James Robert Parrish – Pioneer Books Inc

★ **The Incredible World of 007** (1994),
Lee Pfeiffer and Philip Lisa – Carol Publishing Group

★ **Industrial Light & Magic:
Into the Digital Realm** (1996),
Mark Cotta Vaz and Patricia Rose Duignan –
Virgin Publishing

★ **Industrial Light & Magic:
The Art of Special Effects** (1991),
Thomas G Smith – Virgin Publishing

★ **Inside Oscar The Unofficial History of the
Academy Awards Tenth Anniversary Edition** (1996),
Mason Wiley and Damien Bona – Ballantine Books

★ **International Film Prizes:
An Encyclopaedia** (1991),
Tad Bentley Hammer – St James Press

★ **Leonard Maltin's Movie and
Video Guide 1999 Edition** (1998),
Leonard Maltin – Penguin Books

★ **The Macmillan International
Film Encyclopaedia New Edition** (1994),
Ephraim Katz – Pan Macmillan Ltd

★ **Made in Heaven: The Marriages
and Children of Hollywood Stars** (1991),
Victoria Houseman – Bonus Books, Inc

★ **Movie Psychos and Madmen: Film Psychopaths
from Jekyll and Hyde to Hannibal Lecter** (1994),
John McCarthy – Carol Publishing Group

★ **The Movie List Book** (1994),
Richard B Armstrong and Mary Willems Armstrong –
Betterway Books

★ **The Movie Quote Book** (1981),
Harry Haun – Omnibus Press

★ **Movietalk: Who Said What About
Whom in the Movies** (1988),
David Shipman – Bloomsbury

★ **On Location: The Film Fan's Guide to
Britain & Ireland** (1995),
Brian Pendreigh – Mainstream

★ **Opening Shots : The Unusual, Unexpected,
Potentially Career-Threatening First Roles That
Launched the Careers of 70 Hollywood Stars** (1994),
Damien Bona – Workman Publishing Company

★ **The Playboy Book
The Complete Pictorial History** (1994),
Gretchen Edgren – Benedikt Taschen Verlag GmbH

★ **The Psychotronic Video Guide** (1996),
Michael J Weldon – Titan Books

★ **Questions for the Movie Answer Man** (1997),
Roger Ebert – Andrews McMeel Publishing

★ **Quinlan's Illustrated Directory of Film Stars** (1986),
David Quinlan – Batsford

★ **Quinlan's Illustrated Guide to Film Directors** (1991),
David Quinlan – Batsford

★ **Reel Gags: jokes, sight gags, and director's
tricks from your favourite films** (1998) –
Renaissance Books

★ **Son of Film Flubs:
More Memorable Movie Mistakes** (1991),
Bill Givens – Carol Publishing Group

★ **Sophomore Slumps: Disastrous Second Movies,
Albums, Singles, Books and Other Stuff** (1995),
Christopher Golden – Carol Publishing Group

★ **Those Who Died Young** (1979),
Marianne Sinclair – Plexus Publishing

★ **Too Young to Die** (1991),
Contributing Writers – Mallard Press

★ **The Unauthorized Star Wars Compendium:
The Complete Guide to the Movies,
Comic Books, Novels, and More** (1999),
Ted Edwards – Boxtree

★ **Variety Movie Guide** (Current Edition),
Derek Elley – Hamlyn

★ **Video Movie Guide 1999** (1998),
Mick Martin and Marsha Porter – Ballantine Books

★ **The Wordsworth Dictionary of
Film Quotations** (1994),
Tony Crawley – Wordsworth Reference

★ **You Magazine Movielists** (1992),
John Koski and Mitchell Symons – *You Magazine*

★ **Young Hollywood** (1994),
James Cameron-Wilson – Batsford

Magazines

★ *Empire*
★ *Film Review*
★ *Movieline*
★ *Neon*
★ *Premiere*
★ *Q Magazine*
★ *Screen International*
★ *The Hill* (a magazine specific to *Notting Hill*)
★ *Total Film*
★ *White's Guide to the Movies*

Newspapers

★ The *Guardian*
★ The *Observer*

Internet

★ The Internet Movie Database
(http://www.us.imdb.com)

Other

The authors would like to thank the
following for their help, be it for their knowledge
or spiritual guidance:

★ British Film Institute
★ Christie's South Kensington
★ Iain Johnstone
★ Dennis and Rita Lascelles
★ Benjamin Linsley
★ David Noble
★ Matthew Roberts
★ Paul Robinson at BMG Records
★ Roger and Patricia Rowan
★ Sylvia Salerona
★ Susanne De Simone
★ Beryl Swern

The authors would like to dedicate this
book to the late Alec Swern.